TURKEY
CYPRUS
RUSSIA
KAZAKHSTAN
MONGOLIA
GEORGIA
ARM
AZER
TURKEY
UZBEK
KIRGIZ
TURKMEN
TAJIK
CHINA
N. KOREA
S. KOREA
JAPAN
SYRIA
LEB
ISR
JOR
IRAQ
IRAN
AFGH
KUWAIT
BAH
QATAR
UAE
PAKISTAN
NEPAL
BHU
EGYPT
SAUDI ARABIA
OMAN
B'DESH
INDIA
HONG KONG
TAIWAN
MACAO
MYANMAR
LAOS
THAILAND
VIETNAM
CAMBODIA
PHILIPPINES
SUDAN
ERITREA
YEMEN
DJIB
ETHIOPIA
SOMALIA
SRI LANKA
BRUNEI
MALAYSIA
SING
UGAN
KENYA
CONGO
TANZANIA
INDONESIA
PAPUA NEW GUINEA
ZAMBIA
MALAWI
ZIMB
MOZ
MADAGASCAR
MAURITIUS
BOT
SWAZ
SOUTH AFRICA
LESOTHO
FIJI
AUSTRALIA
NEW ZEALAND

POCKET WORLD IN FIGURES

OTHER TITLES FROM
THE ECONOMIST BOOKS

The Economist Desk Companion
The Economist Economics
The Economist Guide to Economic Indicators
The Economist Guide to the European Union
The Economist Numbers Guide
The Economist Style Guide
Business Ethics
E-Commerce
The Guide to Analysing Companies
Guide to Business Modelling
The Dictionary of Economics
The International Dictionary of Finance
Improving Marketing Effectiveness
Managing Complexity
Measuring Business Performance
Successful Innovation

Pocket Accounting
Pocket Advertising
Pocket Director
Pocket Economics
Pocket Finance
Pocket International Business Terms
Pocket Internet
Pocket Investor
Pocket Law
Pocket Manager
Pocket Marketing
Pocket MBA
Pocket Money
Pocket Negotiator
Pocket Strategy

The Economist Pocket Asia
The Economist Pocket Europe in Figures

POCKET WORLD IN FIGURES

THE ECONOMIST IN ASSOCIATION WITH
PROFILE BOOKS LTD

Published by Profile Books Ltd,
58A Hatton Garden, London EC1N 8LX

This edition published by Profile Books in association with
The Economist, 2001

Material researched and compiled by
Marianne Comparet, Mark Doyle, Lisa Foote, Robert Eves,
Andrew Gilbert, Conrad Heine, Carol Howard, Stella Jones,
David McKelvey, Simon Wright

Typeset in Univers by MacGuru
info@macguru.org.uk

Printed in Italy by
LEGO S.p.a. – Vicenza – Italy

A CIP catalogue record for this book is available
from the British Library

ISBN 1 86197 351 9

Contents

Notes

This 2002 edition of the annual *Economist Pocket World in Figures* has been expanded to include sections on business creativity and the Euro zone, and a number of other rankings. The country profiles cover 64 major countries. The world rankings consider 173: all those with a population of at least 1m or a GDP of at least $1bn; they are listed on page 234. The extent and quality of the statistics available varies from country to country. Every care has been taken to specify the broad definitions on which the data are based and to indicate cases where data quality or technical difficulties are such that interpretation of the figures is likely to be seriously affected. Nevertheless, figures from individual countries will often differ from standard international statistical definitions.

In ex-Yugoslavia, Serbia and Montenegro now constitute the Federal Republic of Yugoslavia, and Macedonia is officially known as the Former Yugoslav Republic of Macedonia. Data for Cyprus normally refer to Greek Cyprus only. Data for China do not include Hong Kong. For other countries such as Morocco they exclude disputed areas. Congo refers to the Democratic Republic of Congo, formerly known as Zaire. Congo-Brazzaville refers to the other Congo. Data for the EU refer to its 15 members following the enlargement of the Union on January 1 1995. The euro area of 11 EU members came into being on January 1 1999. Greece joined on January 1 2001 so is not included in our figures.

Statistical basis

The all-important factor in a book of this kind is to be able to make reliable comparisons between countries. Although this is never quite possible for the reasons stated above, the best route, which this book takes, is to compare data for the same year or period and to use actual, not estimated, figures wherever possible. Where a country's data is excessively out of date, it is excluded. The research for this edition of *The Economist Pocket World in Figures* was carried out in 2001 using the latest available sources that present data on an internationally comparable basis. Data, therefore, unless otherwise indicated, refer to the year ending December 31 1999.

In the country profiles, life expectancy, crude birth, death and fertility rates are based on 1995–2000 averages; human development indices are for 1998 and energy data refer to 1997; household data are latest available and marriage and divorce data refer to the latest year with available figures, 1990–99. In a number of cases, data are shown for the latest year within a range.

Other definitions
Data shown on country profiles may not always be consistent with those shown on the world rankings because the definitions or years covered can differ. Data may also differ between two different rankings.

Most countries' national accounts are now compiled on a GDP basis so, for simplicity, the term GDP has been used interchangeably with GNP or GNI.

Statistics for principal exports and principal imports are normally based on customs statistics. These are generally compiled on different definitions to the visible exports and imports figures shown in the balance of payments section.

Definitions of the statistics shown are given on the relevant page or in the glossary at the end of the book. Figures may not add exactly to totals, or percentages to 100, because of rounding or, in the case of GDP, statistical adjustment. Sums of money have generally been converted to US dollars at the official exchange rate ruling at the time to which the figures refer.

Energy consumption data are not always reliable, particularly for the major oil producing countries. Consumption per head data may therefore be higher than in reality. Energy exports can exceed production and imports can exceed consumption if transit operations distort trade data or oil is imported for refining and re-exported.

Abbreviations

bn	billion (one thousand million)
CIS	Commonwealth of Independent States
EU	European Union
kg	kilogram
km	kilometre
GDP	Gross domestic product
GNI	Gross national income
GNP	Gross national product
GRT	Gross tonnage
m	million
PPP	Purchasing power parity
trn	trillion (one thousand billion)
...	not available

Part I

WORLD RANKINGS

Countries: *natural facts*

Countries: *the largest*[a]

'000 sq km

1	Russia	17,075	31	Nigeria	924
2	Canada	9,971	32	Venezuela	912
3	China	9,561	33	Namibia	824
4	United States	9,373	34	Pakistan	804
5	Brazil	8,512	35	Mozambique	799
6	Australia	7,682	36	Turkey	779
7	India	3,287	37	Chile	757
8	Argentina	2,767	38	Zambia	753
9	Kazakhstan	2,717	39	Myanmar	677
10	Sudan	2,506	40	Afghanistan	652
11	Algeria	2,382	41	Somalia	638
12	Congo	2,345	42	Central African Rep	622
13	Saudi Arabia	2,200	43	Ukraine	604
14	Mexico	1,973	44	Madagascar	587
15	Indonesia[b]	1,904	45	Kenya	583
16	Libya	1,760	46	Botswana	581
17	Iran	1,648	47	France	544
18	Mongolia	1,565	48	Yemen	528
19	Peru	1,285	49	Thailand	513
20	Chad	1,284	50	Spain	505
21	Niger	1,267	51	Turkmenistan	488
22	Angola	1,247	52	Cameroon	475
23	Mali	1,240	53	Papua New Guinea	463
24	South Africa	1,226	54	Sweden	450
25	Colombia	1,142	55	Morocco	447
26	Ethiopia	1,134		Uzbekistan	447
27	Bolivia	1,099	57	Iraq	438
28	Mauritania	1,031	58	Paraguay	407
29	Egypt	1,000	59	Zimbabwe	391
30	Tanzania	945	60	Japan	378

Mountains: *the highest*[c]

	Name	*Location*	*Height (m)*
1	Everest	Nepal-China	8,848
2	K2 (Godwin Austen)	Pakistan	8,611
3	Kangchenjunga	Nepal-Sikkim	8,586
4	Lhotse	Nepal-China	8,516
5	Makalu	Nepal-China	8,463
6	Cho Oyu	Nepal-China	8,201
7	Dhaulagiri	Nepal	8,167
8	Manaslu	Nepal	8,163
9	Nanga Parbat	Pakistan	8,125
10	Annapurna I	Nepal	8,091
11	Gasherbrum I	Pakistan-China	8,068
12	Broad Peak	Pakistan-China	8,047
13	Xixabangma (Gosainthan)	China	8,046
14	Gasherbrum II	Pakistan-China	8,035

a Includes freshwater.
b Excludes East Timor, 14,874 sq km.
c Includes separate peaks which are part of the same massif.

Rivers: *the longest*

	Name	*Location*	*Length (km)*
1	Nile	Africa	6,695
2	Amazon	South America	6,516
3	Yangtze	Asia	6,380
4	Mississippi-Missouri	North America	6,019
5	Ob'-Irtysh	Asia	5,570
6	Yenisey-Angara	Asia	5,550
7	Hwang He (Yellow)	Asia	5,464
8	Congo	Africa	4,667
9	Parana	South America	4,500
10	Mekong	Asia	4,425
11	Amur	Asia	4,416
12	Lena	Asia	4,400
13	Mackenzie	North America	4,250
14	Niger	Africa	4,030
15	Missouri	North America	3,969
16	Mississippi	North America	3,779
17	Murray-Darling	Australia	3,750
18	Volga	Europe	3,688
19	Kolyma	Asia	3,513
20	Madeira	South America	3,200
21	Yukon	North America	3,185
22	Indus	Asia	3,180
23	Syrdar'ya	Asia	3,078
24	Salween	Asia	3,060
25	Sao Francisco	South America	2,900
26	Rio Grande	North America	2,870
27	Danube	Europe	2,850
28	Brahmaputra	Asia	2,840
29	Euphrates	Asia	2,815
30	Para-Tocantis	South America	2,750

Waterfalls: *the highest*

	Name	*Location*	*Height (m)*
1	Angel	Venezuela	979
2	Tugela	South Africa	948
3	Utigard	Norway	800
4	Mongefossen	Norway	774
5	Yosemite	California, USA	739
6	Mardalsfossen	Norway	656
7	Tyssestrengane	Norway	646
8	Cuquenan	Venezuela	609
9	Ribbon	California, USA	491
10	Della	Canada	440

Notes: Estimates of the lengths of different rivers vary widely according to the rules adopted concerning the selection of tributaries to be followed, the path to take through a delta, where different hydrological systems begin and end etc. The Nile is normally taken as the world's longest river but some estimates put the Amazon as longer if a southerly path through its delta leading to the River Para is followed. Likewise, difficulties in waterfall measurements exist depending on which breaks in the fall are counted. The more famous waterfalls, Niagara and Victoria, are surprisingly small, 50m and 108m respectively; their notoriety evolving from their width and accessibility.

Population: *explosions revealed*

Largest populations, 1999

Millions

1	China	1,249.6	32	Tanzania	32.9
2	India	997.5	33	Canada	30.6
3	United States	272.9	34	Algeria	30.0
4	Indonesia	207.0	35	Kenya	29.4
5	Brazil	168.1	36	Sudan	29.0
6	Russia	146.5	37	Morocco	28.2
7	Pakistan	134.8	38	Afghanistan	25.9
8	Bangladesh	127.7	39	Peru	25.2
9	Japan	126.6	40	Uzbekistan	24.6
10	Nigeria	123.9	41	Venezuela	23.7
11	Mexico	97.4	42	Nepal	23.4
12	Germany	82.0		North Korea	23.4
13	Vietnam	77.5	44	Iraq	22.8
14	Philippines	76.8	45	Malaysia	22.7
15	Turkey	64.3	46	Romania	22.5
16	Iran	63.0	47	Taiwan	22.0
17	Ethiopia	62.8	48	Uganda	21.5
18	Egypt	62.4	49	Saudi Arabia	21.4
19	Thailand	61.7	50	Australia	19.0
20	France	60.8		Sri Lanka	19.0
21	United Kingdom	59.1	52	Ghana	18.9
22	Italy	57.6	53	Mozambique	17.3
23	Ukraine	49.9	54	Yemen	17.0
24	Congo	49.8	55	Netherlands	15.8
25	South Korea	46.8	56	Syria	15.7
26	Myanmar	45.0	57	Kazakhstan	15.4
27	South Africa	42.1	58	Madagascar	15.1
28	Colombia	41.4	59	Chile	15.0
29	Spain	39.4	60	Cameroon	14.7
30	Poland	38.7		Côte d'Ivoire	14.7
31	Argentina	36.6			

Largest populations, 2015

Millions

1	China	1,410.2	16	Egypt	84.4
2	India	1,230.5	17	Congo	84.0
3	United States	321.2	18	Germany	80.7
4	Indonesia	250.1	19	Turkey	79.0
5	Pakistan	204.3	20	Thailand	72.5
6	Brazil	201.4	21	France	61.9
7	Bangladesh	183.2	22	United Kingdom	60.6
8	Nigeria	165.3	23	Myanmar	55.3
9	Russia	133.3	24	Italy	55.2
10	Japan	127.5	25	Colombia	52.6
11	Mexico	119.2	26	South Korea	50.6
12	Philippines	95.9	27	Tanzania	49.3
13	Vietnam	94.4	28	South Africa	44.6
14	Ethiopia	89.8	29	Argentina	43.5
15	Iran	87.1	30	Ukraine	43.3

Fastest growing populations, 1995–2000

Average annual growth, %

Rank	Country	%
1	Rwanda	8.5
2	Liberia	7.1
3	Yemen	4.2
4	West Bank and Gaza	3.8
5	Somalia	3.6
6	Niger	3.5
	Saudi Arabia	3.5
8	Oman	3.3
	Togo	3.3
10	Chad	3.2
	Mauritania	3.2
12	Gambia, The	3.1
13	Bosnia	3.0
	Congo-Brazzaville	3.0
	Uganda	3.0
16	Angola	2.9
	Jordan	2.9
	Madagascar	2.9
	Singapore	2.9
20	Cambodia	2.8

Slowest growing populations, 1995–2000

Average annual growth, %

Rank	Country	%
1	Estonia	-1.3
2	Bulgaria	-1.1
3	Ukraine	-0.8
4	Latvia	-0.8
5	Hungary	-0.5
	Kazakhstan	-0.5
7	Russia	-0.4
8	Albania	-0.3
	Belarus	-0.3
	Georgia	-0.3
11	Moldova	-0.2
	Romania	-0.2
13	Czech Republic	-0.1
	Lithuania	-0.1
15	Poland	0.0
	Serbia & Montenegro	0.0
	Slovenia	0.0
	Sweden	0.0
19	Austria	0.1
	Italy	0.1

Fastest growing populations, 2000–2005

Average annual growth, %

Rank	Country	%
1	Liberia	5.5
2	Sierra Leone	4.5
3	Eritrea	4.2
	Somalia	4.2
5	Yemen	4.1
6	Afghanistan	3.7
7	Niger	3.6
	West Bank and Gaza	3.6
9	Congo	3.3
	Oman	3.3
11	Uganda	3.2
12	Chad	3.1
	Saudi Arabia	3.1
14	Angola	3.0
	Burkina Faso	3.0
	Burundi	3.0
	Congo-Brazzaville	3.0
	Mauritania	3.0
19	Mali	2.9
20	Madagascar	2.8

Slowest growing populations, 2000–2005

Average annual growth, %

Rank	Country	%
1	Lithuania	-0.2
2	Estonia	-1.1
3	Bulgaria	-1.0
4	Ukraine	-0.9
5	Latvia	-0.6
	Russia	-0.6
7	Georgia	-0.5
	Hungary	-0.5
9	Belarus	-0.4
	Kazakhstan	-0.4
11	Moldova	-0.3
	Romania	-0.3
13	Serbia, Montenegro	-0.2
14	Austria	-0.1
	Czech Republic	-0.1
	Italy	-0.1
	Poland	-0.1
	Slovenia	-0.1
	Sweden	-0.1
	Switzerland	-0.1

Population density

Highest population density

Population per sq km, 1999

1	Macau	26,301	21	Sri Lanka	294
2	Hong Kong	6,628	22	Haiti	283
3	Singapore	6,384	23	Réunion	279
4	West Bank and Gaza	2,964	24	Netherlands Antilles	271
5	Malta	1,230	25	Guadeloupe	267
6	Bermuda	1,128	26	Burundi	260
7	Bangladesh	981	27	Trinidad & Tobago	252
8	Bahrain	910	28	Philippines	249
9	Barbados	629	29	United Kingdom	246
10	Mauritius	579	30	Jamaica	240
11	South Korea	475	31	Vietnam	238
12	Netherlands	466	32	Germany	235
13	Puerto Rico	439	33	Italy	196
14	Lebanon	418	34	Switzerland	180
15	Rwanda	337	35	Pakistan	175
16	India	336	36	Dominican Republic	174
	Japan	336	37	Nepal	164
18	Belgium	312	38	Nigeria	136
19	El Salvador	297	39	Armenia	135
20	Israel	296	40	China	134

Lowest population density

Population per sq km, 1999

1	Australia	2		Papua New Guinea	10
	Mongolia	2		Turkmenistan	10
	Namibia	2	23	Oman	11
4	Botswana	3	24	Sudan	12
	Canada	3	25	Algeria	13
	Iceland	3		Argentina	13
	Libya	3		Paraguay	13
	Mauritania	3		Zambia	13
9	Suriname	3	29	New Zealand	14
10	Central African Rep	6	30	Norway	15
	Chad	6	31	Finland	17
	Gabon	5	32	Uruguay	19
	Kazakhstan	6	33	Brazil	20
14	Bolivia	8		Chile	20
	Congo-Brazzaville	8		Peru	20
	Niger	8	36	Bahamas	22
17	Mali	9		Congo	22
	Russia	9		Laos	22
	Saudi Arabia	9		Mozambique	22
20	Angola	10		Sweden	22

Note: Estimates of population density refer to the total land area of a country. In countries such as Japan and Canada, where much of the land area is virtually uninhabitable, the effective population densities of the habitable areas are much greater than the figures suggest.

Regional variations

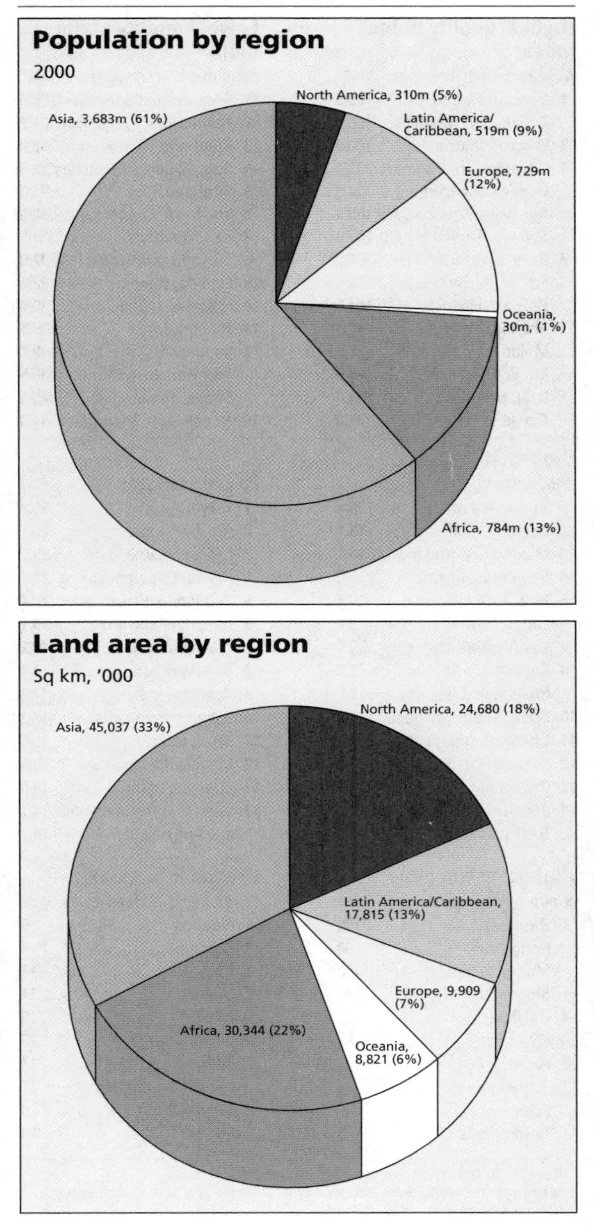

City living

Highest quality of life index[a]

New York=100, November 2000

1	Vancouver, Canada	106.5
	Zurich, Switzerland	106.5
3	Vienna, Austria	106.0
4	Copenhagen, Denmark	105.5
	Geneva, Switzerland	105.5
6	Auckland, New Zealand	105.0
	Sydney, Australia	105.0
8	Bern, Switzerland	104.5
	Frankfurt, Germany	104.5
	Helsinki, Finland	104.5
11	Amsterdam, Neth.	104.0
	Melbourne, Australia	104.0
	Munich, Germany	104.0
	Oslo, Norway	104.0
	Stockholm, Sweden	104.0

Lowest quality of life index[a]

New York=100, November 2000

1	Brazzaville, Congo-Braz.	26.5
2	Pointe Noire, Congo-Braz.	31.5
3	Khartoum, Sudan	32.0
4	Bangui, Cent African Rep	32.5
5	Baghdad, Iraq	33.0
6	Kinshasa, Congo	36.5
7	Bamako, Mali	37.0
	Ouagadougou, Burkina Faso	37.0
9	Luanda, Angola	38.5
10	Ndjamena, Chad	39.0
11	Niamey, Niger	39.5
12	Conakry, Guinea	40.5
	Port Harcourt, Nigeria	40.5
	Sanaa, Yemen	40.5
15	Nouakchott, Mauritania	41.0

Biggest cities[b]

Population m, 2000

1	Tokyo, Japan	26.4
2	Bombay, India	18.1
	Mexico city, Mexico	18.1
4	Sao Paulo, Brazil	17.8
5	New York, US	16.6
6	Lagos, Nigeria	13.4
7	Los Angeles, US	13.1
8	Calcutta, India	12.9
	Shanghai, China	12.9
10	Buenos Aires, Argentina	12.6
11	Dhaka, Bangladesh	12.3
12	Karachi, Pakistan	11.8
13	Delhi, India	11.7
14	Jakarta, Indonesia	11.0
	Osaka, Japan	11.0

Population m, 2015

1	Tokyo, Japan	26.4
2	Bombay, India	26.1
3	Lagos, Nigeria	23.2
4	Dhaka, Bangladesh	21.1
5	Sao Paulo, Brazil	20.4
6	Karachi, Pakistan	19.2
	Mexico city, Mexico	19.2
8	New York, US	17.4
9	Calcutta, India	17.3
	Jakarta, Indonesia	17.3
11	Delhi, India	16.8
12	Manila, Philippines	14.8
13	Shanghai, China	14.6
14	Buenos Aires, Argentina	14.1
	Los Angeles, US	14.1

Highest urban pop.

% pop. living in urban areas, 1999

1	Bermuda	100
	Hong Kong	100
	Macau	100
	Singapore	100
4	Belgium	97
	Kuwait	97
6	Israel	91
7	Argentina	89
	Lebanon	89
	Netherlands	89

Lowest urban pop.

% pop. living in urban areas, 1999

1	Rwanda	6
2	Burundi	9
3	Nepal	12
4	Uganda	14
5	Malawi	15
6	Cambodia	16
7	Ethiopia	17
	Papua New Guinea	17
9	Burkina Faso	18
	Eritrea	18

a Based on 39 factors ranging from recreation to political stability.
b Urban agglomerations. Estimates of cities' populations vary according to where geographical boundaries are defined.

Cities with most car ownership

Cars per 1,000 population

1	Suva, Fiji	668
2	Des Moines, US	657
3	Seattle, US	654
4	Lyon, France	542
5	Hamilton, New Zealand	540
6	Brest, France	525
7	Auckland, New Zealand	500
	Bordeaux, France	500
	Melbourne, Australia	500
	Prague, Czech Republic	500
11	Atlanta, US	473
12	Duisburg, Germany	471
13	Rennes, France	450
14	Cologne, Germany	445
15	Koper, Slovenia	443

Cities with least car ownership

Cars per 1,000 population

1	Kathmandu, Nepal	3
	Mbale, Uganda	3
	Tangail, Bangladesh	3
4	Ibadan, Nigeria	4
	Kano, Nigeria	4
	Lagos, Nigeria	4
7	Mzuzu, Malawi	5
8	Dhaka, Bangladesh	7
	Podgorica, Serbia & Montenegro	7
	Zomba, Malawi	7
11	Monrovia, Liberia	8
	Tamale, Ghana	8

Public transport use

Highest % of work journeys by public transport, selected cities

1	Tbilisi, Georgia	98
	Yervan, Armenia	98
3	Moscow, Russia	85
	Ulan Bator, Mongolia	85
5	Baku, Azerbaijan	80
6	Bombay, India	79
7	Bogota, Colombia	75
	Monrovia, Liberia	75
	Sofia, Bulgaria	75
10	Colombo, Sri Lanka	74
11	Bratislava, Slovakia	72
12	Recife, Brazil	70
13	Nairobi, Kenya	68

Lowest % of work journeys by public transport, selected cities

1	Porto Novo, Benin	0
2	Luanda, Angola	3
3	Lilongwe, Malawi	5
4	Auckland, New Zealand	6
	Yaoundé, Cameroon	6
6	Bangui, Cent African Rep	7
7	Gulbarga, Pakistan	8
8	Windhoek, Nambia	9
9	Douala, Cameroon	11
10	Bamako, Mali	12
11	Cardiff, United Kingdom	13
	Maputo, Mozambique	13
13	Amman, Jordan	14

Tallest habitable buildings

Height[a], m

1	Petronas Towers, Kuala Lumpur	452
2	Sears Tower, Chicago	443
3	World Trade Centre, New York	417
4	Jin Mao Building, Shanghai	382
5	Empire State Building, New York	381
6	T&C Building, Kao-hsiung	348

Cities with most skyscrapers[b]

Number

1	New York	140
2	Chicago	68
3	Hong Kong	36
	Houston	36
5	Kuala Lumpur	25
6	Los Angeles	24
7	Dallas	22
8	San Francisco	20
	Shanghai	20
10	Singapore	18
	Sydney	18

a Excluding spires.
b Habitable buildings of more than 153 metres.

Population: *age and sex*

Youngest populations

% aged under 15, 2000

1	Yemen	50.1	21	Rwanda	44.3
2	Niger	49.9		Senegal	44.3
3	Uganda	49.2		Togo	44.3
4	Congo	48.8	24	Sierra Leone	44.2
5	Burkina Faso	48.7	25	Guinea	44.1
6	Angola	48.2		Mauritania	44.1
7	Somalia	48.0		Oman	44.1
8	Burundi	47.6	28	Cambodia	43.9
9	Chad	46.5		Eritrea	43.9
	Zambia	46.5		Mozambique	43.9
11	Benin	46.4	31	Namibia	43.7
	West Bank and Gaza	46.4	32	Guatemala	43.6
13	Congo-Brazzaville	46.3	33	Afghanistan	43.5
	Malawi	46.3		Guinea-Bissau	43.5
15	Mali	46.1		Kenya	43.5
16	Ethiopia	45.2	36	Cameroon	43.1
	Zimbabwe	45.2	37	Central African Rep	43.0
18	Nigeria	45.1	38	Saudi Arabia	42.9
19	Tanzania	45.0	39	Bhutan	42.7
20	Madagascar	44.7		Laos	42.7

Oldest populations

% aged over 65, 2000

1	Italy	24.1	21	Norway	19.6
2	Greece	23.4	22	Luxembourg	19.4
3	Germany	23.2	23	Slovenia	19.2
	Japan	23.2	24	Belarus	18.9
5	Sweden	22.4	25	Romania	18.8
6	Belgium	22.1	26	Georgia	18.7
7	Spain	21.8	27	Lithuania	18.6
8	Bulgaria	21.7	28	Russia	18.5
9	Switzerland	21.3	29	Czech Republic	18.4
10	Latvia	20.9	30	Netherlands	18.3
11	Portugal	20.8		Serbia & Montenegro	18.3
12	Austria	20.7	32	Uruguay	17.2
13	United Kingdom	20.6	33	Malta	17.0
14	France	20.5	34	Canada	16.7
	Ukraine	20.5	35	Poland	16.6
16	Croatia	20.2	36	Australia	16.3
	Estonia	20.2	37	United States	16.1
18	Denmark	20.0	38	Cyprus	15.7
19	Finland	19.9	39	New Zealand	15.6
20	Hungary	19.7	40	Slovakia	15.4

Median age[a]

Years, 2000

Rank	Country	Years
1	Japan	41.2
2	Italy	40.6
3	Germany	40.0
4	Sweden	39.9
5	Finland	39.4
5	Greece	39.4
7	Belgium	39.3
8	Denmark	39.0
9	Bulgaria	38.8
	Croatia	38.8
11	Switzerland	38.3
12	United Kingdom	38.2
13	Hungary	38.1
	Slovenia	38.1
15	Spain	37.9
16	Austria	37.8
	Luxembourg	37.8
	Netherlands	37.8
19	Latvia	37.7
20	France	37.6
	Ukraine	37.6
22	Czech Republic	37.5
	Estonia	37.5
24	Norway	37.4
25	Portugal	37.3
26	Canada	36.8
27	Russia	36.7
28	Belarus	36.4
29	Malta	36.1
30	Lithuania	36.0
31	Hong Kong	35.9
32	United States	35.8
33	Serbia & Montenegro	35.6
34	Australia	35.3
35	Bosnia	35.1
	Poland	35.1
37	Qatar	35.0
38	Romania	34.9
39	Singapore	34.4
40	Georgia	34.1

Most male populations

No. of men per 100 women[b], 2000

Rank	Country	Men per 100 women
1	United Arab Emirates	195
2	Qatar	184
3	Kuwait	139
4	Bahrain	135
5	Saudi Arabia	115
6	Oman	113
7	Brunei	111
8	Papua New Guinea	109
9	Jordan	108
	Libya	108
11	Afghanistan	107
12	Bangladesh	106
	China	106
	India	106
	Pakistan	106
	Sri Lanka	106
17	Albania	105
	Côte d'Ivoire	105
	Iran	105
	Nepal	105

Most female populations

No. of men per 100 women, 2000

Rank	Country	Men per 100 women
1	Latvia	86
2	Belarus	87
	Estonia	87
	Ukraine	87
5	Russia	88
6	Lithuania	89
7	Georgia	91
	Hungary	91
9	Moldova	92
10	Netherlands Antilles	93
	Portugal	93
	Puerto Rico	93
13	Armenia	94
	Barbados	94
	Burkina Faso	94
	Burundi	94
	Croatia	94
	Italy	94
	Kazakhstan	94
	Martinique	94
	Uruguay	94

a Age at which there are an equal number of people above and below.

b Large numbers of immigrant workers, mostly men, result in the high male ratios of several Middle East countries.

Population: *matters of breeding*

Highest crude birth rates

No. of live births per 1,000 population, 2000–05

1	Liberia	55.4	**21**	Zambia	41.5
2	Niger	55.1	**22**	Madagascar	41.4
3	Somalia	51.8	**23**	Benin	41.0
4	Angola	51.2	**24**	Nigeria	39.4
5	Uganda	50.6	**25**	West Bank and Gaza	38.9
6	Mali	49.6	**26**	Togo	38.6
7	Sierra Leone	49.0	**27**	Eritrea	38.5
8	Yemen	48.7	**28**	Tanzania	37.9
9	Chad	48.4	**29**	Gabon	37.6
10	Afghanistan	47.2	**30**	Central African Rep	37.5
11	Congo	47.1		Senegal	37.5
12	Burkina Faso	46.8	**32**	Gambia, The	37.1
13	Malawi	44.8	**33**	Cameroon	36.3
14	Guinea-Bissau	44.6	**34**	Pakistan	36.2
15	Congo-Brazzaville	44.2	**35**	Oman	35.9
16	Ethiopia	43.7	**36**	Laos	35.7
17	Mauritania	43.6	**37**	Côte d'Ivoire	35.2
18	Burundi	43.4	**38**	Zimbabwe	35.0
19	Guinea	43.3	**39**	Cambodia	34.8
20	Rwanda	42.1	**40**	Bhutan	34.7

Lowest crude birth rates

Number of live births per 1,000 population, 2000–05

1	Latvia	7.7	**21**	Hong Kong	9.5
2	Bulgaria	7.8		Poland	9.5
3	Germany	8.1	**23**	Belgium	9.6
	Ukraine	8.1		Bosnia	9.6
5	Slovenia	8.2	**25**	Finland	9.7
	Sweden	8.2	**26**	Slovakia	10.2
7	Austria	8.3	**27**	Georgia	10.3
8	Italy	8.5	**28**	Romania	10.4
	Russia	8.5	**29**	Netherlands	10.5
	Switzerland	8.5	**30**	United Kingdom	10.6
11	Czech Republic	8.7	**31**	Canada	10.8
	Estonia	8.7		Singapore	10.8
	Lithuania	8.7	**33**	Denmark	11.0
	Macau	8.7		Portugal	11.0
15	Greece	8.8		Serbia & Montenegro	11.0
	Hungary	8.8	**36**	Macedonia	11.3
	Spain	8.8	**37**	Norway	11.4
18	Belarus	9.1	**38**	Croatia	11.5
19	Japan	9.2	**39**	Moldova	11.5
20	Armenia	9.3	**40**	Cuba	11.6

Notes: The crude birth rate is the number of live births in one year per 1,000 population. In addition to the fertility rate (see below) it depends on the population's age structure and will tend to be higher if there is a large proportion of women of childbearing age.

The fertility rate is the average number of children born to a woman who completes her childbearing years.

Highest fertility rates

Average number of children per woman, 1995–2000

1	Niger	8.0
2	Yemen	7.6
3	Angola	7.2
	Somalia	7.2
5	Uganda	7.1
6	Mali	7.0
7	Afghanistan	6.9
	Burkina Faso	6.9
8	Burundi	6.8
	Ethiopia	6.8
	Liberia	6.8
	Malawi	6.8
13	Chad	6.7
	Congo	6.7
15	Sierra Leone	6.5
16	Congo-Brazzaville	6.3
	Guinea	6.3
	Mozambique	6.3
19	Rwanda	6.2
20	Saudi Arabia	6.1

Lowest fertility rates

Average number of children per woman, 1995–2000

1	Bulgaria	1.1
2	Czech Republic	1.2
	Estonia	1.2
	Hong Kong	1.2
	Italy	1.2
	Macau	1.2
	Russia	1.2
	Slovenia	1.2
	Spain	1.2
10	Belarus	1.3
	Germany	1.3
	Greece	1.3
	Romania	1.3
	Ukraine	1.3
15	Armenia	1.4
	Austria	1.4
	Bosnia	1.4
	Hungary	1.4
	Lithuania	1.4

Highest teenage birth rates

No. of births per 1,000 women aged 15–19

1	Angola	219
2	Congo	217
3	Liberia	213
	Somalia	213
5	Sierra Leone	202
6	Niger	199
7	Guinea	193
8	Guinea-Bissau	190
9	Chad	185
10	Mali	181
11	Uganda	180
12	Gabon	172
13	Malawi	162
14	Burkina Faso	157
15	Gambia, The	155
16	Afghanistan	153
17	Ethiopia	152
	Nicaragua	152
19	Central African Rep	142
20	Congo-Brazzaville	141

Lowest teenage birth rates

No. of births per 1,000 women aged 15–19

1	North Korea	2
2	Japan	4
	Netherlands	4
	South Korea	4
	Switzerland	4
6	China	5
7	Hong Kong	7
	Italy	7
	Singapore	7
	Sweden	7
11	Spain	8
12	Denmark	9
	France	9
14	Belgium	11
	Germany	11
16	Luxembourg	12
	Malta	12
18	Greece	13
	Norway	13
	Tunisia	13

The world economy

Biggest economies

GDP, $bn

1	United States	9,152.1	26	Poland	155.2
2	Japan	4,346.9	27	Norway	152.9
3	Germany	2,111.9	28	Indonesia	142.5
4	United Kingdom	1,441.8	29	Saudi Arabia	139.4
5	France[a]	1,432.3	30	South Africa	131.1
6	Italy	1,171.0	31	Finland	129.7
7	China	989.5	32	Greece	125.1
8	Brazil	751.5	33	Thailand	124.4
9	Canada	634.9	34	Portugal	113.7
10	Spain	595.9	35	Iran	110.8
11	Mexico	483.7	36	Venezuela	102.2
12	India	447.3	37	Israel	100.8
13	South Korea	406.9	38	Ireland	93.4
14	Australia	404.0	39	Egypt	89.1
15	Russia	401.4	40	Colombia	86.6
16	Netherlands	393.7	41	Singapore	84.9
17	Taiwan	288.7	42	Malaysia	79.0
18	Argentina	283.2	43	Philippines	76.6
19	Switzerland	258.6	44	Chile	67.5
20	Belgium	248.4	45	Pakistan	58.2
21	Sweden	238.7	46	New Zealand	54.7
22	Austria	208.2	47	Czech Republic	53.1
23	Turkey	185.7	48	Peru	51.9
24	Denmark	174.3	49	Hungary	48.4
25	Hong Kong	158.9	50	Algeria	47.9

Biggest economies by purchasing power

GDP PPP, $bn

1	United States	8,878	21	South Africa	367
2	China	4,452	22	Thailand	358
3	Japan	3,186	23	Iran	347
4	India	2,226	24	Poland	324
5	Germany	1,930	25	Philippines	296
6	France	1,349	26	Belgium	263
7	United Kingdom	1,322	27	Pakistan	250
8	Italy	1,268	28	Colombia	232
9	Brazil	1,163	29	Saudi Arabia	223
10	Russia	1,022	30	Egypt	217
11	Mexico	780	31	Switzerland	205
12	Canada	776	32	Austria	199
13	South Korea	728	33	Bangladesh	196
14	Spain	704		Sweden	196
15	Indonesia	550	35	Malaysia	173
16	Taiwan	467	36	Ukraine	168
17	Australia	452	37	Greece	166
18	Argentina	437	38	Portugal	158
19	Turkey	415	39	Hong Kong	152
20	Netherlands	386	40	Algeria	145

a Includes overseas departments.

For list of all countries with their GDP see pages 234–237.

Regional GDP

$bn, 1999		*% annual growth 1990–99*	
World	30,610	World	3.1
Advanced economies	24,560	Advanced economies	2.6
G7	20,290	G7	2.4
EU15	8,500	EU15	1.9
Asia[a]	2,040	Asia[a]	7.6
Latin America	1,990	Latin America	3.3
Eastern Europe[b]	910	Eastern Europe[b]	-4.1
Middle East and Europe[c]	680	Middle East and Europe[c]	3.5
Africa	420	Africa	2.3

Regional purchasing power

GDP in PPP, % of total		*$ per head*	
World	100.0	World	8,190
Advanced economies	57.1	Advanced economies	25,320
G7	45.4	G7	26,980
EU15	20.0	EU15	22,210
Asia[a]	21.6	Asia[a]	3,680
Latin America	8.4	Latin America	6,870
Eastern Europe[b]	5.9	Eastern Europe[b]	6,230
Middle East and Europe[c]	3.9	Middle East and Europe[c]	5,240
Africa	3.2	Africa	1,790

Regional population and countries

% of total (6.1bn)		*No. of countries[d]*	
Advanced economies	15.4	Advanced economies	29
G7	11.5	G7	7
EU15	6.2	EU15	15
Asia[a]	52.0	Asia[a]	25
Latin America	8.5	Latin America	33
Eastern Europe[b]	6.7	Eastern Europe[b]	28
Middle East and Europe[c]	5.1	Middle East and Europe[c]	16
Africa	12.2	Africa	51

Regional international trade

Exports of goods and services, % of tot.		*Current account balances, $bn*	
Advanced economies	75.7	Advanced economies	-133.1
G7	47.7	G7	-219.1
EU15	36.0	EU15	22.4
Asia[a]	9.2	Asia[a]	46.7
Latin America	4.5	Latin America	-55.7
Eastern Europe[b]	4.3	Eastern Europe[b]	-1.7
Middle East and Europe[c]	4.2	Middle East and Europe[c]	6.0
Africa	2.1	Africa	-15.5

a Excludes Hong Kong, Japan, Singapore, South Korea and Taiwan.
b Includes Russia and other CIS.
c Includes Turkey.
d IMF definition.

Living standards

Highest GDP per head

$

		$			$
1	Luxembourg	42,930	36	Guadeloupe[b]	12,220
2	Bermuda	41,000	37	Cyprus	11,960
3	Switzerland	36,310	38	Greece	11,870
4	Japan	34,340		Réunion[b]	11,870
	Norway	34,340	40	Portugal	11,380
6	United States	33,540	41	Netherlands Antilles[a]	11,160
7	Denmark	32,780	42	Slovenia	10,100
8	Iceland	29,590	43	Bahrain	9,950
9	Sweden	26,950	44	Puerto Rico	9,820
10	Singapore	26,360	45	Malta	9,210
11	Germany	25,750	46	South Korea	8,690
12	Austria	25,740	47	Barbados	8,590
13	Finland	25,090	48	Argentina	7,740
14	Ireland	25,060	49	Oman	6,640
15	Netherlands	24,910	50	Saudi Arabia	6,500
16	United Kingdom	24,390	51	Uruguay	6,280
17	Belgium	24,300	52	Libya	5,960
18	France	23,560	53	Trinidad & Tobago	5,310
19	Hong Kong	23,110	54	Czech Republic	5,170
20	Australia	21,270	55	Mexico	4,970
21	Canada	20,750	56	Hungary	4,810
22	Italy	20,310	57	Croatia	4,580
23	Qatar[a]	18,630	58	Chile	4,490
24	French Polynesia	16,920	59	Brazil	4,470
25	United Arab Emirates	16,780	60	Venezuela	4,310
26	Israel	16,550	61	Costa Rica	4,220
27	Bahamas	15,500	62	Lebanon	4,030
28	Kuwait	15,370	63	Poland	4,010
29	New Caledonia	15,160	64	Suriname[a]	3,870
30	Spain	15,120	65	Botswana	3,780
31	Brunei[a]	15,060	66	Slovakia	3,650
32	Martinique[b]	14,540	67	Estonia	3,630
33	New Zealand	14,300		Mauritius	3,630
34	Taiwan	13,200	69	Gabon	3,600
35	Macau	13,140	70	Malaysia	3,480

Lowest GDP per head

$

		$			$
1	Ethiopia	100	12	Nepal	210
2	Burundi	110	13	Mozambique	230
	Congo	110	14	Burkina Faso	240
4	Liberia[a]	130		Rwanda	240
	Myanmar[a]	130	16	Mali	250
6	Sierra Leone	140		Madagascar	250
7	Eritrea	160	18	Kirgizstan	260
8	Malawi	170	19	Cambodia	270
9	Guinea-Bissau	180		Moldova	270
10	Niger	190		Tanzania	270
11	Chad	200			

a Estimate. b 1998

Highest purchasing power

GDP per head in PPP (USA = 100)

1	Luxembourg	129.2
2	United States	100.0
3	Switzerland	90.1
4	Norway	88.2
5	Iceland	85.3
6	Brunei[b]	85.1
7	Belgium	80.6
8	Denmark	80.2
9	Bermuda[b]	79.7
	Canada	79.7
11	Japan	78.9
12	Austria	77.1
13	Netherlands	76.5
14	Australia	74.7
15	Germany	73.7
16	France	72.1
17	Finland	70.8
18	Hong Kong	70.7
19	Ireland	70.4
20	Singapore	69.9
21	French Polynesia	69.6
	United Kingdom	69.6
23	Euro area	69.5
24	Sweden	69.4
25	Italy	68.9
26	New Caledonia	66.2
27	United Arab Emirates[b]	64.5
28	Cyprus	59.8
29	Israel	56.6
30	Spain	55.9
31	New Zealand	55.2
32	Macau	53.1
33	Slovenia	50.3
34	Portugal	49.7
35	Greece	49.5
36	South Korea	48.7
37	Bahamas	48.6
38	Martinique[b]	46.3
39	Barbados	43.9
40	Guadeloupe[b]	40.6
41	Czech Republic	40.2
42	Bahrain[b]	39.5
43	Réunion[b]	38.7
44	Argentina	37.4
45	Hungary	34.6
	Saudi Arabia	34.6
47	Slovakia	32.7
48	Mauritius	28.0
49	Uruguay	27.4
50	South Africa	27.3
51	Chile	26.4
52	Poland	26.3
53	Estonia	25.7
54	Mexico	25.3
55	Costa Rica	24.7
56	Trinidad & Tobago	24.1
57	Malaysia	23.9
58	Croatia	22.8
59	Russia	21.9
60	Belarus	21.6
61	Brazil	21.4
62	Botswana	20.5
63	Lithuania	20.3
64	Turkey	20.2
65	Latvia	19.5
66	Romania	18.7
67	Thailand	18.6
68	Tunisia	17.9
69	Colombia	17.5
	Namibia	17.5

Lowest purchasing power

GDP per head in PPP (USA = 100)

1	Sierra Leone	1.4
2	Tanzania	1.6
3	Congo-Brazzaville	1.7
4	Burundi	1.8
	Malawi	1.8
6	Ethiopia	1.9
7	Guinea-Bissau	2.0
8	Mali	2.3
	Niger	2.3
	Yemen	2.3
	Zambia	2.3
12	Nigeria	2.4
13	Congo[b]	2.5
	Madagascar	2.5
	Mozambique	2.5
16	Chad	2.6
17	Rwanda	2.8
18	Benin	2.9
19	Burkina Faso	3.0
20	Tajikistan	3.1

Note: for definition of purchasing power parity see page 233.

The quality of life

Human development index

Rank	Country	Index
1	Canada	93.5
2	Norway	93.4
3	Australia	92.9
	United States	92.9
5	Iceland	92.7
6	Sweden	92.6
7	Belgium	92.5
	Netherlands	92.5
9	Japan	92.4
10	United Kingdom	91.8
11	Finland	91.7
	France	91.7
13	Switzerland	91.5
14	Denmark	91.1
	Germany	91.1
16	Austria	90.8
	Luxembourg	90.8
18	Ireland	90.7
19	Italy	90.3
	New Zealand	90.3
21	Spain	89.9
22	Cyprus	88.6
23	Israel	88.3
24	Singapore	88.1
25	Greece	87.5
26	Hong Kong	87.2
27	Malta	86.5
28	Portugal	86.4
29	Slovenia	86.1
30	Barbados	85.8
31	South Korea	85.4
32	Brunei	84.8
33	Bahamas	84.4
34	Czech Republic	84.3
35	Argentina	83.7
36	Kuwait	83.6
37	Chile	82.6
38	Slovakia	82.5
	Uruguay	82.5
40	Bahrain	82.0
41	Qatar	81.9
42	Hungary	81.7
43	Poland	81.4
44	United Arab Emirates	81.0
45	Estonia	80.1
46	Costa Rica	79.7
47	Croatia	79.5
48	Trinidad & Tobago	79.3
49	Lithuania	78.9
50	Mexico	78.4
51	Cuba	78.3
52	Belarus	78.1
53	Panama	77.6
54	Bulgaria	77.2
	Malaysia	77.2
56	Latvia	77.1
	Russia	77.1
58	Romania	77.0
	Venezuela	77.0
60	Fiji	76.9
61	Suriname	76.6
62	Colombia	76.4
63	Macedonia	76.3
64	Georgia	76.2
65	Mauritius	76.1
66	Libya	76.0
67	Kazakhstan	75.4
68	Brazil	74.7
	Saudi Arabia	74.7
70	Thailand	74.5
71	Philippines	74.4
	Ukraine	74.4
73	Peru	73.7
74	Paraguay	73.6
75	Jamaica	73.5
	Lebanon	73.5
77	Sri Lanka	73.3
78	Turkey	73.2
79	Oman	73.0
80	Dominican Republic	72.9

Notes: GDP or GDP per head is often taken as a measure of how developed a country is but its usefulness is limited as it refers only to economic welfare. In 1990 the UN Development Programme published its first estimate of a Human Development Index, which combined statistics on two other indicators – adult literacy and life expectancy – with income levels to give a better, though still far from perfect, indicator of human development. In 1991 average years of schooling was combined with adult literacy to give a knowledge variable. The index is shown here scaled from 0 to 100; countries scoring over 80 are considered to have high human development, those scoring from 50 to 79 have medium human development and those under 50 have low human development.

Economic freedom index

Rank	Country	Score	Rank	Country	Score
1	Hong Kong	1.30		Lithuania	2.55
2	Singapore	1.55		Panama	2.55
3	Ireland	1.65	46	Costa Rica	2.65
4	New Zealand	1.70		Latvia	2.65
5	Luxembourg	1.75	48	Greece	2.70
	United States	1.75		Guatemala	2.70
7	United Kingdom	1.80		Morocco	2.70
8	Netherlands	1.85		Oman	2.70
9	Australia	1.90		Sri Lanka	2.70
	Bahrain	1.90	53	Israel	2.75
	Switzerland	1.90		Poland	2.75
12	El Salvador	1.95	55	Jamaica	2.80
13	Chile	2.00		Malta	2.80
14	Austria	2.05	57	Cambodia	2.85
	Canada	2.05		Dominican Republic	2.85
	Denmark	2.05		Lebanon	2.85
	Estonia	2.05		Slovakia	2.85
	Japan	2.05	61	Benin	2.90
	United Arab Emirates	2.05		Jordan	2.90
20	Belgium	2.10		Slovenia	2.90
	Germany	2.10		Tunisia	2.90
	Taiwan	2.10		Turkey	2.90
23	Bahamas	2.15	66	Armenia	2.95
	Cyprus	2.15		Botswana	2.95
	Finland	2.15		Colombia	2.95
	Iceland	2.15		Mali	2.95
27	Czech Republic	2.20		Mauritius	2.95
	Thailand	2.20		Mexico	2.95
29	Argentina	2.25		Namibia	2.95
	South Korea	2.25	73	Cote d'Ivoire	3.00
	Sweden	2.25		Malaysia	3.00
32	Italy	2.30		Mongolia	3.00
	Portugal	2.30		Saudi Arabia	3.00
34	Uruguay	2.35		Swaziland	3.00
35	Barbados	2.40		Uganda	3.00
	Bolivia	2.40	79	Philippines	3.05
	Spain	2.40		Senegal	3.05
38	Norway	2.45		South Africa	3.05
39	France	2.50	82	Ghana	3.10
	Peru	2.50		Guinea	3.10
	Trinidad & Tobago	2.50		Madagascar	3.10
42	Hungary	2.55	85	Kenya	3.15
	Kuwait	2.55			

Notes: The index of economic freedom, published by the Heritage Foundation, ranks countries on the basis of ten indicators of how government intervention can restrict the economic relations between individuals. The economic indicators are trade policy, taxation, monetary policy, the banking system, foreign-investment rules, property rights, the amount of economic output consumed by the government, regulation policy, the size of the black market and the extent of wage and price controls. A country can score between 1 and 5 in each category, 1 being the most free and 5 being the least free.

Economic growth

Fastest economic growth, 1990–99

Average annual % increase in real GDP

1	Bosnia	35.2
2	China	10.7
3	Sudan	8.2
4	Vietnam	8.1
5	Singapore	8.0
6	Lebanon	7.7
7	Malaysia	7.3
8	Chile	7.2
	Uganda	7.2
10	Ireland	6.9
11	Laos	6.6
12	Myanmar	6.3
13	Mozambique	6.2
	Taiwan	6.2
15	India	6.0
16	Oman	5.9
17	Dominican Republic	5.8
18	South Korea	5.7
	Syria	5.7
20	Jordan	5.3
	Sri Lanka	5.3
22	Israel	5.2
23	Costa Rica	5.1
	Mauritius	5.1
25	El Salvador	5.0
	Eritrea	5.0
	Peru	5.0
28	Argentina	4.9
	Nepal	4.9
30	Cambodia	4.8
31	Bangladesh	4.7
	Benin	4.7
	Indonesia	4.7
	Papua New Guinea	4.7
	Thailand	4.7
36	Ethiopia	4.6
	Tunisia	4.6
38	Poland	4.5
39	Egypt	4.4
	Lesotho	4.4
41	Botswana	4.3
	Ghana	4.3
43	Bolivia	4.2
	Guatemala	4.2
	Guinea	4.2
	Mauritania	4.2
	Panama	4.2
48	Australia	4.1
49	Hong Kong	3.9
50	Burkina Faso	3.8
	Norway	3.8
	Pakistan	3.8
	Turkey	3.8
	Uruguay	3.8

Slowest economic growth, 1990–99

Average annual % increase in real GDP

1	Moldova	-11.0
2	Ukraine	-10.7
3	Azerbaijan	-9.6
4	Turkmenistan	-6.8
5	Russia	-6.1
6	Kazakhstan	-5.9
7	Kirgizstan	-5.4
8	Congo	-5.1
9	Latvia	-4.8
10	Sierra Leone	-4.7
11	Lithuania	-4.0
12	Armenia	-3.2
13	Belarus	-3.0
14	Burundi	-2.9
15	Bulgaria	-2.7
16	Rwanda	-1.5
17	Estonia	-1.3
	Haiti	-1.3
19	Uzbekistan	-1.2
20	Macedonia	-0.8
	Romania	-0.8
22	Congo-Brazzaville	-0.5
23	Croatia	0.2
	Zambia	0.2
25	Guinea-Bissau	0.3
	Jamaica	0.3
27	Angola	0.4
28	Switzerland	0.6
29	Mongolia	0.7
30	Czech Republic	0.8
31	Hungary	1.0
32	Cameroon	1.3
	Germany	1.3
	Japan	1.3
35	Italy	1.4
36	France	1.5
37	Algeria	1.6
	Saudi Arabia	1.6
	Sweden	1.6
40	Belgium	1.7
	Madagascar	1.7
	Venezuela	1.7

Fastest economic growth, 1980–90

Average annual % increase in real GDP

1	Botswana	10.3		Indonesia	6.1
2	China	10.1	13	India	5.8
3	South Korea	9.4	14	Egypt	5.4
4	Oman	8.4		Mongolia	5.4
5	Taiwan	7.9		Turkey	5.4
6	Thailand	7.6	17	Malaysia	5.3
7	Hong Kong	6.9	18	Nepal	4.6
8	Singapore	6.7		Vietnam	4.6
9	Pakistan	6.3	20	Burundi	4.4
10	Mauritius	6.2		Lesotho	4.4
11	Chad	6.1	22	Bangladesh	4.3

Slowest economic growth, 1980–90

Average annual % increase in real GDP

1	Iraq	-6.8	12	Mauritania	0.0
2	Libya	-5.7		Saudi Arabia	0.0
3	United Arab Emirates	-2.1	14	El Salvador	0.2
4	Nicaragua	-1.9	15	Sierra Leone	0.3
5	Trinidad & Tobago	-0.8	16	Georgia	0.4
6	Argentina	-0.7		Sudan	0.4
7	Peru	-0.3		Uruguay	0.4
8	Bolivia	-0.2	19	Panama	0.5
	Haiti	-0.2		Romania	0.5
10	Mozambique	-0.1	21	Myanmar	0.6
	Niger	-0.1	22	Côte d'Ivoire	0.7

Highest industrial growth, 1990–99

Average annual % increase in real terms

1	Bosnia	35.2	6	Laos	11.8
2	China	14.4	7	Myanmar	10.1
3	Uganda	12.7	8	Cambodia	9.6
4	Mozambique	12.6	9	Malaysia	8.8
5	Vietnam	12.5			

Highest services growth, 1990–99

Average annual % increase in real terms

1	Bosnia	46.6	7	India	7.8
2	China	9.2	8	Chile	7.6
3	Uganda	8.1	9	Taiwan	7.5
	Vietnam	8.1	10	Cambodia	6.9
5	Malaysia	8.0	11	Ethiopia	6.8
	Singapore	8.0		Slovakia	6.8

Highest agricultural growth, 1990–99

Average annual % increase in real terms

1	Bosnia	14.8	6	Peru	5.6
2	Sudan	14.3	7	Mozambique	5.5
3	Zambia	9.4	8	Benin	5.3
4	Malawi	7.5		Cameroon	5.3
5	Albania	6.4		Nicaragua	5.3

Trading places

Biggest traders

% of total world exports (visible & invisible)

1	Euro area	16.62	23	Australia	1.13
2	United States	15.16	24	Russia	1.09
3	Germany	8.76	25	Thailand	0.92
4	Japan	8.03	26	Denmark	0.91
5	United Kingdom	6.82	27	Norway	0.83
6	France	5.53	28	Luxembourg	0.78
7	Italy	4.16	29	Saudi Arabia	0.76
8	Canada	3.68	30	Brazil	0.73
9	Netherlands	3.55	31	Indonesia	0.71
10	Belgium	3.21	32	Finland	0.66
11	China	2.82		India	0.66
12	Spain	2.18	34	Turkey	0.59
13	South Korea	2.15	35	Philippines	0.58
14	Switzerland	2.07	36	Poland	0.50
15	Mexico	1.88	37	Israel	0.48
16	Taiwan	1.79	38	Portugal	0.47
17	Sweden	1.57	39	Czech Republic	0.43
18	Singapore	1.33		South Africa	0.43
19	Hong Kong	1.31	41	Argentina	0.42
	Ireland	1.31	42	Hungary	0.35
21	Austria	1.29		United Arab Emirates	0.35
22	Malaysia	1.21	44	Venezuela	0.30

Most trade dependent

Trade as % of GDP[a]

1	Liberia	463.0
2	Malaysia	92.0
3	Singapore	78.8
4	Swaziland	72.3
5	United Arab Emirates	64.9
6	Panama	62.9
7	Malta	60.7
8	Belgium	60.6
	Lesotho	60.6
10	Ireland	58.8
11	Bahrain	57.5
	Mauritania	57.5
13	Gabon	57.0
14	Estonia	55.3
15	Congo-Brazzaville	55.0
16	Slovakia	54.6
17	Mongolia	52.7
18	Luxembourg	51.8
19	Czech Republic	51.2
20	Nicaragua	49.2

Least trade dependent

Trade as % of GDP[a]

1	Somalia	4.7
2	Brazil	6.5
	Sierra Leone	6.5
4	Rwanda	6.8
5	Japan	7.9
6	Argentina	8.4
7	India	9.3
8	United States	9.4
9	Madagascar[b]	10.2
10	Sudan	10.5
11	Burundi	10.7
12	Tanzania	10.9
13	Egypt	11.4
14	Serbia & Montenegro	12.0
15	Iran	12.3
16	Peru	12.4
17	Uganda	12.5
18	Euro area	12.6
19	Colombia	12.9
	Cuba	12.9

Notes: The figures are drawn from balance of payment statistics and, therefore, have differing technical definitions from trade statistics taken from customs or similar sources. The invisible trade figures do not show some countries, notably ex-Soviet republics, due to unavailable data. For Hong Kong and Singapore, domestic exports and retained imports only are used.

Biggest visible traders

% of world visible exports

Rank	Country	%	Rank	Country	%
1	United States	15.91	22	Russia	1.07
2	Euro area	15.25	23	Ireland	1.02
3	Germany	9.40	24	Thailand	0.92
4	Japan	6.34	25	Brazil	0.90
5	United Kingdom	5.38	26	Denmark	0.86
6	France	5.35	27	India	0.77
7	Canada	4.29	28	Indonesia	0.76
8	Italy	4.09	29	Norway	0.74
9	Netherlands	3.45	30	Saudi Arabia	0.71
10	China	3.27	31	Poland	0.70
11	Belgium	2.79	32	Finland	0.67
12	Mexico	2.58	33	Turkey	0.64
13	South Korea	2.43	34	Portugal	0.61
14	Spain	2.33	35	Philippines	0.59
15	Taiwan	2.11	36	United Arab Emirates	0.57
16	Switzerland	1.69	37	Israel	0.51
17	Sweden	1.48	38	Czech Republic	0.50
18	Malaysia	1.35	39	South Africa	0.49
19	Singapore	1.24	40	Hong Kong	0.47
20	Austria	1.23	41	Argentina	0.44
21	Australia	1.13	42	Hungary	0.43

Biggest invisible traders

% of world invisible exports

Rank	Country	%	Rank	Country	%
1	United States	20.02	22	Denmark	0.89
2	Euro area	17.76		Taiwan	0.89
3	United Kingdom	10.46	24	Norway	0.79
4	Japan	9.14	25	Turkey	0.69
5	Germany	6.20	26	Thailand	0.65
6	France	5.56	27	Mexico	0.61
7	Italy	3.94	28	India	0.60
8	Belgium	3.92	29	Malaysia	0.51
9	Netherlands	3.44	30	Israel	0.50
10	Hong Kong	3.10	31	Russia	0.47
11	Switzerland	2.80	32	Philippines	0.47
12	Spain	2.41		Portugal	0.47
13	Canada	2.06	34	Brazil	0.43
14	Luxembourg	2.01		Finland	0.43
15	Austria	1.49	36	Egypt	0.41
16	Ireland	1.46		Saudi Arabia	0.41
	Sweden	1.46	38	Argentina	0.39
18	Singapore	1.43	39	Greece[c]	0.38
19	Australia	1.31		Poland	0.38
20	China	1.26	41	Czech Republic	0.32
21	South Korea	1.09	42	Kuwait	0.29

a Average of imports and exports of goods as % of GDP.
b 1998
c 1997

Current account

Largest surpluses

$m

1	Japan	106,870	25	Libya	2,136
2	France	36,580	26	Ukraine	1,658
3	Switzerland	29,119	27	Luxembourg	1,314
4	Russia	25,302	28	Ecuador	955
5	South Korea	24,477	29	United Arab Emirates	600
6	Singapore	21,254	30	Ireland	595
7	Netherlands	17,275	31	Yemen	577
8	China	15,667	32	Botswana	517
9	Malaysia	12,606	33	Nigeria	506
10	Thailand	12,428	34	Saudi Arabia	412
11	Belgium	11,685	35	Jordan	405
12	Hong Kong	10,540	36	Bermuda	260
13	Taiwan	8,400	37	Syria	201
14	Philippines	7,910	38	Mauritania	140
15	Finland	7,141	39	Namibia	130
16	Italy	6,304	40	Papua New Guinea	95
17	Sweden	5,982	41	Tajikistan	67
18	Norway	5,961	42	Iraq	34
19	Indonesia	5,785	43	Zimbabwe	28
20	Kuwait	5,062	44	Guinea-Bissau	20
21	Iran	4,726	45	Swaziland	17
22	Venezuela	3,689	46	Fiji	13
23	Denmark	2,580	47	Kenya	11
24	Qatar	2,171		Nepal	11

Largest deficits

$m

1	United States	-331,480	22	Croatia	-1,522
2	Brazil	-25,073	23	Panama	-1,376
3	Australia	-23,175	24	Turkey	-1,364
4	Germany	-19,310	25	Romania	-1,297
5	United Kingdom	-15,980	26	Lithuania	-1,194
6	Mexico	-14,166	27	Slovakia	-1,155
7	Spain	-12,621	28	Vietnam[b]	-1,067
8	Poland	-12,487	29	Czech Republic	-1,032
9	Argentina	-12,312	30	Guatemala	-1,026
10	Portugal	-10,169	31	Algeria[b]	-910
11	Euro area	-6,050	32	Bosnia	-884
12	Austria	-5,747	33	Slovenia	-782
13	Greece[a]	-4,860	34	Malawi	-770
14	New Zealand	-4,341	35	Mozambique	-770
15	India	-2,784	36	Ghana	-766
16	Canada	-2,273	37	Tanzania	-765
17	Pakistan	-2,187	38	Serbia & Montenegro[b]	-703
18	Hungary	-2,101	39	Bulgaria	-685
19	Israel	-1,881	40	Bahamas	-672
20	Peru	-1,822	41	Congo[a]	-658
21	Egypt	-1,635	42	Nicaragua	-652

a 1997
b 1998

Largest surpluses as % of GDP

%

Rank	Country	%	Rank	Country	%
1	Singapore	25.0	25	Namibia	4.2
2	Kuwait	17.1	26	Indonesia	4.1
3	Malaysia	15.9	27	Norway	3.9
4	Qatar	15.4	28	Tajikistan	3.6
5	Mauritania	14.6		Venezuela	3.6
6	Switzerland	11.3	30	Taiwan	2.9
7	Philippines	10.3	31	France	2.6
8	Thailand	10.0		Papua New Guinea	2.6
9	Bermuda	9.9	33	Japan	2.5
10	Guinea-Bissau	9.2		Sweden	2.5
11	Botswana	8.6	35	China	1.6
12	Yemen	8.5	36	Denmark	1.5
13	Luxembourg	7.1	37	Nigeria	1.4
14	Hong Kong	6.6	38	United Arab Emirates	1.3
	Libya	6.6	39	Swaziland	1.2
16	Russia	6.3	40	Syria	1.0
17	South Korea	6.0	41	Fiji	0.7
18	Finland	5.5	42	Ireland	0.6
19	Ecuador	5.0	43	Italy	0.5
	Jordan	5.0		Zimbabwe	0.5
21	Belgium	4.7	45	Saudi Arabia	0.3
22	Netherlands	4.4	46	Iraq	0.2
23	Iran	4.3		Nepal	0.2
	Ukraine	4.3	48	Kenya	0.1

Largest deficits as % of GDP

%

Rank	Country	%	Rank	Country	%
1	Eritrea	-43.7	22	Latvia	-10.3
2	Malawi	-42.5	23	Honduras	-10.0
3	Lesotho	-32.1	24	Ghana	-9.9
4	Nicaragua	-28.8	25	Trinidad & Tobago	-9.4
5	Bosnia	-20.2	26	Togo	-9.0
	Kirgizstan	-20.2	27	Portugal	-8.9
7	Mozambique	-19.4	28	Mali	-8.8
8	Turkmenistan	-17.8	29	Tanzania	-8.7
9	Armenia	-16.6	30	Niger	-8.6
10	Azerbaijan	-15.0		Uganda	-8.6
11	Bahamas	-14.5	32	Laos	-8.5
12	Panama	-14.4	33	Madagascar[b]	-8.0
13	Mongolia	-12.2		Poland	-8.0
14	Burkina Faso	-12.1	35	New Zealand	-7.9
15	Gambia, The	-11.7	36	Croatia	-7.5
16	Suriname	-11.4	37	Iceland	-7.3
17	Lithuania	-11.2	38	Georgia	-7.2
18	Congo-Brazzaville[a]	-11.0	39	Bolivia	-6.7
19	Congo[a]	-10.8	40	Benin	-6.6
20	Chad	-10.5	41	Senegal	-6.4
	Liberia[b]	-10.5	42	Malta	-6.3

a 1997
b 1998

Inflation

Highest inflation, 1999–2000

% consumer price inflation

Rank	Country	%	Rank	Country	%
1	Angola	325.0	31	Macedonia	10.6
2	Belarus	168.6	32	Bulgaria	10.4
3	Suriname[a]	98.9	33	Poland	10.1
4	Ecuador	96.1	34	Madagascar[a]	9.9
5	Zimbabwe	55.7	35	Hungary	9.7
6	Turkey	54.9	36	Colombia	9.5
7	Romania	45.7		Mexico	9.5
8	Moldova	31.2	38	Namibia	9.2
9	Malawi	29.6	39	Paraguay	8.9
10	Ukraine	28.2	40	Botswana	8.7
11	Zambia	26.0	41	Jamaica	8.2
12	Ghana	25.2	42	Nepal[a]	8.0
13	Laos	25.1	43	Mongolia[a]	7.6
14	Uzbekistan	24.9	44	Brazil	7.1
15	Burundi	24.3	45	Nigeria	6.9
16	Russia	20.8	46	Jordan	6.7
17	Georgia[a]	19.1	47	Bangladesh[a]	6.2
18	Kirgizstan	18.7	48	Guatemala	6.0
19	Swaziland	16.7	49	Tanzania	5.9
20	Venezuela	16.2	50	Kenya	5.8
21	Sudan	16.0	51	Ireland	5.6
22	Papua New Guinea	15.6	52	Croatia	5.4
23	Iran	14.5	53	Cameroon[a]	5.3
24	Haiti	13.7		South Africa	5.3
25	Kazakhstan	13.1	55	Iceland	5.1
26	Slovakia	12.0	56	Uruguay	4.8
27	Nicaragua	11.5	57	Sri Lanka[a]	4.7
28	Honduras	11.1	58	Bolivia	4.6
29	Costa Rica	11.0	59	Australia	4.5
30	Slovenia	10.9	60	Philippines	4.4

Highest inflation, 1990–2000

% average annual consumer price inflation

Rank	Country	%	Rank	Country	%
1	Congo[b]	1,710.5	16	Bulgaria	108.8
2	Turkmenistan[b]	668.4	17	Romania	105.9
3	Angola	597.8	18	Croatia	92.6
4	Tajikistan[b]	467.6	19	Lithuania	91.1
5	Belarus	330.3	20	Macedonia	87.0
6	Georgia[c]	323.0	21	Suriname[c]	77.5
7	Armenia	265.5	22	Sudan[c]	76.3
8	Ukraine	240.2	23	Turkey	76.1
9	Brazil	199.9	24	Estonia	70.6
10	Kazakhstan	197.7	25	Latvia	63.9
11	Azerbaijan	177.1	26	Zambia	60.3
12	Russia	166.4	27	Mongolia[c]	59.3
13	Uzbekistan	163.9	28	Nicaragua	57.1
14	Moldova	135.9	29	Venezuela	43.3
15	Kirgizstan	116.4	30	Ecuador	42.4

Lowest inflation, 1999–2000

% consumer price inflation

1	Hong Kong	-3.6		Israel	1.1
2	Vietnam	-1.6	27	Taiwan	1.3
3	Central Africa[a]	-1.5	28	Panama	1.4
4	Argentina	-0.9		Singapore	1.4
5	Armenia	-0.8	30	Bahamas	1.6
	Cambodia	-0.8		Malaysia	1.6
	Congo-Brazzaville	-0.8		Switzerland	1.6
	Saudi Arabia	-0.8		Thailand	1.6
	Sierra Leone	-0.8	34	France	1.7
10	Guinea-Bissau[a]	-0.7	35	Azerbaijan	1.8
	Japan	-0.7	36	Morocco	1.9
	Mali	-0.7		Togo	1.9
13	Bahrain[d]	-0.4	38	Germany	2.0
14	Syria	-0.5		Mozambique[a]	2.0
15	Burkina Faso	-0.3	40	Qatar[a]	2.1
16	Myanmar	-0.1	41	El Salvador	2.3
17	Albania	0.1		South Korea	2.3
	Algeria	0.1	43	Austria	2.4
19	China	0.3		Barbados	2.4
20	Latvia	0.7		Côte d'Ivoire	2.4
21	Dominican Republic	0.8		Malta	2.4
	Senegal	0.8	47	Belgium	2.5
23	Lithuania	1.0		Italy	2.5
	Sweden	1.0		Uganda	2.5
25	Fiji	1.1	50	Netherlands Antilles	2.6

Lowest inflation, 1990–2000

% average annual consumer price inflation

1	Japan	0.8		Netherlands Antilles	2.3
2	Bahrain[e]	1.0		Norway	2.3
	Saudi Arabia	1.0		Sweden	2.3
4	Panama	1.2	19	Germany	2.4
5	France	1.7		Kuwait[c]	2.4
6	New Zealand	1.8	21	Bahamas	2.5
	Singapore	1.8		Ireland	2.5
8	Finland	1.9	23	Taiwan	2.6
	Switzerland	1.9	24	Barbados	2.8
10	Canada	2.0		Qatar[c]	2.8
11	Belgium	2.1		United States	2.8
	Denmark	2.1	27	Malta	2.9
13	Australia	2.2	28	United Kingdom	3.0
	Luxembourg	2.2	29	Iceland	3.2
15	Austria	2.3	30	Fiji	3.5

a 1998–99 d 1997–98
b 1990–97 e 1990–98
c 1990–99

Notes: Inflation is measured as the % increase in the consumer price index between two dates. The figures shown are based on the average level of the index during the relevant years.

Debt

Highest foreign debt[a]

$m

1	Brazil	244,673	24	Vietnam	23,260
2	Russia	173,940	25	Czech Republic	22,582
3	Mexico	166,960	26	Syria	22,369
4	China	154,223	27	Morocco	19,060
5	Indonesia	150,096	28	Bangladesh	17,534
6	Argentina	147,880	29	Sudan	16,132
7	South Korea	129,784	30	Ecuador	14,506
8	Turkey	101,796	31	Ukraine	14,136
9	Thailand	96,335	32	Côte d'Ivoire	13,170
10	India	94,393	33	Serbia & Montenegro	12,949
11	Poland	54,268	34	Congo	11,906
12	Philippines	52,022	35	Tunisia	11,872
13	Malaysia	45,939	36	Angola	10,871
14	Chile	37,762	37	Iran	10,357
15	Venezuela	35,852	38	Bulgaria	9,872
16	Colombia	34,538	39	Sri Lanka	9,472
17	Pakistan	34,423	40	Cameroon	9,443
18	Peru	32,284		Croatia	9,443
19	Egypt	30,404	42	Romania	9,367
20	Nigeria	29,358	43	Slovakia	9,150
21	Hungary	29,042	44	Jordan	8,947
22	Algeria	28,015	45	Lebanon	8,441
23	South Africa	24,158	46	Tanzania	7,967

Highest debt service[b]

$m

1	Brazil	63,777	22	Morocco	3,101
2	Mexico	32,658	23	Romania	2,921
3	South Korea	29,924	24	Pakistan	2,716
4	Argentina	23,141	25	Peru	2,387
5	China	19,515	26	Ukraine	2,112
6	Indonesia	16,492	27	Croatia	1,640
7	Thailand	15,237	28	Slovakia	1,570
8	Turkey	12,241	29	Egypt	1,502
9	India	9,630	30	Ecuador	1,488
10	Poland	8,046	31	Tunisia	1,401
11	Hungary	7,382	32	Côte d'Ivoire	1,368
12	Russia	6,524	33	Vietnam	1,347
13	Colombia	6,326	34	Kazakhstan	1,147
14	Philippines	6,290	35	Angola	1,099
15	Venezuela	5,011	36	Bulgaria	969
16	Algeria	4,885	37	Uruguay	947
17	Chile	4,852	38	Nigeria	884
18	Iran	4,358	39	Lebanon	882
19	Malaysia	4,290	40	Oman	711
20	South Africa	4,208	41	Bangladesh	675
21	Czech Republic	3,169	42	Jamaica	673

a Foreign debt is debt owed to non-residents and repayable in foreign currency; the figures shown include liabilities of government, public and private sectors. Developed countries have been excluded.

Highest foreign debt burden

Foreign debt as % of GDP

1	Guinea-Bissau	456.4	23	Mongolia	103.4
2	Angola	366.5	25	Honduras	102.0
3	Nicaragua	341.4	26	Guinea	97.6
4	Congo	302.7	27	Nigeria	93.4
5	Mauritania	272.8	28	Tanzania	91.3
6	Zambia	195.5	29	Ghana	90.8
7	Sierra Leone	191.7	30	Central African Rep	88.3
8	Mozambique	186.6	31	Zimbabwe	87.2
9	Sudan	182.9	32	Ethiopia	86.9
10	Laos	181.4	33	Papua New Guinea	83.0
11	Burundi	160.6	34	Panama	82.4
12	Malawi	155.1	35	Niger	81.4
13	Syria	148.9	36	Ecuador	81.2
14	Kirgizstan	144.6	37	Vietnam	81.1
15	Côte d'Ivoire	126.3	38	Bulgaria	81.0
16	Mali	124.2	39	Thailand	79.9
17	Madagascar	120.3	40	Moldova	78.9
18	Gambia, The	119.0	41	Senegal	78.3
19	Indonesia	113.3	42	Bolivia	75.8
20	Jordan	113.0	43	Chad	75.5
21	Togo	108.7	44	Yemen	74.7
22	Cameroon	108.3	45	Cambodia	73.3
23	Gabon	104.4	46	Benin	70.6

Highest debt service ratios[b]

%

1	Brazil	110.9	21	Ecuador	25.7
2	Argentina	75.8	22	Chile	25.4
3	Zambia	46.6	23	Zimbabwe	25.3
4	Burundi	45.6	24	Mexico	25.1
5	Colombia	43.5	25	Uruguay	25.0
6	Algeria	37.8	26	Moldova	24.9
7	Peru	32.7	27	South Korea	24.6
8	Bolivia	32.0	28	Morocco	24.4
9	Romania	31.3	29	Cameroon	24.3
10	Turkmenistan	31.1	30	Uganda	23.7
11	Pakistan	30.5	31	Venezuela	23.2
12	Indonesia	30.3	32	Iran	22.6
13	Macedonia	29.9	33	Thailand	22.0
	Sierra Leone	29.9	34	Kirgizstan	21.8
15	Rwanda	29.6	35	Angola	21.1
16	Mauritania	28.4	36	Poland	20.4
17	Kenya	26.7	37	Mozambique	20.0
18	Hungary	26.6	38	Ghana	19.9
19	Côte d'Ivoire	26.2	39	Croatia	19.5
	Turkey	26.2	40	Kazakhstan	19.4

b Debt service is the sum of interest and principal repayments (amortization) due on outstanding foreign debt. The debt service ratio is debt service expressed as a percentage of the country's exports of goods and services.

Aid

Largest bilateral and multilateral donors[a]

$m

1	Japan	15,323	13	Australia	982
2	United States	9,145	14	Switzerland	969
3	France	5,637	15	Belgium	760
4	Germany	5,515	16	Austria	527
5	United Kingdom	3,401	17	Finland	416
6	Netherlands	3,134	18	South Korea	317
7	Italy	1,806	19	Portugal	276
8	Denmark	1,733	20	Ireland	245
9	Canada	1,699	21	Greece	194
10	Sweden	1,630	22	Saudi Arabia	185
11	Norway	1,370	23	Kuwait	147
12	Spain	1,363	24	New Zealand	134

Largest recipients of bilateral and multilateral aid

$m

1	China	2,324	34	Angola	388
2	Indonesia	2,206	35	Romania	373
3	Russia	1,816		Rwanda	373
4	Egypt	1,579	37	Madagascar	358
5	India	1,484	38	Mali	354
6	Vietnam	1,421	39	Nepal	344
7	Bangladesh	1,203	40	Czech Republic	318
8	Bosnia	1,063		Slovakia	318
9	Thailand	1,003	42	Kenya	308
10	Tanzania	990	43	Colombia	301
11	Israel	906	44	Laos	294
12	Honduras	817	45	Guatemala	293
13	West Bank and Gaza[b]	800	46	Cambodia	279
14	Pakistan	732	47	Macedonia	273
15	Philippines	690	48	Kirgizstan	267
16	Morocco	678	49	Bulgaria	265
17	Nicaragua	675	50	Haiti	263
18	Ethiopia	633	51	Sri Lanka	251
19	Zambia	623	52	Hungary	248
20	Ghana	607	53	Tunisia	244
21	Uganda	590		Zimbabwe	244
22	Bolivia	569	55	Sudan	243
23	South Africa	539	56	Georgia	239
24	Senegal	534	57	Guinea	238
25	Albania	480	58	Syria	228
	Ukraine	480	59	Mauritania	219
27	Yemen	456		Mongolia	219
28	Peru	452	61	Papua New Guinea	216
29	Côte d'Ivoire	447	62	Benin	211
30	Malawi	446	63	Armenia	208
31	Cameroon	434	64	North Korea	201
32	Jordan	430	65	Dominican Republic	195
33	Burkina Faso	398	66	Lebanon	194

a China also provides aid, but does not disclose amounts.
b Estimate.

Largest bilateral and multilateral donors[a]

% of GDP

1	Denmark	0.99	13	Canada	0.28
2	Norway	0.94	14	Germany	0.27
3	Netherlands	0.81	15	Portugal	0.26
4	Sweden	0.72	16	Australia	0.25
5	Luxembourg	0.68		Austria	0.25
6	Kuwait	0.50		New Zealand	0.25
7	France	0.40		United Kingdom	0.25
8	Switzerland	0.37	20	Spain	0.24
9	Japan	0.35	21	United Arab Emirates	0.19
10	Finland	0.33	22	Greece	0.16
11	Belgium	0.31		Italy	0.16
12	Ireland	0.29	24	Saudi Arabia	0.14

Largest recipients of bilateral and multilateral aid

$ per head

1	Netherlands Antilles	591		Latvia	40
2	West Bank and Gaza[b]	282	35	Bahamas	39
3	Bosnia	274	36	Botswana	38
4	Israel	149	37	Eritrea	37
5	Albania	142	38	Burkina Faso	36
6	Nicaragua	137		Mauritius	36
7	Macedonia	135	40	Benin	35
8	Honduras	129		Lithuania	35
9	Namibia	105	42	Haiti	34
10	Jordan	92	43	Central African Rep	33
11	Suriname	87		Guinea	33
12	Bhutan	86	45	Bulgaria	32
13	Mauritania	84		Ghana	32
14	Mongolia	83		Mali	32
15	Bolivia	70	48	Angola	31
16	Cyprus	66		Czech Republic	31
	Malta	66		Liberia	31
18	Zambia	63	51	Cameroon	30
19	Slovakia	59		Côte d'Ivoire	30
20	Laos	58		El Salvador	30
	Senegal	58		Tanzania	30
22	Estonia	57	55	Swaziland	28
23	Kirgizstan	56	56	Uganda	27
24	Armenia	55		Yemen	27
25	Congo-Brazzaville	49	58	Gambia, The	26
26	Papua New Guinea	46		Guatemala	26
27	Lebanon	45		Tunisia	26
	Rwanda	45	61	Chad	25
29	Georgia	44		Egypt	25
	Guinea-Bissau	44		Hungary	25
31	Fiji	42	64	Madagascar	24
32	Malawi	41		Moldova	24
33	Gabon	40		Morocco	24

a China also provides aid, but does not disclose amounts.
b Estimate.

Industry and services

Largest industrial output

$bn

1	United States	2,613	26	Poland	48
2	Japan	1,582	27	Norway	45
3	Germany	583		Turkey	45
4	China	486	29	South Africa	42
5	United Kingdom	343	30	Denmark	37
6	France	324		Venezuela	37
7	Italy	299	32	Finland	35
8	Brazil	236	33	Malaysia	34
9	South Korea	179	34	Iran	31
10	Spain	157		Singapore	31
11	Canada	153	36	Egypt	30
12	Russia	143	37	Ireland	29
13	Mexico	133		Portugal	29
14	India	120	39	Greece	25
15	Australia	97	40	Algeria	24
16	Taiwan	93		Chile	24
17	Netherlands	92		Czech Republic	24
18	Argentina	79		Hong Kong	24
19	Switzerland	70	44	Colombia	23
20	Sweden	68		Philippines	23
21	Saudi Arabia	62	46	Peru	22
22	Austria	61	47	Hungary	16
	Belgium	61		Ukraine	16
	Indonesia	61	49	Nigeria	14
25	Thailand	50		Pakistan	14

Highest growth in industrial output

Average annual real % growth, 1990–99[a]

1	Bosnia	35.2		Yemen	7.9
2	China	14.4	12	Bangladesh	7.4
3	Uganda	12.7	13	Nepal	7.2
4	Mozambique	12.6	14	Dominican Republic	6.9
5	Vietnam	12.5	15	India	6.7
6	Laos	11.8		Papua New Guinea	6.7
7	Myanmar	10.1	17	Indonesia	6.5
8	Cambodia	9.6		Mali	6.5
9	Malaysia	8.8	19	Côte d'Ivoire	6.4
10	Singapore	7.9	20	Lesotho	6.3

Lowest growth in industrial output

Average annual real % growth, 1990–99[a]

1	Tajikistan	-17.2	11	Burundi	-6.7
2	Moldova	-15.9	12	Turkmenistan	-5.5
3	Ukraine	-13.5	13	Bulgaria	-4.7
4	Kirgizstan	-12.3		Macedonia	-4.7
5	Congo-Brazzaville	-11.7	15	Sierra Leone	-4.6
6	Latvia	-10.5	16	Estonia	-4.2
7	Kazakhstan	-10.1	17	Uzbekistan	-4.0
8	Russia	-9.6	18	Zambia	-3.9
9	Lithuania	-8.1	19	Belarus	-3.8
10	Armenia	-7.0	20	Croatia	-3.6

Largest manufacturing output

$bn

1	United States	1,393	21	Belgium	44
2	Japan	1,055	22	Austria	40
3	Germany	437		Thailand	40
4	China	377	24	Indonesia	35
5	France	287	25	Czech Republic	30
6	United Kingdom	273		Ireland	30
7	Italy	218	27	Poland	28
8	Brazil	175		Turkey	28
9	Russia[b]	132	29	Portugal	27
10	South Korea	122	30	Finland	26
11	Canada	110	31	South Africa	25
12	Mexico	100	32	Denmark	24
13	Spain	90		Malaysia	24
14	India	74	34	Singapore	22
	Taiwan	74	35	Egypt	18
16	Switzerland	65		Norway	18
17	Netherlands	62	37	Iran	17
18	Argentina	51		Israel	17
	Australia	51	39	Philippines	16
20	Sweden	48	40	Venezuela	15

Largest services output

$bn

1	United States	5,966	26	Poland	100
2	Japan	2,725	27	Norway	97
3	Germany	1,478	28	Greece	89
4	France	1,044	29	Finland	86
5	United Kingdom	1,016	30	South Africa	84
6	Italy	816	31	Portugal	74
7	Brazil	464	32	Thailand	62
8	Canada	412	33	Venezuela	61
9	Spain	388	34	Israel	59
10	China	327	35	Saudi Arabia	58
11	Mexico	318	36	Colombia	54
12	Netherlands	285		Singapore	54
13	Australia	281	38	Ireland	53
14	India	211	39	Indonesia	52
15	Russia	210	40	Iran	49
16	South Korea	208	41	Egypt	47
17	Switzerland	197	42	Chile	41
18	Argentina	189	43	Philippines	39
19	Taiwan	180	44	New Zealand	36
20	Belgium	179	45	Malaysia	32
21	Sweden	149		Peru	32
22	Austria	144	47	Czech Republic	30
23	Hong Kong	135	48	Hungary	29
24	Denmark	133		Pakistan	29
25	Turkey	113			

a Or nearest available years.
b 1997

Agriculture

Most economically dependent on agriculture

% of GDP from agriculture

Rank	Country	%
1	Guinea-Bissau	62
2	Myanmar	60
3	Congo-Brazzaville	58
4	Central African Rep	55
5	Albania	53
	Laos	53
7	Burundi	52
	Ethiopia	52
9	Cambodia	51
10	Mali	47
11	Rwanda	46
12	Tanzania	45
13	Cameroon	44
	Uganda	44
15	Sierra Leone	43
16	Nepal	42
17	Niger	41
	Togo	41
19	Sudan	40
20	Nigeria	39
21	Benin	38
	Kirgizstan	38
	Malawi	38
24	Chad	36
	Georgia	36
	Ghana	36
27	Mozambique	33
	Uzbekistan	33
29	Mongolia	32
	Nicaragua	32
31	Burkina Faso	31
	Gambia, The	31
33	Madagascar	30
	Papua New Guinea	30
35	Armenia	29
	Haiti	29
	Paraguay	29
38	India	28
39	Pakistan	27
	Turkmenistan	27
41	Côte d'Ivoire	26
42	Bangladesh	25
	Mauritania	25
	Moldova	25
	Vietnam	25
	Zambia	25

Least economically dependent on agriculture

% of GDP from agriculture

Rank	Country	%
1	Hong Kong	0
	Singapore	0
3	Belgium	1
	Germany	1
	United Kingdom	1
6	Austria	2
	Canada	2
	Denmark	2
	Japan	2
	Jordan	2
	Norway	2
	Trinidad & Tobago	2
	United States	2
14	Australia	3
	Finland	3
	France	3
	Italy	3
	Netherlands	3
	Poland	3
	Taiwan	3
21	Botswana	4
	Czech Republic	4
	Latvia	4
	Portugal	4
	Slovakia	4
	Slovenia	4
	South Africa	4
	Spain	4
29	Argentina	5
	Ireland	5
	Mexico	5
	South Korea	5
	Venezuela	5
34	Estonia	6
	Hungary	6
	Mauritius	6
	Uruguay	6
38	Angola	7
	Greece	7
	Jamaica	7
	Panama	7
	Peru	7
	Russia	7
	Saudi Arabia	7
45	Chile	8
	Gabon	8

Fastest growth

Average annual real % growth, 1990–99[a]

1	Bosnia	14.8	9	Benin	5.3
2	Sudan	14.3		Cameroon	5.3
3	Zambia	9.4		Nicaragua	5.3
4	Malawi	7.5	12	Mauritania	5.0
5	Albania	6.4		Yemen	5.0
6	Peru	5.6	14	Myanmar	4.9
7	Georgia	5.5		Vietnam	4.9
	Mozambique	5.5			

Slowest growth

Average annual real % growth, 1990–99[a]

1	Moldova	-16.0	10	Haiti	-3.8
2	Kazakhstan	-13.4		West Bank and Gaza	-3.8
3	Tajikistan	-12.2	12	Estonia	-3.7
4	Latvia	-8.2	13	Hungary	-3.1
	Turkmenistan	-8.2	14	Angola	-3.0
6	Russia	-7.9	15	Croatia	-2.5
7	Ukraine	-6.3		Spain	-2.5
8	Belarus	-5.4	17	Burundi	-2.0
9	Rwanda	-3.9		Colombia	-2.0

Biggest producers

'000 tonnes

Cereals

1	China	455,188	6	Russia	53,845
2	United States	335,556	7	Canada	53,785
3	India	232,487	8	Brazil	47,493
4	France	64,817	9	Germany	44,461
5	Indonesia	60,070	10	Bangladesh	35,975

Meat

1	China	61,468	6	Spain	4,962
2	United States	37,251	7	India	4,759
3	Brazil	13,744	8	Mexico	4,312
4	France	6,608	9	Russia	4,291
5	Germany	6,398	10	Italy	4,156

Fruit

1	China	62,799	6	Spain	15,447
2	India	38,561	7	France	11,701
3	Brazil	37,506	8	Iran	11,572
4	United States	28,090	9	Mexico	11,390
5	Italy	18,428	10	Turkey	10,389

Vegetables

1	China	259,619	6	Iran	14,168
2	India	59,395	7	Egypt	13,517
3	United States	39,019	8	Japan	12,794
4	Turkey	21,777	9	Russia	12,706
5	Italy	15,367	10	Spain	12,092

a Or nearest available years.

Commodities

Wheat

Top 10 producers '000 tonnes			Top 10 consumers '000 tonnes		
1	China	113,900	1	China	117,600
2	EU15	96,100	2	EU15	86,800
3	India	70,800	3	India	69,900
4	United States	62,700	4	United States	35,400
5	Russia	31,000	5	Russia	35,100
6	Canada	26,900	6	Pakistan	21,600
7	Australia	25,000	7	Turkey	15,800
8	Pakistan	17,900	8	Iran	14,800
9	Turkey	16,500	9	Egypt	13,300
10	Argentina	15,300	10	Ukraine	12,300

Rice

Top 10 producers[a] '000 tonnes			Top 10 consumers[b] '000 tonnes		
1	China	198,480	1	China	137,000
2	India	134,233	2	India	82,500
3	Indonesia	52,919	3	Indonesia	35,900
4	Bangladesh	32,298	4	Bangladesh	22,100
5	Vietnam	31,435	5	Vietnam	17,417
6	Thailand	25,000	6	Thailand	9,600
7	Myanmar	17,000	7	Japan	9,450
8	Philippines	11,957	8	Myanmar	9,330
9	Brazil	11,534	9	Philippines	8,400
10	Japan	11,470	10	Brazil	8,260

Sugar[c]

Top 10 producers '000 tonnes			Top 10 consumers '000 tonnes		
1	Brazil	20,600	1	India	15,800
2	EU15	19,300	2	EU15	15,000
3	India	17,400	3	Brazil	9,500
4	China	9,300	4	United States	9,200
5	United States	8,200	5	China	8,700
6	Australia	5,500	6	Russia	5,600
	Thailand	5,500	7	Mexico	4,500
8	Mexico	5,000	8	Pakistan	3,300
9	Cuba	3,800	9	Indonesia	2,800
10	Pakistan	3,700	10	Japan	2,500

Coarse grains[d]

Top 5 producers '000 tonnes			Top 5 consumers '000 tonnes		
1	United States	263,400	1	United States	211,700
2	China	137,900	2	China	133,000
3	EU15	102,800	3	EU15	91,400
4	Brazil	33,000	4	Mexico	35,000
5	India	31,500	5	Brazil	34,200

Tea

Top 10 producers '000 tonnes			Top 10 consumers '000 tonnes		
1	India	806	**1**	India	655
2	China	676	**2**	China	478
3	Sri Lanka	284	**3**	Turkey	166
4	Kenya	249	**4**	Russia	153
5	Turkey	171	**5**	Britain	137
6	Indonesia	165		Japan	137
7	Japan	89	**7**	Pakistan	108
8	Iran	60	**8**	United States	93
9	Argentina	50	**9**	Iran	91
10	Bangladesh	47	**10**	Egypt	73

Coffee

Top 10 producers '000 tonnes			Top 10 consumers '000 tonnes		
1	Brazil	1,941	**1**	United States	1,121
2	Vietnam	676	**2**	Brazil	765
3	Colombia	560	**3**	Germany	567
4	Mexico	387	**4**	Japan	404
5	Indonesia	361	**5**	France	319
6	Côte d'Ivoire	328	**6**	Italy	307
7	India	324	**7**	Spain	188
8	Guatemala	312	**8**	United Kingdom	138
9	Ethiopia	210	**9**	Ethiopia	98
10	Uganda	186	**10**	Netherlands	95

Cocoa

Top 10 producers '000 tonnes			Top 10 consumers '000 tonnes		
1	Côte d'Ivoire	1,163	**1**	United States	656
2	Ghana	398	**2**	Germany	285
3	Indonesia	390	**3**	United Kingdom	218
4	Nigeria	198	**4**	France	186
5	Brazil	138	**5**	Japan	132
6	Cameroon	124	**6**	Brazil	125
7	Ecuador	75	**7**	Italy	97
7	Malaysia	75	**8**	Russia	93
9	Colombia	38	**9**	Spain	68
10	Papua New Guinea	35	**10**	Canada	64

a Paddy (unmilled rice, in the husk).
b Milled rice.
c Raw.
d Includes: maize (corn), barley, sorghum, rye, oats and millet.

Copper

Top 10 producers[a]
'000 tonnes

1	Chile	4,383
2	United States	1,601
3	Indonesia	790
4	Australia	711
5	Canada	614
6	Peru	536
7	China	520
8	Russia	510
9	Poland	464
10	Mexico	381

Top 10 consumers[b]
'000 tonnes

1	United States	2,988
2	China	1,484
3	Japan	1,294
4	Germany	1,133
5	South Korea	784
6	Taiwan	655
7	Italy	635
8	France	550
9	Mexico	395
10	Belgium	353

Lead

Top 10 producers[a]
'000 tonnes

1	Australia	681
2	China	549
3	United States	514
4	Peru	271
5	Canada	161
6	Mexico	126
7	Sweden	116
8	South Africa	80
9	Morocco	69
10	Poland	68

Top 10 consumers[b]
'000 tonnes

1	United States	1,745
2	China	525
3	Germany	374
4	Japan	318
5	Unite Kingdom	283
6	Italy	265
7	France	264
8	South Korea	256
9	Mexico	203
10	Spain	192

Zinc

Top 10 producers[a]
'000 tonnes

1	China	1,476
2	Australia	1,163
3	Canada	1,009
4	Peru	900
5	United States	843
6	Mexico	354
7	Kazakhstan	288
8	Ireland	226
9	Sweden	175
10	India	161

Top 10 consumers[c]
'000 tonnes

1	United States	1,341
2	China	1,196
3	Japan	634
4	Germany	564
5	South Korea	472
6	Italy	338
7	France	331
8	Belgium	275
	Taiwan	275
10	India	229

Tin

Top 5 producers[a]
'000 tonnes

1	China	80.1
2	Indonesia	47.8
3	Peru	29.7
4	Brazil	13.2
5	Bolivia	11.9

Top 5 consumers[b]
'000 tonnes

1	United States	55.6
2	China	39.5
3	Japan	23.2
4	Germany	18.0
5	South Korea	11.9

Nickel

Top 10 producers[a] *'000 tonnes*			*Top 10 consumers*[b] *'000 tonnes*		
1	Russia	252.9	**1**	Japan	159.1
2	Canada	186.2	**2**	United States	158.0
3	Australia	124.9	**3**	Taiwan	103.5
4	New Caledonia	90.3	**4**	Germany	97.4
5	Indonesia	83.9	**5**	South Korea	89.5
6	Cuba	66.5	**6**	Italy	54.6
7	China	49.5	**7**	France	49.0
8	South Africa	35.8	**8**	Finland	45.5
9	Brazil	32.4	**9**	China	38.5
10	Colombia	28.3	**10**	Belgium	35.1

Aluminium

Top 10 producers[d] *'000 tonnes*			*Top 10 consumers*[e] *'000 tonnes*		
1	United States	3,779	**1**	United States	6,203
2	Russia	3,149	**2**	China	2,926
3	China	2,599	**3**	Japan	2,100
4	Canada	2,390	**4**	Germany	1,520
5	Australia	1,719	**5**	South Korea	814
6	Brazil	1,250	**6**	France	786
7	Norway	1,020	**7**	Canada	774
8	South Africa	687	**8**	Italy	735
9	Germany	634	**9**	United Kingdom	581
10	India	614	**10**	Russia	563

Precious metals

Gold[a] *Top 10 producers* *tonnes*			*Silver*[a] *Top 10 producers* *tonnes*		
1	South Africa	447.2	**1**	Mexico	2,467
2	United States	341.0	**2**	Peru	2,217
3	Australia	300.4	**3**	United States	1,952
4	China	170.0	**4**	Australia	1,720
5	Canada	159.0	**5**	Chile	1,380
6	Indonesia	129.0	**6**	China	1,330
7	Peru	128.1	**7**	Canada	1,231
8	Russia	125.9	**8**	Poland	1,093
9	Uzbekistan	82.0	**9**	Kazakhstan	816
10	Papua New Guinea	65.8	**10**	Bolivia	424

a Mine production.
b Refined consumption.
c Slab consumption.
d Primary refined production.
e Primary refined consumption.

Rubber (natural and synthetic)

Top 10 producers
'000 tonnes

1	United States	2,354
2	Thailand	2,240
3	Indonesia	1,634
4	Japan	1,577
5	China	1,139
6	Malaysia	769
7	Russia	737
8	Germany	720
9	India	686
10	South Korea	655

Top 10 consumers
'000 tonnes

1	United States	3,230
2	China	2,112
3	Japan	1,867
4	Germany	830
5	India	783
6	South Korea	725
7	France	687
8	Brazil	482
9	Russia	451
10	Italy	421

Raw wool

Top 10 producers[a]
'000 tonnes

1	Australia	673
2	China	290
3	New Zealand	256
4	Russia	133
5	Turkey	72
6	United Kingdom	64
7	Argentina	63
	Iran	63
9	Pakistan	57
10	South Africa	55

Top 10 consumers[b]
'000 tonnes

1	China	324
2	Italy	145
3	Russia	67
4	India	61
	Turkey	61
6	Japan	48
7	United Kingdom	46
8	South Korea	42
9	Iran	34
10	United States	29

Cotton

Top 10 producers
'000 tonnes

1	China	3,829
2	United States	3,694
3	India	2,652
4	Pakistan	1,700
5	Uzbekistan	1,128
6	Turkey	791
7	Australia	712
8	Brazil	700
9	Greece	428
10	Syria	306

Top 10 consumers
'000 tonnes

1	China	4,800
2	India	2,939
3	United States	2,229
4	Pakistan	1,600
5	Turkey	1,200
6	Brazil	885
7	Mexico	530
8	Indonesia	480
9	Thailand	371
10	South Korea	337

Major oil seeds[c]

Top 5 producers
'000 tonnes

1	United States	81,894
2	China	41,269
3	Brazil	35,317
4	Argentina	27,543
5	India	20,490

Top 5 consumers
'000 tonnes

1	United States	56,689
2	China	53,733
3	EU 15	33,627
4	Brazil	24,111
5	Argentina	23,632

Oil[d]

Top 15 producers
'000 barrels per day

1	Saudi Arabia[e]	8,595
2	United States	7,760
3	Russia	6,180
4	Iran[e]	3,550
5	Mexico	3,345
6	China	3,195
	Norway	3,195
8	Venezuela[e]	3,125
9	United Kingdom	2,895
10	Canada	2,595
11	Iraq[e]	2,580
12	United Arab Emirates[e]	2,505
13	Nigeria[e]	2,030
14	Kuwait[e]	2,025
15	Indonesia[e]	1,445

Top 15 consumers
'000 barrels per day

1	United States	18,490
2	Japan	5,650
3	China	4,370
4	Germany	2,825
5	Russia	2,535
6	South Korea	2,165
7	France	2,045
8	India	2,010
9	Italy	1,955
10	Brazil	1,805
11	Canada	1,800
12	Mexico	1,775
13	United Kingdom	1,705
14	Spain	1,405
15	Saudi Arabia[e]	1,335

Natural gas

Top 10 producers
Billion cubic metres

1	Russia	551.0
2	United States	540.5
3	Canada	162.3
4	United Kingdom	99.6
5	Algeria	82.2
6	Indonesia	66.4
7	Netherlands	60.1
8	Iran	52.5
9	Uzbekistan	51.9
10	Norway	51.0

Top 10 consumers
Billion cubic metres

1	United States	617.0
2	Russia	363.6
3	United Kingdom	91.6
4	Germany	80.1
5	Japan	74.6
6	Ukraine	73.0
7	Canada	71.5
8	Italy	61.7
9	Uzbekistan	49.3
10	Saudi Arabia	46.2

Coal

Top 10 producers
Million tonnes oil equivalent

1	United States	580.5
2	China	512.1
3	Australia	149.8
4	India	144.1
5	South Africa	116.7
6	Russia	112.6
7	Poland	73.1
8	Germany	59.6
9	Ukraine	42.3
10	Indonesia	40.1

Top 10 consumers
Million tonnes oil equivalent

1	United States	543.3
2	China	511.0
3	India	150.0
4	Russia	109.3
5	Japan	91.5
6	South Africa	81.7
7	Germany	80.6
8	Poland	61.7
9	Australia	45.5
10	Ukraine	38.5

a Greasy basis.
b Clean basis.
c Soybeans, sunflower seed, cottonseed, groundnuts and rapeseed.
d Includes crude oil, shale oil, oil sands and natural gas liquids.
e Opec members.

Energy

Largest producers

Million tonnes coal equivalent, 1997

1	United States	2,506.4	16	Algeria	193.5
2	Russia	1,365.4	17	South Africa	184.1
3	China	1,271.2	18	France	168.4
4	Saudi Arabia	664.5	19	Kuwait	163.2
5	Canada	521.7	20	Japan	143.4
6	United Kingdom	381.9	21	Nigeria	141.9
7	India	344.8	22	Poland	136.1
8	Iran	333.6	23	Ukraine	117.4
9	Mexico	314.4	24	Argentina	111.4
10	Venezuela	313.3	25	Brazil	108.8
11	Indonesia	305.7	26	Libya	107.9
12	Norway	303.4	27	Malaysia	103.3
13	Australia	286.7	28	Netherlands	101.3
14	United Arab Emirates	208.6	29	Kazakhstan	93.6
15	Germany	195.0	30	Colombia	89.4

Largest consumers

Million tonnes coal equivalent, 1997

1	United States	3,123.6	16	Poland	142.3
2	China	1,208.8	17	Iran	139.8
3	Russia	832.2	18	Spain	132.9
4	Japan	654.0	19	Indonesia	129.8
5	Germany	467.1	20	South Africa	127.7
6	India	406.5	21	Saudi Arabia	123.8
7	Canada	338.7	22	Netherlands	118.5
8	France	322.2	23	Venezuela	111.0
9	United Kingdom	320.1	24	North Korea	95.9
10	Italy	238.1	25	Thailand	86.7
11	Ukraine	220.9	26	Turkey	85.6
12	South Korea	210.6	27	Argentina	78.8
13	Mexico	184.5	28	Belgium	72.8
14	Brazil	165.2	29	Uzbekistan	64.5
15	Australia	144.3	30	Malaysia	60.3

Energy efficiency

Most efficient

GDP[a] per kg of energy, 1998, $

1	Albania	10.3
2	Morocco	10.2
3	Uruguay	9.9
4	Costa Rica	9.5
5	Bangladesh	8.9
6	Hong Kong	8.5
7	Sri Lanka	8.0
8	Colombia	7.9
9	Peru	7.8
10	Dominican Republic	7.5
11	Italy	7.4
12	Argentina	7.3
13	Georgia	7.1

Least efficient

GDP[a] per kg of energy, 1998, $

1	Tanzania	1.1
	Trinidad & Tobago	1.1
	Uzbekistan	1.1
4	Nigeria	1.2
	Turkmenistan	1.2
	Ukraine	1.2
	Zambia	1.2
8	Azerbaijan	1.5
9	Russia	1.7
10	Congo-Brazzaville	1.8
	Kazakhstan	1.8
	United Arab Emirates	1.8

Largest exporters

Million tonnes coal equivalent, 1997

1	Russia	524.2	14	Nigeria	126.9
2	Saudi Arabia	495.8	15	United States	124.2
3	Norway	271.7	16	Netherlands	119.7
4	Canada	249.7	17	Libya	88.8
5	Venezuela	206.4	18	China	73.5
6	Iran	190.8	19	South Africa	71.8
7	Australia	165.6	20	Oman	61.4
8	United Arab Emirates	163.7	21	Singapore	59.0
9	Indonesia	155.4	22	Colombia	56.0
10	United Kingdom	147.9	23	Malaysia	55.0
11	Algeria	137.9	24	Iraq	48.3
12	Mexico	134.9	25	Angola	47.6
13	Kuwait	129.6			

Largest importers

Million tonnes coal equivalent, 1997

1	United States	847.0	14	China	90.6
2	Japan	575.1	15	Canada	78.0
3	Germany	326.5	16	Brazil	74.8
4	South Korea	256.1	17	Turkey	63.6
5	Italy	223.1	18	Thailand	59.0
6	France	210.0	19	Poland	43.6
7	Netherlands	151.2	20	Sweden	42.9
8	Singapore	122.2	21	Belarus	38.7
9	Spain	121.4	22	Australia	33.2
10	Ukraine	112.7	23	Hong Kong	32.5
11	United Kingdom	105.2		Philippines	32.5
12	Belgium	99.1	25	Greece	32.3
13	India	92.1			

Largest consumption per head

Kg coal equivalent, 1997

1	Qatar	44,155	16	Belgium	7,191
2	United Arab Emirates	21,203	17	Sweden	6,491
3	Bahrain	19,488	18	Saudi Arabia	6,358
4	Kuwait	13,446	19	Netherlands Antilles	5,918
5	United States	11,493	20	New Zealand	5,914
6	Canada	11,191	21	Germany	5,692
7	Brunei	11,144	22	Russia	5,636
8	Luxembourg	10,914	23	Czech Republic	5,529
9	Singapore	10,324	24	France	5,507
10	Trinidad & Tobago	9,920	25	Estonia	5,452
11	Norway	7,886	26	United Kingdom	5,446
12	Australia	7,873	27	Japan	5,189
13	Netherlands	7,588	28	Venezuela	4,873
14	Iceland	7,497	29	Ireland	4,694
15	Finland	7,390	30	Denmark	4,653

a At purchasing-power parity exchange rates.

Note: Consumption data for small countries, especially oil producers, can be unreliable, often leading to unrealistically high consumption per head rates.

Workers of the world

Highest % of population in labour force

1999 or latest

1	Kuwait	64.6	26	Slovakia	47.4
2	Singapore	58.0	27	Azerbaijan	47.0
3	China	56.0	28	Netherlands	46.8
4	Switzerland	55.9	29	Hong Kong	46.5
5	Thailand	53.8	30	Indonesia	46.3
6	Japan	53.6	31	South Korea	46.2
7	Iceland	53.4	32	Bahrain	46.1
8	Bahamas	52.5	33	Austria	46.0
9	Norway	52.4		Belarus	46.0
10	Canada	51.4	35	Brazil	45.7
11	United States	51.1		Kazakhstan	45.7
12	Czech Republic	50.9	37	Ukraine	45.6
13	Denmark	50.6	38	Ireland	45.3
14	Lithuania	50.3	39	Estonia	44.6
15	Australia	49.9	40	Bangladesh	43.9
	Finland	49.9	41	Cambodia	43.5
17	United Kingdom	49.4	42	Ethiopia	43.4
18	New Zealand	49.1	43	Trinidad & Tobago	43.2
19	Germany	48.6	44	Belgium	42.9
	Slovenia	48.6		Macau	42.9
	Sweden	48.6	46	Greece	42.2
22	Romania	48.3	47	Luxembourg	42.0
23	Latvia	47.6	48	Philippines	41.7
	Portugal	47.6		Spain	41.7
	Russia	47.6	50	Mexico	40.8

Most male workforce

Highest % men in workforce

1	Iran	87.3
2	Algeria	87.0
3	Pakistan	86.7
4	Bahrain	82.6
5	Guatemala	81.0
6	Saudi Arabia	80.7
7	Egypt	79.1
8	Kuwait	76.8
9	Tunisia	75.7
10	Dominican Republic	75.1
11	Mauritania	72.0
12	Malta	71.9
13	India	71.4
14	Morocco	70.8
15	Nicaragua	70.5
16	Sudan	69.4
17	Turkey	69.1
18	Costa Rica	66.9
19	Sri Lanka	66.6
20	Mexico	66.5

Most female workforce

Highest % women in workforce

1	Belarus	53.5
2	Cambodia	51.6
3	Bahamas	49.4
4	Ukraine	48.4
5	Lithuania	48.3
6	Estonia	48.2
7	Georgia	48.0
8	Chad	47.9
9	Azerbaijan	47.8
10	Kenya	47.7
	Mongolia	47.7
	Russia	47.7
	Sweden	47.7
14	Finland	47.4
15	Latvia	47.3
16	Croatia	46.9
17	Iceland	46.6
18	Colombia	46.5
	United States	46.5
20	Norway	46.4

Lowest % of population in labour force

1999 or latest

1	Colombia	17.1	26	Sri Lanka	35.3
2	Bolivia	17.4	27	Kirgizstan	35.9
3	Saudi Arabia	21.1	28	Chad	36.3
4	Suriname	21.8	29	Jamaica	36.7
5	Guatemala	22.3	30	Georgia	36.8
6	Mauritania	22.5	31	Turkey	37.0
7	Netherlands Antilles	25.2	32	France	37.3
8	Ecuador	25.4	33	Bulgaria	37.8
	Iran	25.4		Honduras	37.8
10	Pakistan	26.1	35	Morocco	38.2
11	Algeria	26.4	36	Israel	38.5
12	Sudan	27.5		Malta	38.5
13	Gambia, The	27.6	38	Costa Rica	38.6
14	Egypt	28.9	39	El Salvador	38.8
15	Mongolia	30.2		Panama	38.8
16	Dominican Republic	30.4		Venezuela	38.8
17	Armenia	30.5	42	Croatia	39.3
18	Peru	31.1		Moldova	39.3
19	India	31.5	44	Chile	39.5
	Tunisia	31.5	45	Poland	39.7
21	Kenya	31.6	46	Macedonia	39.9
22	Puerto Rico	33.4	47	Malaysia	40.3
23	Uruguay	33.6	48	Italy	40.5
24	Nicaragua	34.5	49	Hungary	40.7
25	Madagascar	35.2	50	Mexico	40.8

Highest rate of unemployment

% of labour force[a]

1	Armenia	36.4	21	Argentina	12.8
2	Algeria	28.7	22	France	11.9
3	Morocco	22.0		Ukraine	11.9
4	Colombia	20.1	24	Panama	11.8
5	Barbados	19.7		Puerto Rico	11.8
6	Netherlands Antilles	16.7	26	Estonia	11.7
7	Slovakia	16.2	27	Ecuador	11.5
8	Jamaica	16.0	28	Italy	11.4
9	Dominican Republic	15.9	29	Uruguay	11.3
	Spain	15.9	30	Suriname	11.0
11	Venezuela	14.9	31	Greece	10.8
12	Latvia	14.5	32	Sri Lanka	10.6
13	Bulgaria	14.4	33	Poland	10.5
14	Trinidad & Tobago	14.2	34	Finland	10.1
15	Lithuania	14.1	35	Philippines	9.4
16	Georgia	13.8	36	Brazil	9.0
17	Kazakhstan	13.7		Czech Republic	9.0
18	Croatia	13.5	38	Israel	8.9
19	Russia	13.4	39	Germany	8.8
20	Nicaragua	13.3	40	Belgium	8.6

a ILO definition.

The business world

Global competitiveness

	Overall	*Government*	*Trade blocks*
1	United States	Singapore	Finland
2	Singapore	Finland	Austria
3	Finland	Ireland	Ireland
4	Luxembourg	Hong Kong	Mexico
5	Netherlands	Australia	Luxembourg
6	Hong Kong	Switzerland	Germany
7	Ireland	Luxembourg	Denmark
8	Sweden	United States	Netherlands
9	Canada	Iceland	Belgium
10	Switzerland	Canada	Greece
11	Australia	Austria	Spain
12	Germany	Netherlands	Singapore
13	Iceland	Denmark	Sweden
14	Austria	Sweden	Hong Kong
15	Denmark	Israel	Portugal
16	Israel	Estonia	Canada
17	Belgium	New Zealand	France
18	Taiwan	Germany	Italy
19	United Kingdom	Chile	Chile
20	Norway	Taiwan	United States
21	New Zealand	Spain	United Kingdom
22	Estonia	Hungary	Iceland
23	Spain	Norway	Israel
24	Chile	United Kingdom	Malaysia
25	France	Belgium	Taiwan
26	Japan	Malaysia	South Korea
27	Hungary	Mexico	China
28	South Korea	Slovakia	Estonia
29	Malaysia	Japan	Switzerland
30	Greece	Czech Republic	Hungary
31	Brazil	South Korea	Japan
32	Italy	Portugal	South Africa
33	China	Greece	New Zealand
34	Portugal	France	Australia
35	Czech Republic	China	Thailand
36	Mexico	Brazil	Colombia
37	Slovakia	Philippines	Turkey
38	Thailand	South Africa	Philippines
39	Slovenia	Thailand	Slovakia
40	Philippines	Italy	Slovenia
41	India	Argentina	Indonesia
42	South Africa	Colombia	Brazil
43	Argentina	India	Czech Republic
44	Turkey	Slovenia	Norway

Notes: Rankings reflect assessments for the ability of a country to achieve sustained high rates of GDP growth per head. Column 1 is based on 259 criteria covering: the openness of an economy, the role of the government, the development of financial markets, the quality of infrastructure, technology, business management and judicial and political institutions and labour-market flexibility. Column 2 looks at the extent to which government policies are conducive to competitiveness. Column 3 is based on the extent to which a country is integrated into regional trade blocks.

The business environment

		2001–05 score	*1996–2000 score*	*1996–2000 ranking*
1	United States	8.80	8.72	1
2	Netherlands	8.79	8.67	2
3	Canada	8.77	8.59	5
4	United Kingdom	8.76	8.62	4
5	Switzerland	8.67	8.31	8
6	Finland	8.64	8.27	9
7	Ireland	8.61	8.33	7
8	Singapore	8.54	8.47	6
9	Sweden	8.53	8.11	10
10	Germany	8.50	7.93	13
11	Denmark	8.41	8.00	12
12	Hong Kong	8.40	8.63	3
13	Belgium	8.29	7.92	14
14	France	8.28	7.76	16
15	Australia	8.18	7.89	15
16	New Zealand	8.17	8.06	11
17	Taiwan	8.12	7.37	20
18	Norway	8.06	7.58	17
19	Spain	8.04	7.42	19
20	Austria	7.98	7.57	18
21	Italy	7.89	6.91	23
22	Chile	7.85	7.33	21
23	Portugal	7.66	7.00	22
24	Israel	7.64	6.75	25
25	Japan	7.43	6.73	26
26	South Korea	7.36	6.33	29
27	Hungary	7.24	6.42	28
28	Greece	7.18	6.12	33
29	Thailand	7.16	6.29	30
30	Mexico	7.11	6.09	34
	Poland	7.11	6.20	31
32	Czech Republic	7.03	6.18	32
33	Argentina	7.01	6.54	27
34	Malaysia	6.76	6.80	24
35	Slovakia	6.49	5.46	37
36	Brazil	6.40	5.44	39
37	Philippines	6.39	5.52	35
38	South Africa	6.35	5.51	36
39	Peru	6.32	5.40	41
40	India	6.16	5.19	45
41	Saudi Arabia	6.13	5.45	38
42	China	6.09	5.35	42
43	Egypt	6.07	5.44	39
44	Colombia	6.05	5.35	42
45	Indonesia	6.02	5.15	46
	Turkey	6.02	5.35	42

Note: Scores reflect the opportunities for, and hindrances to, the conduct of business, measured by countries' rankings in ten categories including market potential, tax and labour-market policies, infrastructure, skills and the political environment. Scores reflect average and forecast average over given date range.

Creativity and research

Economic Creativity Index

2000

		Economic Creativity	*Technology Index*	*Startup Index*
1	United States	2.0	2.0	2.0
2	Finland	1.7	2.0	1.4
3	Singapore	1.6	2.0	1.3
4	Luxembourg	1.4	1.4	1.5
5	Sweden	1.4	1.5	1.2
6	Irael	1.4	1.6	1.2
7	Ireland	1.3	1.7	0.9
8	Netherlands	1.3	1.2	1.3
9	United Kingdom	1.2	1.1	1.4
10	Iceland	1.2	0.8	1.5
11	Switzerland	1.1	1.6	0.6
12	Hong Kong	1.1	0.6	1.6
13	Denmark	1.1	1.3	0.9
14	Germany	1.0	1.7	0.4
15	Canada	1.0	1.2	0.8
16	Australia	1.0	0.9	1.0
17	Taiwan	1.0	0.9	1.0
18	Belgium	1.0	1.0	0.9
19	Norway	0.8	0.6	1.0
20	Japan	0.7	1.6	-0.2
21	Hungary	0.7	1.1	0.3
22	New Zealand	0.6	0.7	0.6
23	Malaysia	0.6	1.1	0.1
24	France	0.6	1.4	-0.2
25	Poland	0.6	1.1	0.0
26	South Africa	0.5	0.5	0.5
27	South Korea	0.5	0.8	0.2
28	Austria	0.5	1.0	-0.1
29	Turkey	0.4	0.7	0.2
30	Spain	0.3	0.5	0.0
31	Brazil	0.2	1.0	-0.6
32	Portugal	0.1	0.5	-0.2
33	Chile	0.1	0.4	-0.2
34	Egypt	0.0	0.2	-0.2
35	Mexico	0.0	1.3	-1.2
36	Philippines	0.0	0.5	-0.5
37	Greece	0.0	0.0	0.0
38	India	0.0	0.3	-0.4
39	Italy	-0.1	0.3	-0.4
40	Thailand	-0.1	-0.1	-0.2
41	Czech Republic	-0.2	0.4	-0.7
42	Slovakia	-0.3	-0.1	-0.5
43	Indonesia	-0.3	-0.7	0.0
44	Mauritius	-0.4	-0.7	-0.2
45	Argentina	-0.4	0.0	-0.8

Notes: The Economic Creativity Index is based on observed data and survey results. It is an average of the Technology Index which measures innovation and technological transfer, and the Startup Index which measures the ease of starting new enterprises.

Total expenditure on R&D

% of GDP

1	Sweden	3.7	**24**	New Zealand	1.1
2	Finland	3.1	**25**	Italy	1.0
	Japan	3.1		Russia	1.0
4	Israel	2.8	**27**	Spain	0.9
5	Switzerland	2.7	**28**	Brazil	0.8
6	United States	2.6		China	0.8
7	South Korea	2.5	**30**	Hungary	0.7
8	Germany	2.4		Poland	0.7
9	France	2.2		Slovakia	0.7
10	Taiwan	2.1	**33**	Chile	0.6
11	Denmark	2.0		Estonia	0.6
12	Iceland	1.9		India	0.6
	Netherlands	1.9		Portugal	0.6
	Singapore	1.9		South Africa	0.6
15	Austria	1.8	**38**	Argentina	0.5
	Belgium	1.8		Greece	0.5
	United Kingdom	1.8		Turkey	0.5
18	Norway	1.7	**41**	Colombia	0.4
19	Canada	1.6		Malaysia	0.4
	Ireland	1.6		Mexico	0.4
21	Australia	1.5	**44**	Hong Kong	0.3
	Slovenia	1.5		Venezuela	0.3
23	Czech Republic	1.3			

Patents

No. of patents granted to residents
Total, 1998

1	Japan	125,704
2	United States	80,292
3	South Korea	35,900
4	Germany	19,271
5	Russia	19,215
6	Taiwan	16,417
7	France	12,068
8	United Kingdom	4,838
9	Netherlands	2,972
10	Sweden	2,400
11	Spain	1,684
12	China	1,653
13	Australia	1,398
14	Austria	1,337
15	Switzerland	1,313
16	Poland	1,174
17	Finland	964
18	Canada	949
19	South Africa	884
20	Italy	743

No. of patents in force
Per 100,000 inhabitants, 1998

1	Luxembourg	7,135.1
2	Switzerland	1,231.0
3	Sweden	1,101.0
4	Belgium	871.2
5	Ireland	855.3
6	Canada	779.9
7	Netherlands	747.6
8	Japan	740.3
9	Taiwan	706.4
10	Denmark	555.3
11	France	554.7
12	Spain	503.1
13	Australia	445.4
14	United States	433.6
15	Germany	432.7
16	Finland	393.7
17	Singapore	384.3
18	Norway	354.4
19	Israel	201.3
20	Austria	168.6

Businesses and banks

Largest businesses

By sales, $bn

1	General Motors	United States	176.6
2	Wal-Mart Stores	United States	166.8
3	Exxon Mobil	United States	163.9
4	Ford Motor	United States	162.6
5	DaimlerChrysler	United States	160.0
6	Mitsui	Japan	118.6
7	Mitsubishi	Japan	117.8
8	Toyota Motor	Japan	115.7
9	General Electric	United States	111.6
10	Itochu	Japan	109.1
11	Royal Dutch/Shell Group	United Kingdom/Netherlands	105.4
12	Sumitomo	Japan	95.7
13	Nippon Telegraph & Telephone[a]	Japan	93.6
14	Marubeni	Japan	91.8
15	AXA	France	87.6
16	Intl. Business Machines	United States	87.5
17	BP Amoco	United Kingdom	83.6
18	Citigroup	United States	82.0
19	Volkswagen	Germany	80.1
20	Nippon Life Insurance	Japan	78.5
21	Siemens	Germany	75.3
22	Allianz	Germany	74.2
23	Hitachi	Japan	71.9
24	Matsushita Electric Industrial	Japan	65.6
25	Nissho Iwai	Japan	65.4
26	U.S. Postal Service[a]	United States	62.7
27	ING Group	Netherlands	62.5
28	AT&T	United States	62.4
29	Philip Morris	United States	61.8
30	Sony	Japan	60.1
31	Deutsche Bank	Germany	58.6
32	Boeing	United States	58.0
33	Dai-ichi Mutual Life Insurance	Japan	55.1
34	Honda Motor	Japan	54.8
35	Assicurazioni Generali	Italy	53.7
35	Nissan Motor	Japan	53.7
37	E. ON	Germany	52.2
38	Toshiba	Japan	51.6
39	Bank of America Corp.	United States	51.4
40	Fiat	Italy	51.3
41	Nestlé	Switzerland	49.7
42	SBC Communications	United States	49.5
43	Credit Suisse	Switzerland	49.4
44	Hewlett-Packard	United States	48.3
45	Fujitsu	Japan	47.2

a Government owned.

Notes: Industrial and service corporations. Figures refer to the year ended December 31, 1999, except for Japanese companies, where figures refer to year ended March 31, 2000. They include sales of consolidated subsidiaries but exclude excise taxes, thus differing, in some instances, from figures published by the companies themselves.

Largest banks

By capital, $m

1	Citigroup	United States	47,699
2	Bank of America Corp	United States	38,176
3	HSBC Holdings	United Kingdom	28,533
4	Bank of Tokyo-Mitsubishi	Japan	26,019
5	Chase Manhattan Corp	United States	25,504
6	Dai-Ichi Kangyo Bank	Japan	23,525
7	Crédit Agricole Groupe	France	23,335
8	Sakura Bank	Japan	23,057
9	Fuji Bank	Japan	22,654
10	Industrial and Commercial Bank of China	China	21,919
11	Sanwa Bank	Japan	21,391
12	Sumitomo Bank	Japan	20,821
13	Bank One Corp	United States	20,367
14	BNP Paribas	France	19,939
15	UBS	Switzerland	18,460
16	ABN-Amro Bank	Netherlands	17,817
17	Credit Suisse Group	Switzerland	17,668
18	Deutsche Bank	Germany	17,418
19	Industrial Bank of Japan	Japan	17,000
20	Agricultural Bank of China	China	16,286
21	Bank of China	China	15,270
22	Tokai Bank	Japan	15,150
23	Norinchukin Bank	Japan	14,795
24	HypoVereinsbank	Germany	14,708
25	Banco Bilbao Vizcaya Argentaria	Spain	14,481
26	National Westminster Bank	United Kingdom	14,446
27	First Union Corp	United States	14,202
28	Barclays Bank	United Kingdom	14,055
29	ING Bank	Netherlands	13,964
30	Lloyds TSB Group	United Kingdom	13,674
31	Wells Fargo & Co.	United States	13,335
32	China Construction Bank	China	13,196
33	Rabobank Nederland	Netherlands	13,067
34	Dresdner Bank	Germany	12,968
35	FleetBoston Financial Corp	United	12,767
36	Banco Santander Central Hispano	Spain	12,514
37	Société Générale	France	12,256
38	Banca Intesa	Italy	12,249
39	Ashai Bank	Japan	11,873
40	J.P. Morgan & Co.	United States	11,551
41	Commerzbank	Germany	11,201
42	Fortis Bank	Belgium	11,057
43	National Australia Bank	Australia	10,003
44	Halifax	United Kingdom	10,002
45	Groupe Caisse d'Epargne	France	9,798
46	Crédit Mutuel	France	9,690

Notes: Capital is essentially equity and reserves.
Figures for Japanese banks refer to the year ended March 31, 2000. Figures for all other countries refer to the year ended December 31, 1999.

Stockmarkets

Largest market capitalisation

$m, end 1999

1	United States	16,635,114	27	Argentina	83,887
2	Japan	4,546,937	28	Russia	72,205
3	United Kingdom	2,933,280	29	Chile	68,226
4	France	1,475,457	30	Portugal	66,488
5	Germany	1,432,190	31	Indonesia	64,087
6	Italy	728,273	32	Israel	63,820
7	Netherlands	695,209	33	Norway	63,696
8	Switzerland	693,127	34	Saudi Arabia	60,440
9	Hong Kong	609,090	35	Thailand	58,365
10	Spain	431,668	36	Philippines	48,105
11	Australia	427,683	37	Ireland	42,458
12	Taiwan	375,991	38	Luxembourg	35,940
13	Sweden	373,278	39	Austria	33,025
14	Finland	349,409	40	Egypt	32,838
15	China	330,703	41	Poland	29,577
16	South Korea	308,534	42	New Zealand	28,352
17	South Africa	262,478	43	Iran	21,830
18	Brazil	227,962	44	Kuwait	18,814
19	Greece	204,213	45	Hungary	16,317
20	Singapore	198,407	46	Morocco	13,695
21	Belgium	184,942	47	Peru	13,392
22	India	184,605	48	Czech Republic	11,796
23	Mexico	154,044	49	Colombia	11,590
24	Malaysia	145,445	50	Cyprus	8,075
25	Turkey	112,716	51	Venezuela	7,471
26	Denmark	105,293	52	Pakistan	6,965

Highest growth in market capitalisation, $ terms

% increase, 1990–99

1	Russia[a]	29,492	21	Honduras[f]	1,045
2	Poland[a]	20,440	22	Iceland[e]	893
3	China[a]	16,207	23	Armenia[b]	733
4	Latvia[b]	3,810	24	Colombia	719
5	Namibia[c]	3,190	25	Philippines	712
6	Hungary[c]	3,131	26	Indonesia	693
7	Argentina	2,467	27	Hong Kong	630
8	Israel	1,820	28	Lithuania[b]	625
9	Egypt	1,761	29	Portugal	623
10	Paraguay[d]	1,663	30	Barbados	612
11	Romania[e]	1,579	31	Malta[e]	540
12	Peru	1,549	32	Trinidad and Tobago	527
13	Panama[c]	1,486	33	Cyprus[a]	526
14	Finland	1,438	34	Mauritius	513
15	Zambia[b]	1,432	35	Ecuador[c]	501
16	Morocco	1,318	36	Turkey	491
17	Brazil	1,294	37	Netherlands	480
18	Greece	1,241	38	Singapore	478
19	Ghana[c]	1,105	39	Swaziland	459
20	Bulgaria[b]	1,057	40	United States	444

Highest growth in value traded, $ terms

% increase, 1990–99

1	China[a]	45,888	23	Brazil	1,459
2	Poland[a]	39,718	24	Turkey	1,291
3	Bangladesh	13,050	25	Sweden	1,256
4	Hungary[c]	12,203	26	Bulgaria[b]	1,225
5	Romania[e]	10,467	27	Nigeria	1,218
6	Pakistan	9,016	28	Mauritius	1,167
7	Egypt	7,073	29	Italy	1,160
8	Panama[c]	5,100	30	Luxembourg	1,066
9	Greece	4,709	31	Ireland[e]	1,054
10	Morocco	3,981	32	United States	961
11	Bolivia[e]	3,700	33	Russia[e]	959
12	Cyprus[a]	3,123	34	Colombia	892
13	Finland	2,737	35	Belgium	820
14	Macedonia[g]	2,600	36	Iceland[e]	816
15	Portugal	2,318	37	Argentina	813
16	Netherlands	2,243	38	South Africa	794
17	Peru	2,212	39	Chile	778
18	Tunisia	2,111	40	Lithuania[b]	684
19	Costa Rica[c]	1,864	41	Switzerland	683
20	Spain	1,717	42	Kenya	640
21	Mongolia[b]	1,650	43	Malta[e]	633
22	Philippines	1,518	44	Hong Kong	607

Highest growth in number of listed companies

% increase, 1990–99

1	Romania[e]	145,525	24	Turkey	159
2	China[a]	6,686	25	Oman[c]	155
3	Bulgaria[b]	5,275	26	Hong Kong	145
4	Slovakia[e]	4,594	27	India	141
5	Poland[a]	2,356	28	Panama[c]	138
6	Paraguay[d]	1,733	29	Singapore	137
7	Russia[a]	1,492	30	Iceland[e]	133
8	Armenia[g]	850	31	Taiwan	132
9	Bolivia[e]	800	32	Germany	126
10	Swaziland	600	33	Fiji[e]	125
11	Namibia[c]	367	34	Indonesia	122
12	Lebanon[b]	333	35	Croatia[e]	103
13	Lithuania	315	36	Finland	101
14	Latvia[b]	312	37	Greece	94
15	Zambia[b]	300	38	Thailand	83
16	Tunisia	238	39	Spain	83
17	Canada	229	40	Colombia	81
18	Mauritius	215	41	Egypt	80
19	Hungary[c]	214	42	Malta[e]	75
20	Iran[c]	204	43	Norway	74
21	Israel	198	44	Ghana[c]	69
22	Honduras[f]	173	45	France	67
23	Malaysia	168	45	Botswana[a]	67

a 1991–1999 b 1995–1999 c 1992–1999
d 1993–1999 e 1994–1999 f 1992–1998 g 1996–1999

Transport: *roads and cars*

Longest road networks

Km, 1999 or latest

Rank	Country	Km	Rank	Country	Km
1	United States	6,348,227	21	Sweden	210,907
2	India	3,319,644	22	Bangladesh	201,182
3	Brazil	1,724,924	23	Austria	200,000
4	China	1,210,000	24	Philippines	199,950
5	Japan	1,152,207	25	Romania	198,589
6	Russia	948,000	26	Nigeria	194,394
7	Australia	913,000	27	Hungary	188,203
8	Canada	901,903	28	Ukraine	168,674
9	France	893,500	29	Iran	167,157
10	Spain	663,795	30	Congo	157,000
11	Germany	656,140	31	Saudi Arabia	151,470
12	Italy	654,676	32	Belgium	145,850
13	South Africa	534,131	33	Czech Republic	127,854
14	Turkey	385,960	34	Greece	117,000
15	Poland	381,046	35	Netherlands	116,500
16	United Kingdom	371,913	36	Colombia	112,988
17	Indonesia	342,700	37	Kazakhstan	109,445
18	Mexico	323,977	38	Algeria	104,000
19	Pakistan	254,410	39	Sri Lanka	99,200
20	Argentina	215,471	40	Venezuela	96,155

Densest road networks

Km of road per km² land area, 1999 or latest

Rank	Country	Km/km²	Rank	Country	Km/km²
1	Macau	15.82	21	Puerto Rico	1.58
2	Malta	5.51	22	United Kingdom	1.53
3	Singapore	4.80	23	Sri Lanka	1.51
4	Belgium	4.78	24	Bangladesh	1.40
5	Bahrain	4.67	25	Ireland	1.32
6	Barbados	3.72		Spain	1.32
7	Japan	3.05	27	Poland	1.22
8	Netherlands	2.81	28	Cyprus	1.19
9	Austria	2.39	29	Latvia	1.15
10	Italy	2.17	30	Lithuania	1.13
11	Hungary	2.02	31	Estonia	1.12
12	Luxembourg	2.01	32	India	1.01
13	Germany	1.83	33	Slovenia	0.99
14	Switzerland	1.72		Taiwan	0.99
15	Hong Kong	1.70	35	Mauritius	0.94
	Jamaica	1.70	36	Greece	0.89
17	Denmark	1.66	37	South Korea	0.88
18	France	1.64	38	Slovakia	0.87
19	Czech Republic	1.62	39	Romania	0.84
	Trinidad & Tobago	1.62	40	Israel	0.78

Most crowded road networks

Number of vehicles per km of road network, 1999 or latest

1	Hong Kong	287	**26**	Luxembourg	55
2	United Arab Emirates	232	**27**	Switzerland	53
3	Macau	199	**28**	Italy	52
4	Lebanon	191	**29**	Guatemala	45
5	Singapore	169		Mexico	45
6	Kuwait	156		Slovenia	45
7	Qatar	154	**32**	Barbados	43
8	Taiwan	144	**33**	Croatia	42
9	South Korea	128	**34**	France	37
10	Malta	126		Jordan	37
11	Israel	102	**36**	El Salvador	36
12	Thailand	97	**37**	Belgium	35
13	Brunei	77		Macedonia	35
14	Puerto Rico	74	**37**	Serbia	35
15	Malaysia	69	**40**	Cyprus	34
16	Germany	66	**41**	Slovakia	33
17	Bahrain	63	**42**	United States	32
	Portugal	63	**43**	Denmark	31
	Uruguay	63		Finland	31
20	United Kingdom	62		Greece	31
21	Japan	61	**46**	Argentina	30
22	Mauritius	60		Dominican Republic	30
23	Bulgaria	58	**48**	Czech Republic	29
	Netherlands	58		Poland	29
25	Sri Lanka	56		Spain	29

Most used road networks

'000 vehicle-km per year per km of road network, 1999 or latest

1	Indonesia	8,134.1	**16**	Japan	647.5
2	Hong Kong	5,888.0	**17**	Denmark	627.5
3	Taiwan	2,793.2	**18**	Finland	590.6
4	Bahrain	2,755.6	**19**	France	577.8
5	Israel	2,131.2	**20**	Macedonia	489.1
6	Portugal	1,353.4	**21**	Croatia	471.6
7	United Kingdom	1,243.3	**22**	Poland	456.6
8	Belgium	1,085.3	**23**	Slovenia	449.3
9	Netherlands	943.8	**24**	El Salvador	423.2
10	Germany	898.4	**25**	United States	399.6
11	Pakistan	859.9	**26**	Oman	391.2
12	South Korea	773.3	**27**	Ecuador	378.2
13	Switzerland	760.9	**28**	Colombia	368.1
14	Luxembourg	739.8	**29**	Ukraine	362.8
15	Greece	691.9	**30**	China	360.3

Highest car ownership

Number of cars per 1,000 people, 1999 or latest

Rank	Country	Cars
1	Lebanon	732
2	Luxembourg	576
3	Brunei	576
4	Italy	545
5	Iceland	543
6	Germany	516
7	Austria	495
8	Australia	488
9	United States	486
10	Switzerland	485
11	France	470
	New Zealand	470
13	Malta	462
14	Canada	458
15	Belgium	440
16	Sweden	428
17	Slovenia	417
18	Spain	408
19	Norway	405
20	Finland	403
21	Japan	394
22	Cyprus	385
23	Netherlands	384
	United Kingdom	384
25	Kuwait	359
26	Denmark	353
27	Czech Republic	334
28	Portugal	321
29	Estonia	319
30	Ireland	309
31	Lithuania	295
32	Greece	254
33	Poland	240
34	Hungary	237
35	Bulgaria	233
	Croatia	233
37	Puerto Rico	230
38	Slovakia	229
39	Qatar	219
40	Latvia	217
41	Israel	216
42	Bahrain	205
43	Taiwan	205
44	South Korea	167
45	Bahamas	161
46	Libya	154
	Uruguay	154
48	Malaysia	145
	Serbia & Montenegro	145
50	Macedonia	142

Lowest car ownership

Number of cars per 1,000 people, 1999 or latest

Rank	Country	Cars
1	Somalia	0.1
	Tajikistan	0.1
3	Armenia	0.3
	Central African Rep	0.3
	Mozambique	0.3
6	Bangladesh	0.5
7	Myanmar	0.6
8	Tanzania	0.8
9	Ethiopia	0.9
10	Afghanistan	1.4
	Rwanda	1.4
12	Eritrea	1.5
13	Uganda	1.8
14	Guinea	2.0
15	Malawi	2.3
16	Liberia	2.6
	Nicaragua	2.6
18	Burundi	2.8
19	Mali	2.9
20	Chad	3.2
	China	3.2
22	Laos	3.4
23	Burkina Faso	3.6
24	Niger	3.8
25	Sierra Leone	3.9
26	Madagascar	4.1
27	Haiti	4.4
28	India	4.5
29	Ghana	4.7
30	Cambodia	4.8

Most accidents

Number of people injured per 100m vehicle-km, 1999 or latest

1	Malawi	2,730
2	Rwanda	1,764
3	South Korea	510
4	Costa Rica	406
5	Kenya	363
6	India	333
7	Honduras	317
8	Turkey	228
9	Egypt	222
10	Sri Lanka	205
11	Portugal	194
12	Hong Kong	176
13	Morocco	168
14	Kirgizstan	134
15	Japan	133
16	Israel	130
17	South Africa	129
18	Colombia	126
19	Latvia	125
20	Italy	122
21	Canada	121
22	Czech Republic	113
23	Belgium	108
24	United Kingdom	94
25	Saudi Arabia	89
26	Mongolia	86
	Philippines	86
28	Germany	81
	Macedonia	81
30	Slovenia	79
31	Iceland	76
	United States	76
33	Spain	73
34	Mexico	66
35	Yemen	59
36	Hungary	57
37	Senegal	56
	Switzerland	56
39	Iran	53
	Oman	53
41	Thailand	40
42	Slovakia	39
43	Ireland	38
44	Norway	35
45	France	32
	Mauritius	32
	New Zealand	32
	Sweden	32
	Zimbabwe	32
50	Bahrain	31

Most deaths

Number of people killed per 100m vehicle-km, 1999 or latest

1	Malawi	1,117
2	India	65
3	Egypt	44
4	Kenya	41
5	Latvia	25
6	Kirgizstan	24
7	Sri Lanka	23
8	Mongolia	21
9	Colombia	17
	South Korea	17
11	Honduras	16
12	Morocco	15
13	Philippines	14
14	Thailand	13
15	Costa Rica	11
	Saudi Arabia	11
	Yemen	11
18	Mexico	10
	South Africa	10
20	Turkey	9
21	Albania	8
22	Portugal	6
23	Czech Republic	5
	Ecuador	5
	Iran	5
	Romania	5
27	Estonia	4
	Macedonia	4
	Oman	4
	Senegal	4

Transport: *planes and trains*

Most air travel

Million passenger-km[a] per year

1	United States	1,041,042	**16**	Russia	39,446
2	Japan	165,170	**17**	Thailand	38,624
3	United Kingdom	158,003	**18**	Malaysia	33,442
4	Germany	97,153	**19**	Switzerland	29,515
5	France	96,128	**20**	Mexico	27,586
6	China	93,032	**21**	India	25,842
7	Australia	78,520	**22**	New Zealand	20,386
8	Netherlands	73,512	**23**	Saudi Arabia	20,178
9	Canada	66,585	**24**	United Arab Emirates	18,574
10	Singapore	63,988	**25**	Belgium	17,953
11	Hong Kong	53,095	**26**	South Africa	17,716
12	South Korea	52,956	**27**	Indonesia	17,232
13	Brazil	50,404	**28**	Argentina	15,188
14	Spain	41,632	**29**	Turkey	14,979
15	Italy	40,914	**30**	Austria	13,250

Busiest airports

Total passengers, m			*International passengers, m*		
1	Atlanta, Hartsfield	80.1	**1**	London, Heathrow	54.8
2	Chicago, O'Hare	72.1	**2**	Paris, Charles de Gaulle	38.9
3	Los Angeles Intl.	68.5	**3**	Frankfurt/Main	37.2
4	London, Heathrow	64.6	**4**	Amsterdam, Schipol	36.3
5	Dallas/Ft. Worth	60.7	**5**	Hong Kong Intl.	29.1
6	Tokyo, Haneda	56.4	**6**	London, Gatwick	27.6
7	Frankfurt/Main	49.4	**7**	Singapore, Changi	24.5
8	Paris, Charles de Gaulle	48.2	**8**	Tokyo, Narita	22.5
9	San Francisco Intl.	41.2	**9**	Brussels, Zaventem	20.0
10	Amsterdam. Schipol	39.6	**10**	Zurich	19.4
11	Denver Intl.	37.7	**10**	Bangkok Intl.	18.9
12	Las Vegas Intl.	36.9	**12**	New York, Kennedy	17.9

Average daily aircraft movements, take-offs and landings

1	Atlanta, Hartsfield	2,509	**12**	Cincinnati Intl.	1,333
2	Chicago, O'Hare	2,490	**13**	Philadelphia Intl.	1,327
3	Dallas/Ft. Worth	2,295	**14**	Houston George Bush Intercont.	1,325
4	Phoenix, Skyharbor	1,745	**15**	Lambert/St Louis Intl.	1,318
5	Los Angeles Intl.	1,537	**16**	Boston, Logan Intl.	1,310
6	Detroit, Metro	1,522	**17**	London, Heathrow	1,279
7	Minneapolis, St Paul	1,433	**18**	Frankfurt/Main	1,257
8	Paris, Charles de Gaulle	1,418	**19**	Washington Intl.	1,253
	Miami Intl.	1,418	**20**	Seattle/Tacoma	1,247
10	Las Vegas Intl.	1,412			
11	Denver Intl.	1,395			

a Air passenger–km data refer to the distance travelled by each aircraft of national origin.

Longest railway networks

'000 km, 1999

1	United States	234.1	**21**	Australia	9.5
2	Russia	86.0	**22**	Czech Republic	9.3
3	China	67.4	**23**	Turkey	8.7
4	India	59.4	**24**	Hungary	7.8
5	Germany	37.5		Pakistan	7.8
6	Argentina	34.2	**26**	Iran	6.4
7	France	31.6	**27**	Finland	5.8
8	Mexico	26.5	**28**	Austria	5.7
9	Poland	22.9	**29**	Belarus	5.5
10	South Africa	22.7	**30**	Egypt	5.0
11	Ukraine	22.5	**31**	Philippines	4.9
12	Brazil	22.1	**32**	Cuba	4.8
13	Japan	20.2	**33**	Sudan	4.6
14	United Kingdom	17.8	**34**	North Korea	4.5
15	Italy	16.1	**35**	Bulgaria	4.3
16	Spain	14.1		Serbia & Montenegro	4.3
17	Canada	14.0	**37**	Indonesia	4.2
18	Kazakhstan	13.6		Norway	4.2
19	Romania	11.4	**39**	Algeria	4.0
20	Sweden	10.8	**40**	New Zealand	3.9

Most rail passengers

Km per person per year, 1999

1	Japan	1,905	**11**	Germany	884
2	Switzerland	1,849	**12**	Sweden	840
3	Belarus	1,656	**13**	Luxembourg	738
4	France	1,130	**14**	Belgium	722
5	Egypt	1,096	**15**	Italy	711
6	Denmark	1,050	**16**	Hungary	676
7	Austria	1,004	**17**	Czech Republic	673
8	Russia	962	**18**	Finland	663
9	Ukraine	943	**19**	United Kingdom	659
10	Netherlands	913	**20**	South Korea	611

Most rail freight

Million tonnes-km per year, 1999

1	United States	2,010,027	**11**	Australia	30,449
2	China	1,226,152	**12**	Belarus	30,370
3	Russia	901,381	**13**	Japan	22,681
4	India	284,249	**14**	Italy	22,454
5	Ukraine	158,693	**15**	Czech Republic	18,286
6	South Africa	103,866	**16**	United Kingdom	18,175
7	Kazakhstan	99,877	**17**	Romania	17,854
8	Germany	73,613	**18**	Uzbekistan	15,672
9	Poland	60,937	**19**	Austria	14,487
10	France	53,959	**20**	Sweden	14,313

Transport: *sail away*

Largest merchant fleets

Number of vessels not less than 100 GRT and built before end of 2000[a]
By country of:

		registration	ownership			registration	ownership
1	Japan	8,012	2,922	**45**	United Arab Emirates	350	179
2	Panama	6,184	5	**46**	Portugal	326	84
3	United States	5,792	1,440	**47**	Bangladesh	310	29
4	Russia	4,755	2,525	**48**	Iceland	309	60
5	China	3,319	2,214	**49**	Nigeria	296	38
6	South Korea	2,502	903	**50**	Azerbaijan	284	152
7	Indonesia	2,480	591	**51**	Finland	280	149
8	Norway	2,349	1,688	**52**	Saudi Arabia	276	124
9	Philippines	1,865	355	**53**	Romania	264	123
10	Singapore	1,728	755	**54**	Venezuela	262	62
11	Liberia	1,557	0	**55**	Croatia	246	111
12	Spain	1,554	325	**56**	Syria	219	73
13	Greece	1,529	3,251	**57**	Ghana	210	19
14	Malta	1,505	13	**58**	Estonia	209	90
15	Cyprus	1,475	74	**59**	Kuwait	205	35
16	Italy	1,457	631	**60**	Senegal	200	2
17	United Kingdom	1,448	819	**61**	South Africa	198	29
18	Honduras	1,407	6	**62**	Lithuania	185	86
19	Netherlands	1,317	755	**63**	Belgium	182	156
20	Bahamas	1,295	10	**64**	Netherlands Antilles	177	0
21	Turkey	1,153	553	**65**	North Korea	176	93
22	Denmark	1,081	732	**66**	New Zealand	173	41
23	Germany	994	2,103	**67**	Ireland	172	59
24	India	987	407	**68**	Ecuador	171	27
25	Ukraine	894	444	**69**	Bulgaria	164	111
26	Malaysia	865	295	**70**	Latvia	163	99
27	Canada	861	309	**71**	Mauritania	144	0
28	France	808	270	**72**	Algeria	142	71
29	Peru	721	22	**73**	Libya	142	22
30	Vietnam	691	150	**74**	Bermuda	129	0
31	Taiwan	680	519	**75**	Mozambique	127	1
32	Mexico	631	95	**76**	Angola	125	14
33	Australia	631	89	**77**	Myanmar	123	35
34	Sweden	565	361	**78**	Bahrain	121	15
35	Thailand	561	267	**79**	Namibia	119	3
36	Hong Kong	560	548	**80**	Georgia	118	10
37	Brazil	505	177	**81**	Papua New Guinea	112	16
38	Argentina	493	90	**82**	Colombia	111	23
39	Morocco	493	49	**83**	Lebanon	105	52
40	Chile	471	84	**84**	Madagascar	105	11
41	Poland	429	150	**85**	Cuba	99	85
42	Cambodia	405	0	**86**	Iraq	99	41
43	Iran	395	168				
44	Egypt	372	133				

a Gross Tonnage (GRT) = total volume within the hull and above deck. 1 GRT=100 cu ft.

Tourism

Most tourist arrivals

Number of arrivals, '000

1	France	73,042	**21**	Malaysia	7,931
2	Spain	51,772	**22**	Ukraine	7,500
3	United States	48,491	**23**	Turkey	6,893
4	Italy	36,097	**24**	Ireland	6,511
5	China	27,047	**25**	Belgium	6,369
6	United Kingdom	25,740	**26**	Singapore	6,258
7	Canada	19,557	**27**	South Africa	6,253
8	Mexico	19,043	**28**	Brazil	5,107
9	Russia	18,496	**29**	Macau	5,050
10	Poland	17,950	**30**	Tunisia	4,832
11	Austria	17,467	**31**	Indonesia	4,700
12	Germany	17,116	**32**	South Korea	4,660
13	Czech Republic	16,031	**33**	Egypt	4,489
14	Hungary	12,930	**34**	Norway	4,481
15	Greece	12,000	**35**	Australia	4,459
16	Portugal	11,600	**36**	Japan	4,438
17	Hong Kong	11,328	**37**	Morocco	3,824
18	Switzerland	10,800	**38**	Croatia	3,443
19	Netherlands	9,881	**39**	Romania	3,209
20	Thailand	8,651	**40**	Puerto Rico	3,024

Biggest tourist spenders

$m

1	United States	74,400	**9**	Canada	10,000
2	Spain	32,900	**10**	Greece	8,800
3	France	31,700	**11**	Russia	7,800
4	Italy	28,400	**12**	Mexico	7,600
5	United Kingdom	21,000	**13**	Australia	7,500
6	Germany	16,800	**14**	Switzerland	7,400
7	China	14,100	**15**	Hong Kong	7,200
8	Austria	11,100			

Largest tourist receipts

$m

1	United States	74,448	**16**	Netherlands	7,092
2	Spain	32,913	**17**	South Korea	6,802
3	France	31,699	**18**	Thailand	6,695
4	Italy	28,357	**19**	Poland	6,100
5	United Kingdom	20,972	**20**	Singapore	5,974
6	Germany	16,828	**21**	Turkey	5,203
7	China	14,098	**22**	Portugal	5,169
8	Austria	11,088	**23**	Brazil	3,994
9	Canada	10,025	**24**	Egypt	3,903
10	Greece	8,765	**25**	Sweden	3,894
11	Russia	7,771	**26**	Denmark	3,682
12	Australia	7,525	**27**	Taiwan	3,571
13	Switzerland	7,355	**28**	Japan	3,428
14	Mexico	7,223	**29**	Hungary	3,394
15	Hong Kong	7,210	**30**	Ireland	3,306

Education

Highest primary enrolment

Number enrolled as % of relevant age group, 1997

1	Gabon	162		Mexico	114
2	Malawi	134		Vietnam	114
3	South Africa	133	18	Cambodia	113
4	Namibia	131		Colombia	113
5	Portugal	128		Indonesia	113
6	Ecuador	127		Nepal	113
7	Brazil	125	22	Laos	112
8	China	123		Zimbabwe	112
	Peru	123	24	Argentina	111
10	Myanmar	121		Honduras	111
11	Togo	120		Lebanon	111
12	Tunisia	118		Libya	111
13	Philippines	117		Paraguay	111
14	United Kingdom	115	29	Sri Lanka	109
15	Congo-Brazzaville	114		Uruguay	109

Lowest primary enrolment

Number enrolled as % of relevant age group, 1997

1	Niger	29	15	Côte d'Ivoire	71
2	Burkina Faso	40		Jordan	71
3	Ethiopia	43		Senegal	71
4	Mali	49	18	Congo	72
5	Burundi	51	19	Pakistan	74
	Sudan	51		Uganda	74
7	Eritrea	53	21	Oman	76
8	Guinea	54		Saudi Arabia	76
9	Chad	58	23	Gambia, The	77
10	Mozambique	60		Kuwait	77
11	Guinea-Bissau	62	25	Benin	78
12	Tanzania	67		Uzbekistan	78
13	Serbia & Montenegro	69	27	Ghana	79
14	Yemen	70		Mauritania	79

Highest tertiary enrolment[a]

Number enrolled as % of relevant age group, 1997

1	Canada	90	12	Sweden	50
2	United States	81	13	Austria	48
3	Australia	80	14	Germany	47
4	Finland	74		Greece	47
5	South Korea	68		Italy	47
6	New Zealand	63		Netherlands	47
7	Norway	62	18	Denmark	45
8	Belgium	57		Estonia	45
9	United Kingdom	52	20	Belarus	44
10	France	51		Israel	44
	Spain	51	22	Japan	43

Notes: The gross enrolment ratios shown are the actual number enrolled as a percentage of the number of children in the official primary age group. They may exceed 100 when children outside the primary age group are receiving primary education either because they have not moved on to secondary education or because they have started primary education early.

Least literate

% adult literacy rate, 1997

1	Niger	14.3	16	Pakistan	40.9
2	Burkina Faso	20.7	17	Central African Rep	42.4
3	Gambia, The	33.1	18	Yemen	42.5
4	Afghanistan	33.4	19	Côte d'Ivoire	42.6
5	Guinea-Bissau	33.6	20	Bhutan	44.2
6	Benin	33.9	21	Burundi	44.6
7	Sierra Leone	34.3	22	Haiti	45.8
8	Senegal	34.6	23	Morocco	45.9
9	Ethiopia	35.4	24	Liberia	48.4
10	Mali	35.5	25	Chad	50.3
11	Guinea	37.9	26	Egypt	52.7
12	Nepal	38.1	27	Togo	53.2
13	Mauritania	38.4	28	Sudan	53.3
14	Bangladesh	38.9	29	India	53.5
15	Mozambique	40.5	30	Malawi	57.7

Highest education spending

% of GDP, 1997

1	Moldova	10.6		Saudi Arabia	7.5
2	Namibia	9.1	15	Jamaica	7.4
3	Zimbabwe	9.0		Norway	7.4
4	Botswana	8.6	17	New Zealand	7.3
5	Lesotho	8.4		Swaziland	7.3
6	Sweden	8.3		Ukraine	7.3
7	Denmark	8.1	20	Barbados	7.2
8	South Africa	7.9		Estonia	7.2
9	Tunisia	7.7	22	Yemen	7.0
	Uzbekistan	7.7	23	Canada	6.9
11	Israel	7.6	24	Jordan	6.8
12	Finland	7.5	25	Cuba	6.7
	Poland	7.5	26	Kenya	6.5

Lowest education spending

% of GDP, 1997

1	Nigeria	0.7	14	Bangladesh	2.2
2	Sudan	0.9		Mali	2.2
3	Myanmar	1.2		Tajikistan	2.2
4	Indonesia	1.4		Turkey	2.2
5	Burkina Faso	1.5		Zambia	2.2
6	Chad	1.7	19	China	2.3
	Guatemala	1.7		Dominican Republic	2.3
8	Eritrea	1.8		Niger	2.3
	United Arab Emirates	1.8	22	El Salvador	2.5
10	Guinea	1.9		Lebanon	2.5
	Madagascar	1.9	24	Uganda	2.6
12	Armenia	2.0	25	Pakistan	2.7
13	Laos	2.1			

a Tertiary education includes all levels of post-secondary education including courses leading to awards not equivalent to a university degree, courses leading to a first university degree and postgraduate courses.

Life: *the chances*

Highest life expectancy

Years, 2000–05

Rank	Country	Years
1	Japan	81.5
2	Sweden	80.1
3	Hong Kong	79.9
4	Iceland	79.4
5	Australia	79.2
	Israel	79.2
7	Martinique	79.1
	Switzerland	79.1
9	Canada	79.0
	France	79.0
11	Norway	78.9
12	Belgium	78.8
	Spain	78.8
14	Italy	78.7
15	Austria	78.5
	Greece	78.5
	Malta	78.5
18	Cyprus	78.3
	Guadeloupe	78.3
	Netherlands	78.3
21	Germany	78.2
	United Kingdom	78.2
23	Singapore	78.1
24	Finland	78.0
	New Zealand	78.0
26	Luxembourg	77.9
27	United States	77.5
28	Barbados	77.2
29	Ireland	77.0
30	Costa Rica	76.7
31	Denmark	76.6
32	Kuwait	76.5
33	Cuba	76.4
34	Brunei	76.3
	Netherlands Antilles	76.3
36	Portugal	76.2
37	Slovenia	76.1
38	Jamaica	75.7
39	Chile	75.6
	Puerto Rico	75.6
41	South Korea	75.5
42	Czech Republic	75.4
	United Arab Emirates	75.4
44	Uruguay	75.0
45	Réunion	74.9
46	Trinidad & Tobago	74.8
47	Taiwan[a]	74.7
48	Panama	74.5

Highest male life expectancy

Years, 2000–05

Rank	Country	Years
1	Japan	77.8
2	Sweden	77.6
3	Hong Kong	77.3
4	Iceland	77.1
	Israel	77.1
6	Macau	76.9
7	Australia	76.4
8	Canada	76.2
9	Cyprus	76.0
	Norway	76.0
11	Greece	75.9
	Malta	75.9
	Singapore	75.9
	Switzerland	75.9
15	Martinique	75.8
16	Belgium	75.7
	United Kingdom	75.7
18	Netherlands	75.6

Highest female life expectancy

Years, 2000–05

Rank	Country	Years
1	Japan	85.0
2	France	82.8
	Hong Kong	82.8
4	Sweden	82.6
5	Martinique	82.3
	Spain	82.3
	Switzerland	82.3
8	Australia	82.0
9	Belgium	81.9
	Italy	81.9
	Norway	81.9
12	Canada	81.8
	Iceland	81.8
14	Guadeloupe	81.7
15	Macau	81.6
16	Austria	81.5
	Finland	81.5
18	Greece	81.2
19	Germany	81.1

a 1998

Lowest life expectancy

Years, 2000–05

1	Botswana	36.1	**26**	Kenya	49.3
2	Mozambique	38.0	**27**	Cameroon	50.0
3	Swaziland	38.1	**28**	Tanzania	51.1
4	Malawi	39.3	**29**	Congo-Brazzaville	51.6
5	Lesotho	40.2	**30**	Congo	52.1
6	Sierra Leone	40.5		Mali	52.1
7	Burundi	40.6		Nigeria	52.1
8	Rwanda	40.9	**33**	Togo	52.2
9	Zambia	42.2	**34**	Eritrea	52.4
10	Zimbabwe	42.9	**35**	Mauritania	52.5
11	Afghanistan	43.2	**36**	Gabon	52.9
12	Central African Rep	43.3	**37**	Haiti	53.3
	Ethiopia	44.3	**38**	Madagascar	53.6
	Namibia	44.3	**39**	Benin	54.0
15	Guinea-Bissau	45.4	**40**	Senegal	54.3
16	Angola	45.8	**41**	Laos	54.5
17	Uganda	46.0	**42**	Liberia	55.6
18	Niger	46.2	**43**	Cambodia	56.2
19	Chad	46.3		Myanmar	56.2
20	Gambia, The	47.1	**45**	Sudan	57.0
21	South Africa	47.4	**46**	Ghana	57.2
22	Côte d'Ivoire	47.9	**47**	Papua New Guinea	57.7
23	Burkina Faso	48.1	**48**	Nepal	59.8
24	Guinea	48.5	**49**	Bangladesh	60.7
25	Somalia	48.9	**50**	Pakistan	61.0

Lowest male life expectancy

Years, 2000–05

1	Botswana	36.5	**11**	Ethiopia	42.8
2	Mozambique	37.3	**12**	Afghanistan	43.0
3	Swaziland	38.1	**13**	Zimbabwe	43.3
4	Sierra Leone	39.2	**14**	Guinea-Bissau	44.0
5	Malawi	39.6	**15**	Namibia	44.3
6	Burundi	39.8	**16**	Angola	44.5
7	Rwanda	40.2	**17**	Chad	45.1
8	Lesotho	40.9	**18**	Uganda	45.3
9	Zambia	42.6	**19**	Gambia, The	45.7
10	Central African Rep	42.7	**20**	Niger	45.9

Lowest female life expectancy

Years, 2000–05

1	Botswana	35.6	**10**	Zimbabwe	42.4
2	Swaziland	38.1	**11**	Afghanistan	43.5
3	Mozambique	38.6	**12**	Ethiopia	43.8
4	Malawi	39.0	**13**	Namibia	44.1
5	Lesotho	39.6	**14**	Central African Rep	46.0
6	Burundi	41.4	**15**	Niger	46.5
7	Rwanda	41.7	**16**	Uganda	46.8
	Zambia	41.7	**17**	Guinea-Bissau	46.9
9	Sierra Leone	41.8	**18**	Angola	47.1

Death: *the chances*

Highest death rates

Number of deaths per 1,000 population, 2000–05

Rank	Country	Rate
1	Botswana	24.5
2	Mozambique	23.9
3	Sierra Leone	23.3
4	Swaziland	23.0
5	Malawi	22.6
6	Lesotho	21.9
7	Afghanistan	21.4
8	Burundi	20.8
9	Rwanda	20.6
10	Ethiopia	19.4
11	Guinea-Bissau	19.3
12	Niger	19.1
13	Angola	19.0
14	Zambia	18.8
15	Central African Rep	18.6
	Chad	18.6
17	Namibia	17.8
	Zimbabwe	17.8
19	Mali	17.3
20	Uganda	17.2
21	South Africa	17.1
22	Gambia, The	17.0
	Somalia	17.0
24	Guinea	16.8
25	Burkina Faso	15.9
26	Ukraine	15.4
27	Côte d'Ivoire	15.3
	Russia	15.3
29	Gabon	15.2
30	Bulgaria	15.1
31	Cameroon	14.6
32	Mauritania	14.2
33	Belarus	14.1
34	Congo-Brazzaville	14.0
35	Kenya	13.7
36	Congo	13.6
37	Hungary	13.5
38	Latvia	13.4
39	Eritrea	13.3
	Estonia	13.3
	Nigeria	13.3
42	Madagascar	13.2
	Togo	13.2
44	Tanzania	13.1
45	Romania	12.8
46	Haiti	12.6
	Laos	12.6
48	Benin	12.3
	Moldova	12.3
50	Liberia	12.2
51	Myanmar	11.6
	Senegal	11.6
53	Croatia	11.3
	Denmark	11.3
55	Lithuania	11.2
56	Sudan	11.1
57	Italy	10.9
58	Czech Republic	10.8
	Germany	10.8
	Portugal	10.8
61	Serbia & Montenegro	10.7
62	Cambodia	10.6
	Sweden	10.6
64	United Kingdom	10.5
65	Ghana	10.4
	Greece	10.4
67	Kazakhstan	10.1
68	Belgium	10.0
	Norway	10.0
70	Austria	9.9
	Georgia	9.9
	Nepal	9.9
	North Korea	9.9
	Poland	9.9
	Slovenia	9.9
76	Finland	9.8
	Slovakia	9.8
	Spain	9.8
	Switzerland	9.8
80	Pakistan	9.7
81	Papua New Guinea	9.6
82	France	9.4
83	Uruguay	9.3
84	Luxembourg	9.1
85	Netherlands	9.0
86	Bangladesh	8.7
87	Bhutan	8.6
88	India	8.4
	Macedonia	8.4
	United States	8.4
91	Japan	8.3
	Yemen	8.3
93	Bolivia	8.2
	Ireland	8.2
95	Bosnia	8.1
96	Argentina	7.8
	Barbados	7.8
	Malta	7.8

Note: Both death and, in particular, infant mortality rates can be underestimated in certain countries where not all deaths are officially recorded.

Highest infant mortality

Number of deaths per 1,000 live births, 2000–05

1	Afghanistan	161.3	**21**	Madagascar	91.5
2	Sierra Leone	146.3	**22**	Laos	88.0
3	Malawi	130.1	**23**	Myanmar	87.2
4	Mozambique	127.7	**24**	Burkina Faso	86.6
5	Niger	125.7	**25**	Pakistan	86.5
6	Guinea-Bissau	121.2	**26**	Eritrea	82.4
7	Mali	120.5	**27**	Côte d'Ivoire	80.8
8	Rwanda	119.2	**28**	Benin	80.6
9	Angola	117.7	**29**	Gabon	80.0
10	Chad	116.1	**30**	Zambia	79.6
11	Gambia, The	115.0	**31**	Liberia	79.3
12	Guinea	114.4		Cameroon	79.3
13	Somalia	112.7	**33**	Nigeria	78.5
14	Burundi	111.5	**34**	Sudan	77.7
15	Lesotho	111.2	**35**	Congo	77.2
16	Ethiopia	106.1	**36**	Togo	74.8
17	Mauritania	96.7	**37**	Tanzania	72.7
18	Uganda	93.9	**38**	Cambodia	72.5
19	Central African Rep	93.3	**39**	Nepal	70.9
20	Swaziland	91.7	**40**	Botswana	67.2

Lowest death rates

No. deaths per 1,000 pop., 2000–05

1	Kuwait	2.7
2	Brunei	3.2
3	Bahrain	3.7
4	Costa Rica	4.0
	Syria	4.0
	United Arab Emirates	4.0
7	Oman	4.1
	Qatar	4.1
	Saudi Arabia	4.1
10	Jordan	4.3
	West Bank and Gaza	4.3
12	Macau	4.6
13	Malaysia	4.7
	Venezuela	4.7
15	Libya	4.8
16	Iran	5.0
17	Mexico	5.1
	Panama	5.1
	Paraguay	5.1
20	Nicaragua	5.2
	Philippines	5.2

Lowest infant mortality

No. deaths per 1,000 live births, 2000–05

1	Japan	3.3
2	Sweden	3.4
3	Finland	4.0
4	Hong Kong	4.1
5	Belgium	4.2
6	Iceland	4.5
	Netherlands	4.5
	Norway	4.5
9	Germany	4.6
	Singapore	4.6
11	Austria	4.7
12	Switzerland	4.8
13	Denmark	5.0
	France	5.0
15	Australia	5.2
16	Spain	5.3
17	Canada	5.4
	Czech Republic	5.4
	Italy	5.4
	United Kingdom	5.4
21	Luxembourg	5.6
	Slovenia	5.6
23	Israel	5.9
24	Ireland	6.0
25	Portugal	6.1
26	New Zealand	6.2

Death and diseases

Cancer[a]

	%	
1	Netherlands	25.3
2	Belgium	24.6
	Canada	24.6
	France	24.6
5	Italy	24.0
6	Australia	23.9
7	United Kingdom	23.6
8	Ireland	22.9
9	Germany	22.7
10	Austria	22.5
	Norway	22.5
12	Singapore	22.3
13	United States	22.2
14	Spain	22.0
15	Israel	21.7
16	Slovenia	21.4
17	Hungary	21.2
18	Sweden	21.0
19	Costa Rica	20.7
20	Chile	19.9

Heart attack[a]

	%	
1	Azerbaijan	44.8
2	Lithuania	38.4
3	Macedonia	36.8
4	Austria	36.5
5	Estonia	34.6
6	Sweden	33.7
7	Israel	32.8
8	United States	32.7
9	Argentina	32.3
	Finland	32.3
11	Germany	32.1
12	Ireland	31.9
13	Australia	31.7
14	Kazakhstan	31.6
15	Moldova	31.4
16	Latvia	30.9
	Romania	30.9
18	Greece	30.6
19	Cuba	29.9
20	Mauritius	29.4
	Norway	29.4

Infectious disease[a]

	%	
1	Ecuador	6.7
2	Venezuela	4.8
3	Tajikistan	4.1
4	Argentina	3.4
5	Mexico	3.3
6	Kazakhstan	2.6
	Singapore	2.6
8	Chile	2.5
9	Azerbaijan	2.3
	Kirgizstan	2.3
11	Colombia	2.2
12	Costa Rica	2.0
13	Mauritius	1.8
14	Cuba	1.6
	Israel	1.6
16	France	1.4
	United States	1.4
18	Trinidad & Tobago	1.3
19	Latvia	1.2
	Russia	1.2

Motor accident[a]

	%	
1	Ecuador	2.1
2	Venezuela	2.0
3	Costa Rica	1.9
4	Colombia	1.7
	Greece	1.7
	Latvia	1.7
	Portugal	1.7
8	Estonia	1.5
	Mexico	1.5
	Slovenia	1.5
11	Cuba	1.4
	Mauritius	1.4
13	Lithuania	1.3
	Poland	1.3
	Russia	1.3
16	United States	1.2
17	Belgium	1.1
	Chile	1.1
	France	1.1
	Hungary	1.1
	Italy	1.1
	Moldova	1.1
	Spain	1.1

a Data refer to the chances a newborn baby has of eventually dying from one of the causes shown. Statistics are available for only a limited number of countries and many less developed countries are excluded. Latest available.

Least access to essential drugs

% of population, 1997

Rank	Country	%	Rank	Country	%
1	Nigeria	10		Yemen	50
2	Sudan	15	23	Tunisia	51
3	Angola	20	24	Eritrea	57
	Burundi	20	25	Albania	60
	Nepal	20		Burkina Faso	60
6	Moldova	25		Mali	60
7	Cambodia	30		Mongolia	60
	Gabon	30		Myanmar	60
	Georgia	30		Peru	60
	Haiti	30		Rwanda	60
11	India	35	32	Congo-Brazzaville	61
	Kenya	35	33	Bangladesh	65
13	Armenia	40		Madagascar	65
	Brazil	40		Pakistan	65
	Ecuador	40	36	Argentina	70
	Honduras	40		Belarus	70
17	Chad	46		Bolivia	70
	Nicaragua	46		Malaysia	70
19	Central African Rep	50		Togo	70
	Guatemala	50		Uganda	70
	Mozambique	50		Zimbabwe	70

AIDS

Cases per 100,000 population[a]

Rank	Country	Cases	Rank	Country	Cases
1	Congo-Brazzaville	1,421.6	21	Trinidad & Tobago	202.1
2	Namibia	1,142.9	22	Central African Rep	198.2
3	Bahamas	1,039.6	23	Rwanda	191.4
4	Botswana	640.9	24	Guadeloupe	175.6
5	Zimbabwe	628.2	25	Eritrea	172.2
6	Bermuda	540.6	26	Chad	150.9
7	Malawi	472.5	27	Spain	143.3
8	Zambia	454.8	28	Gabon	137.4
9	Barbados	390.6	29	Honduras	129.9
10	Côte d'Ivoire	379.9	30	Cameroon	129.2
11	Burundi	379.8	31	Burkina Faso	122.9
12	Lesotho	347.6	32	Netherlands Antilles	119.5
13	Swaziland	346.6	33	Jamaica	114.5
14	Tanzania	340.3	34	Haiti	114.0
15	Kenya	277.1	35	Martinique	111.2
16	United States	268.8	36	Guinea-Bissau	97.9
17	Togo	263.8	37	Congo	95.5
18	Uganda	254.7	38	Switzerland	95.2
19	Ghana	211.2	39	Brazil	86.5
20	Thailand	208.5	40	Mozambique	85.8

a AIDS data refer to the total number of cases reported to the World Health Organisation up to November 15 2000. The number of cases diagnosed and reported depends on the quality of medical practice and administration and is likely to be under-recorded in a number of countries.

Health

Highest health spending

As % of GDP[a]

1	United States	13.0
2	Nicaragua	12.2
3	Germany	10.6
4	Switzerland	10.4
5	Argentina	10.3
6	Lebanon	9.8
7	Croatia	9.6
	France	9.6
9	Israel	9.5
10	Colombia	9.3
11	Canada	9.2
12	Cuba	9.1
	Jordan	9.1
	Uruguay	9.1
15	Belgium	8.9
	Norway	8.9
17	Honduras	8.6
	Netherlands	8.6
	West Bank and Gaza	8.6
20	Australia	8.5
21	Moldova	8.4
22	Austria	8.3
	Denmark	8.3
	Greece	8.3
25	Italy	8.2
	United Arab Emirates	8.2
27	New Zealand	8.1
28	Iceland	8.0
	Saudi Arabia	8.0
	Sweden	8.0

Lowest health spending

As % of GDP[a]

1	Indonesia	1.6
2	Azerbaijan	1.8
	Myanmar	1.8
4	Eritrea	2.0
5	Madagascar	2.1
6	Georgia	2.2
7	Syria	2.4
8	Malaysia	2.5
9	Laos	2.6
	Niger	2.6
	Togo	2.6
12	Nigeria	2.8
	Qatar	2.8
14	Chad	2.9
15	Central African Rep	3.0
	Tanzania	3.0
17	Gabon	3.1
	Sri Lanka	3.1
19	Benin	3.2
	Papua New Guinea	3.2
	Singapore	3.2
22	Kuwait	3.3
23	Fiji	3.4
	Mauritius	3.4
	Sudan	3.4
26	Bermuda	3.5
	Mozambique	3.5
	Oman	3.5

Highest population per doctor

Latest available year

1	Chad	50,000
	Eritrea	50,000
	Gambia, The	50,000
	Malawi	50,000
5	Mozambique	33,333
	Niger	33,333
7	Angola	25,000
	Ethiopia	25,000
	Ghana	25,000
	Rwanda	25,000
	Somalia	25,000
	Tanzania	25,000
	Uganda	25,000
14	Nepal	20,000
15	Benin	16,667
	Burundi	16,667
	Central African Rep	16,667
18	Cameroon	14,286
	Senegal	14,286
20	Cambodia	10,000
	Congo	10,000
	Côte d'Ivoire	10,000
	Kenya	10,000
	Lesotho	10,000
	Mali	10,000
	Mauritania	10,000
	Papua New Guinea	10,000
	Sudan	10,000
	Togo	10,000
	Zambia	10,000
	Zimbabwe	10,000

Most hospital beds

Beds per 1,000 pop.

1	Switzerland	18.1	32	Israel	6.0
2	Japan	16.5	33	Croatia	5.9
3	Norway	14.7	34	Slovenia	5.7
4	Belarus	12.2	35	Poland	5.3
5	Moldova	12.1		Serbia & Montenegro	5.3
	Russia	12.1	37	Macedonia	5.2
7	Ukraine	11.8	38	Cuba	5.1
8	Mongolia	11.5		South Korea	5.1
	Turkmenistan	11.5		Trinidad & Tobago	5.1
10	Netherlands	11.3	41	Greece	5.0
11	Bulgaria	10.6	42	Georgia	4.8
12	Latvia	10.3	43	Denmark	4.6
13	Azerbaijan	9.7	44	Uruguay	4.4
14	Lithuania	9.6	45	Libya	4.3
15	Kirgizstan	9.5	46	Canada	4.2
16	Germany	9.3		United Kingdom	4.2
17	Austria	8.9	48	Papua New Guinea	4.0
18	Tajikistan	8.8		Portugal	4.0
19	Czech Republic	8.7	50	Spain	3.9
20	Australia	8.5	51	Sweden	3.8
	France	8.5	52	Ireland	3.7
	Kazakhstan	8.5		United States	3.7
23	Hungary	8.3	54	Singapore	3.6
	Uzbekistan	8.3	55	Congo-Brazzaville	3.4
25	Finland	7.8	56	Argentina	3.3
26	Romania	7.6		Puerto Rico	3.3
27	Slovakia	7.5	58	Albania	3.2
28	Estonia	7.4		Gabon	3.2
29	Belgium	7.2	60	Brazil	3.1
30	Italy	6.5		Mauritius	3.1
31	New Zealand	6.2			

Lowest population per doctor

Latest available year

1	Italy	169		Hungary	286
2	Cuba	189		Kazakhstan	286
3	Israel	217	18	Belgium	294
	Russia	217		Latvia	294
5	Ukraine	222	20	Uzbekistan	303
6	Belarus	233	21	Estonia	323
7	Spain	238		Kirgizstan	323
8	Greece	250		Portugal	323
9	Lithuania	256		Sweden	323
10	Azerbaijan	263	25	Armenia	333
	Georgia	263		Austria	333
12	Uruguay	270		Czech Republic	333
13	Moldova	278		Finland	333
14	Bulgaria	286		France	333
	Germany	286		Slovakia	333

a Latest available year.

Till death us do part

Highest marriage rates[a]

Number of marriages per 1,000 population

Rank	Country	Rate
1	Bermuda	15.7
2	Barbados	13.5
3	Cyprus	11.0
4	United Kingdom	10.7
5	Egypt	9.9
	Fiji	9.9
7	Bangladesh	9.7
8	Bahamas	9.3
	Sri Lanka	9.3
10	Denmark	9.1
11	Puerto Rico	8.7
12	Mauritius	8.6
	United States	8.6
14	Syria	8.4
15	Turkey	8.0
16	Taiwan	7.9
	Uzbekistan	7.9
18	Iran	7.8
19	Jamaica	7.4
20	Macedonia	7.0
	Mexico	7.0
	Thailand	7.0
23	Australia	6.9
	Belarus	6.9
	Costa Rica	6.9
	Philippines	6.9
27	Albania	6.8
	South Korea	6.8
	Tajikistan	6.8
30	China	6.7
	Portugal	6.7
32	Singapore	6.6
33	Japan	6.2
	Kazakhstan	6.2
	Réunion	6.2
36	Brunei	6.1
	Malta	6.1
	Ukraine	6.1
39	Kirgizstan	6.0
	Moldova	6.0
	Mongolia	6.0
	Romania	6.0
43	Turkmenistan	5.9
44	Bahrain	5.7
	Croatia	5.7
46	Ecuador	5.6
	Iceland	5.6
	Trinidad & Tobago	5.6
49	Algeria	5.5
	Greece	5.5
	Jordan	5.5
	Suriname	5.5
	Tunisia	5.5
	Uruguay	5.5
55	Cuba	5.4
	Germany	5.4
	Netherlands	5.4
58	Chile	5.3
	Norway	5.3
60	Netherlands Antilles	5.2
	Russia	5.2
	Spain	5.2
	Switzerland	5.2

Lowest marriage rates[a]

Number of marriages per 1,000 population

Rank	Country	Rate
1	Dominican Republic	1.9
2	Ireland	2.2
3	Qatar	2.9
4	Armenia	3.0
5	Saudi Arabia	3.1
6	Latvia	3.3
7	Panama	3.4
8	Estonia	3.6
	Georgia	3.6
	United Arab Emirates	3.6
11	Poland	3.7
	Slovenia	3.7
13	Argentina	3.8
	Belgium	3.8
	Venezuela	3.8
16	South Africa	4.0
17	Bulgaria	4.1
	Martinique	4.1
	Peru	4.1
20	Hong Kong	4.4

a Latest available year.

Note: Marriage rates refer to registered marriages only and, therefore, reflect the customs surrounding registry and efficiency of administration. The data are based on latest available figures and hence will be affected by the population age structure at the time.

Highest divorce rates[a]

Number of divorces per 1,000 population

Rank	Country	Rate
1	Cuba	5.9
2	Belarus	4.7
	United States	4.7
4	Puerto Rico	3.7
5	Ukraine	3.6
6	Lithuania	3.4
	United Kingdom	3.4
8	Estonia	3.3
9	New Zealand	3.2
	Russia	3.2
11	Czech Republic	3.1
12	Moldova	3.0
13	Australia	2.7
	Belgium	2.7
15	Finland	2.6
	Hungary	2.6
	Latvia	2.6
	Netherlands Antilles	2.6
	Switzerland	2.6
20	Denmark	2.5
21	Germany	2.4
	Norway	2.4
23	Sweden	2.3
24	Canada	2.2
	Kazakhstan	2.2
	Uruguay	2.2
27	Austria	2.1
28	France	2.0
	Guadeloupe	2.0
	Israel	2.0
	Netherlands	2.0
	Suriname	2.0
33	Romania	1.9
	Singapore	1.9
35	Iceland	1.8
	Japan	1.8
	Luxembourg	1.8
	Taiwan	1.8
39	Bahamas	1.7
	Hong Kong	1.7
41	Egypt	1.6
	Portugal	1.6
	Slovakia	1.6
44	Kuwait	1.5
	South Korea	1.5
	Uzbekistan	1.5
47	Barbados	1.4
	Bulgaria	1.4
	Cyprus	1.4
	Georgia	1.4
51	Jordan	1.3
	Réunion	1.3
	Turkmenistan	1.3
54	Bahrain	1.2
	Kirgizstan	1.2
	Poland	1.2
	Thailand	1.2
58	Costa Rica	1.1
	Slovenia	1.1
	Tunisia	1.1
	United Arab Emirates	1.1
62	Venezuela	1.0

Lowest divorce rates[a]

Number of divorces per 1,000 population

Rank	Country	Rate
1	Colombia	0.2
	Guatemala	0.2
	Nicaragua	0.2
4	Macedonia	0.3
5	Armenia	0.4
	Bosnia	0.4
7	Iran	0.5
	Jamaica	0.5
	Mexico	0.5
	Turkey	0.5
11	Bermuda	0.6
	Chile	0.6
	Libya	0.6
	Macau	0.6
15	Azerbaijan	0.7
	Ecuador	0.7
	Italy	0.7
	Mauritius	0.7
19	Albania	0.8
	Brazil	0.8
	Brunei	0.8
	Spain	0.8
	Syria	0.8
24	China	0.9
	Croatia	0.9
	Greece	0.9
	Martinique	0.9
	Panama	0.9
	Qatar	0.9
	South Africa	0.9
	Tajikistan	0.9
	Trinidad & Tobago	0.9

Households and prices

Biggest households[a]

Population per dwelling

Rank	Country		Rank	Country	
1	Saudi Arabia	8.0	27	Bangladesh	5.5
2	Gabon	7.2		Laos	5.5
3	Pakistan	7.1		Mexico	5.5
4	Bosnia	6.8		Sri Lanka	5.5
5	Swaziland	6.3	31	Central African Rep	5.4
6	Rwanda	6.2		Croatia	5.4
	Sudan	6.2		Gambia, The	5.4
8	Congo-Brazzaville	6.1		Guinea	5.4
	North Korea	6.1		Guinea-Bissau	5.4
	Togo	6.1		Tanzania	5.4
	United Arab Emirates	6.1		Uganda	5.4
12	Burundi	6.0	38	Afghanistan	5.3
13	Ghana	5.9		Chad	5.3
	Malawi	5.9		Fiji	5.3
	Niger	5.9		Haiti	5.3
	Papua New Guinea	5.9		India	5.3
	Uzbekistan	5.9		Iran	5.3
18	Réunion	5.8		Iraq	5.3
	Senegal	5.8	45	Egypt	5.2
	Sierra Leone	5.8		Kirgizstan	5.2
21	South Africa	5.7		Madagascar	5.2
	Yemen	5.7	48	Azerbaijan	5.1
23	Lesotho	5.6		Kazakhstan	5.1
	Mozambique	5.6		Mauritius	5.1
	Nigeria	5.6		Netherlands Antilles	5.1
	Philippines	5.6		Turkmenistan	5.1

Highest cost of living[b]

December 2000, USA=100

Rank	Country		Rank	Country	
1	Japan	160	17	Mexico	87
2	Serbia & Montenegro	122	18	Denmark	85
3	Hong Kong	117		Russia	85
4	South Korea	102		Sweden	85
	Taiwan	102	21	Austria	84
6	United States	100		Jordan	84
7	Israel	99	23	Nigeria	82
	Norway	99	24	Bahrain	81
	United Kingdom	99		Egypt	81
10	Gabon	98	26	Finland	79
11	Singapore	97	27	United Arab Emirates	78
12	Switzerland	96	28	Côte d'Ivoire	77
13	China	94	29	Canada	76
14	Iceland	93		Netherlands	76
15	Argentina	92		Venezuela	76
16	France	88			

a Latest available year.

b The cost of living index shown is compiled by The Economist Intelligence Unit for use by companies in determining expatriate compensation: it is a comparison of the cost of maintaining a typical international lifestyle in the country rather than a comparison of the purchasing power of a citizen of the country. The index is based on typical urban prices an international executive and family will face abroad. The

Smallest households[a]

Population per dwelling

1	Sweden	2.1		Portugal	2.9
2	Germany	2.2		Romania	2.9
3	Denmark	2.3	**29**	Cyprus	3.0
	Finland	2.3		Greece	3.0
	Netherlands	2.3		Ireland	3.0
	United Kingdom	2.3		Japan	3.0
7	Belgium	2.4	**33**	Albania	3.1
	France	2.4		Myanmar	3.1
	Iceland	2.4	**35**	Belarus	3.2
	Norway	2.4		Malta	3.2
	Switzerland	2.4		Poland	3.2
12	Austria	2.5		Spain	3.2
	Hungary	2.5	**39**	Macau	3.3
14	Canada	2.6	**40**	Serbia & Montenegro	3.4
	Ukraine	2.6	**41**	Estonia	3.6
	Uruguay	2.6		Zimbabwe	3.6
17	Argentina	2.7	**43**	Cameroon	3.7
	Australia	2.7		Hong Kong	3.7
	Bulgaria	2.7		Lithuania	3.7
	United States	2.7		Slovenia	3.7
21	Russia	2.8	**47**	Botswana	3.8
	Slovakia	2.8		China	3.8
23	Czech Republic	2.9		Congo	3.8
	Italy	2.9		Oman	3.8
	Luxembourg	2.9		Taiwan	3.8
	New Zealand	2.9			

Lowest cost of living[b]

December 2000, USA=100

1	Tehran	26		Paraguay	56
2	India	40		Sri Lanka	56
3	Libya	44		Ukraine	56
4	Hungary	46	**19**	Bangladesh	57
	Pakistan	46		Thailand	57
	Philippines	46	**21**	Kenya	58
	Romania	46	**22**	Croatia	59
	Zimbabwe	46		New Zealand	59
9	South Africa	51		Poland	59
10	Czech Republic	52	**25**	Malaysia	60
	Tunisia	52	**26**	Ecuador	61
12	Zambia	53		Indonesia	61
13	Uzbekistan	54		Turkey	61
14	Colombia	56	**29**	Cameroon	62
	Costa Rica	56		Senegal	62

prices are for products of international comparable quality found in a supermarket or department store. Prices found in local markets and bazaars are not used unless the available merchandise is of the specified quality and the shopping area itself is safe for executive and family members. New York City prices are used as the base, so United States = 100.

Consumer goods: *ownership*

TV

Colour TVs per 100 households

Rank	Country	Value	Rank	Country	Value
1	Taiwan	99.4	26	Denmark	92.0
2	Hong Kong	99.2	27	Australia	91.2
	Japan	99.2	28	Jordan	91.1
	United States	99.2	29	Greece	90.8
5	Ireland	99.1	30	Slovenia	90.5
6	Canada	98.7	31	Malaysia	90.3
7	Belgium	98.5	32	Venezuela	89.2
8	Singapore	98.4	33	Mexico	88.5
9	United Kingdom	98.3	34	Argentina	88.4
10	Netherlands	98.2	35	Czech Republic	87.1
11	Spain	98.1	36	Croatia	86.8
12	Saudi Arabia	97.3	37	Kuwait	86.7
13	Austria	97.2	38	Slovakia	85.7
	Portugal	97.2	39	Brazil	85.4
15	Sweden	97.1	40	Hungary	85.2
16	Finland	97.0	41	Tunisia	84.9
16	Switzerland	97.0	42	Colombia	84.5
18	Germany	96.9	43	Poland	81.9
19	New Zealand	96.8	44	Thailand	80.3
20	France	95.8	45	Russia	79.5
21	Italy	95.4	46	Estonia	77.6
22	United Arab Emirates	95.2	47	Belarus	76.5
23	Israel	94.4	48	Ukraine	71.4
24	Norway	92.8	49	Algeria	67.9
25	South Korea	92.5	50	Ecuador	65.1

Telephone

Telephone lines per 100 people

Rank	Country	Value	Rank	Country	Value
1	Bermuda	85.7	23	Ireland	47.8
2	Norway	72.9	24	Israel	47.1
3	Luxembourg	72.4	25	South Korea	46.4
4	Switzerland	69.9	26	Italy	46.2
5	Iceland	67.7	27	Guadeloupe	44.7
6	United States	67.3	28	Martinique	43.8
7	Sweden	66.5	29	Barbados	42.7
8	Canada	65.5	30	Portugal	42.3
9	Denmark	63.8	31	Spain	42.1
10	Cyprus	63.0	32	Macau	40.8
11	Netherlands	60.7	33	United Arab Emirates	40.7
12	Germany	60.1	34	Réunion	38.9
13	Hong Kong	57.6	35	Slovenia	37.8
14	United Kingdom	56.7	36	Czech Republic	37.1
15	Japan	55.8	37	Netherlands Antilles	36.8
16	Taiwan	54.5	38	Croatia	36.5
17	Australia	52.4	39	Estonia	35.7
18	Malta	51.2	40	Bulgaria	35.4
19	Belgium	49.9	41	Puerto Rico	33.3
20	New Zealand	49.6	42	Lithuania	31.2
21	Singapore	48.2	43	Slovakia	30.7
22	Austria	48.1	44	Latvia	30.0

Video cassette recorder

VCRs per 100 households

1	Canada	89.9	13	Belgium	73.5
2	United Kingdom	85.3	14	Switzerland	72.9
3	United States	82.2	15	Hong Kong	72.4
4	Denmark	82.1	16	South Korea	67.8
5	New Zealand	80.0	17	Finland	67.3
6	Singapore	79.3	18	Malaysia	66.6
7	Ireland	78.6	19	Israel	65.1
8	Japan	76.9	20	Italy	65.0
	Sweden	76.9	21	Spain	64.9
10	Australia	76.5	22	France	59.8
11	Netherlands	76.1	23	Taiwan	58.1
12	Poland	74.4	24	Austria	56.9

Computer

Computers per 100 people

1	United States	58.5	18	United Kingdom	33.8
2	Sweden	50.7	19	Germany	33.6
3	Switzerland	50.3	20	Japan	31.5
4	Norway	49.1	21	France	30.5
5	Singapore	48.3	22	Austria	27.7
6	Australia	46.5	23	Israel	25.4
7	Luxembourg	45.9	24	Slovenia	25.1
8	Bermuda	43.7	25	Taiwan	22.5
9	Denmark	43.2	26	Italy	20.9
10	Finland	39.6	27	Cyprus	19.3
11	Netherlands	39.5	28	Guadeloupe	18.9
12	Iceland	39.2	29	Spain	14.3
13	Canada	39.0	30	Bahrain	14.0
14	Ireland	36.5	31	Macau	13.7
15	New Zealand	36.0	32	Qatar	13.6
16	Hong Kong	34.7	33	Estonia	13.5
17	Belgium	34.5	34	United Arab Emirates	12.5

Mobile telephone

Subscribers per 100 people

1	Luxembourg	87.2	16	South Korea	56.7
2	Austria	78.6	17	Greece	55.9
3	Italy	73.7	18	Belgium	54.9
4	Finland	72.6	19	Taiwan	52.2
5	Norway	70.3	20	France	49.4
6	Netherlands	67.1	21	Israel	47.2
7	United Kingdom	67.0	22	Japan	44.9
8	Portugal	66.5	23	Ireland	44.7
9	Hong Kong	63.6	24	Australia	44.6
	Switzerland	63.6	25	Martinique	41.0
11	Iceland	61.9	26	Guadeloupe	37.3
12	Denmark	61.4	27	Réunion	36.8
13	Singapore	60.8	28	New Zealand	36.6
14	Sweden	58.3	29	United Arab Emirates	34.7
15	Germany	57.9	30	United States	31.6

Books and newspapers

Book sales

$m, 1999

1	United States	26,786
2	Japan	9,913
3	Germany	9,806
4	United Kingdom	4,611
5	France	2,840
6	Italy	2,658
7	Brazil	2,506
8	Spain	2,411
9	China	2,387
10	South Korea	1,740
11	Canada	1,489
12	Australia	1,165
13	Netherlands	983
14	Belgium	977
15	Argentina	702
16	Sweden	666
17	Switzerland	639
18	Taiwan	622
19	Mexico	614
20	Norway	566
21	Finland	504
22	Poland	495
23	Austria	387
24	South Africa	383
25	Denmark	374
26	Portugal	350
27	Vietnam	339

Per head, $

1	Norway	127
2	Germany	120
3	United States	98
4	Finland	97
5	Belgium	96
6	Switzerland	90
7	Japan	78
	United Kingdom	78
9	Sweden	75
10	Denmark	70
	Singapore	70
12	New Zealand	65
13	Netherlands	62
14	Australia	61
	Spain	61
16	Ireland	56
17	Canada	49
18	Austria	48
19	France	47
20	Italy	46
21	South Korea	37
22	Portugal	35
23	Israel	28
	Taiwan	28
25	Greece	22
26	Argentina	19

Daily newspapers

Copies per '000 population, latest year

1	Hong Kong	762
2	Macau	533
3	Norway	499
4	Sweden	466
5	Finland	456
6	Japan	423
7	Kuwait	346
8	Switzerland	343
9	Singapore	332
10	Poland	320
11	United Kingdom	315
12	Germany	309
13	Denmark	302
14	Netherlands	287
15	Bermuda	250
16	Uruguay	226
17	Thailand	207
18	United States	203
19	Hungary	197
20	Belgium	172
	Puerto Rico	172
22	Canada	167
23	Barbados	154
24	France	147
25	Ireland	146
26	Trinidad & Tobago	135
27	Lebanon	117
28	Malaysia	115
29	United Arab Emirates	107
30	Qatar	106
31	Suriname	104
32	Greece	94
33	Guadeloupe	78
34	Portugal	68
35	Bolivia	63
	Egypt	63
37	Jamaica	62
38	Ecuador	60
39	Slovakia	58
40	Panama	57

Music and the Internet

Music sales[a]

$m, 2000			*$ per head*		
1	United States	14,042	1	Iceland	55
2	Japan	6,497	2	Norway	52
3	United Kingdom	2,829	3	Japan	51
4	Germany	2,421		United States	51
5	France	1,695	5	United Kingdom	48
6	Canada	819	6	Denmark	44
7	Brazil	725	7	Ireland	38
8	Mexico	666	8	Switzerland	37
9	Spain	563	9	Austria	36
10	Australia	561		Sweden	36
11	Italy	532	11	Australia	30
12	Netherlands	455		Germany	30
13	Sweden	323	13	Netherlands	29
14	South Korea	300	14	France	28
15	Austria	289	15	Canada	27
16	Belgium	267	16	Belgium	26
17	Switzerland	264	17	New Zealand	23
18	Taiwan	244	18	Cyprus	22
19	India	237		Finland	22
20	Denmark	233	20	Hong Kong	16
21	Norway	232			
22	Russia	197			

Internet hosts

By country, January 2001			*Per 1,000 pop., January 2001*		
1	United States[b]	72,616,479	1	United States[b]	266.11
2	Japan	4,640,863	2	Iceland	158.99
3	Canada	2,364,014	3	Finland	149.36
4	United Kingdom	2,291,369	4	Norway	117.88
5	Germany	2,163,326	5	New Zealand	90.27
6	Italy	1,630,526	6	Sweden	86.26
7	Australia	1,615,939	7	Australia	85.08
8	Netherlands	1,309,911	8	Netherlands	82.90
9	France	1,229,763	9	Denmark	81.92
10	Taiwan	1,095,718	10	Canada	77.25
11	Brazil	876,596	11	Switzerland	64.81
12	Finland	771,725	12	Austria	62.35
13	Sweden	764,011	13	Singapore	54.55
14	Spain	663,553	14	Taiwan	50.10
15	Mexico	559,165	15	Belgium	40.80
16	Norway	525,030	16	United Kingdom	38.76
17	Austria	504,144	17	Japan	36.67
18	Switzerland	461,456	18	Hong Kong	33.30
19	Denmark	435,556	19	Israel	29.59
20	Belgium	417,130	20	Italy	28.28
21	South Korea	397,809	21	Estonia	27.80
22	Poland	371,943	22	Germany	26.37
23	New Zealand	345,107	23	Ireland	23.72

a Vinyl, tape and compact disc sales.
b Includes all hosts ending ".com", ".net" and ".org", which exaggerates the numbers.

Nobel prize winners: *1901–2000*

Peace

1	United States	16
2	United Kingdom	11
3	France	9
4	Sweden	5
5	Germany	4
	Belgium	4
7	Norway	3
	South Africa	3
9	Argentina	2
	Austria	2
	Israel	2
	Russia	2
	Switzerland	2

Economics[a]

1	United States	24
2	United Kingdom	8
3	Norway	2
	Sweden	2
5	France	1
	Germany	1
	Netherlands	1
	Russia	1

Literature

1	France	13
2	United States	12
3	United Kingdom	8
4	Germany	7
5	Spain	6
	Sweden	6
7	Italy	5
8	Norway	3
	Poland	3
	Russia	3

Physiology or medicine

1	United States	45
2	United Kingdom	18
3	Germany	14
4	Sweden	7
5	France	6
	Switzerland	6
7	Austria	5
	Denmark	5
9	Belgium	3
	Italy	3

Physics

1	United States	42
2	United Kingdom	19
3	Germany	17
4	France	8
5	Netherlands	6
6	Russia	5
7	Sweden	4
	Switzerland	4
9	Austria	3
	Italy	3
	Japan	3

Chemistry

1	United States	37
2	United Kingdom	22
3	Germany	14
4	France	6
5	Sweden	5
	Switzerland	5
7	Canada	4
8	Japan	2
9	Argentina	1
	Austria	1
	Belgium	1
	Czech Republic	1
	Denmark	1
	Finland	1
	Italy	1
	Netherlands	1
	Norway	1
	Russia	1

a Since 1969.

Prizes by country of residence at time awarded. When prizes have been shared in the same field, one credit given to each country. Only top rankings in each field are included.

Olympic medal winners

Summer games, 1896–2000

		Gold	Silver	Bronze
1	United States	872	659	581
2	Soviet Union[a]	517	423	382
3	Germany	374	392	417
4	United Kingdom	188	243	232
5	France	189	195	216
6	Italy	179	144	155
7	Hungary	150	134	158
8	Sweden	138	157	176
9	Finland	101	81	114
10	Japan	98	97	103
11	Australia	103	110	139
12	Romania	74	83	108
13	China	80	79	64
14	Poland	56	72	113
15	Canada	52	80	99
16	Netherlands	61	66	85
17	Cuba	57	47	41
18	Switzerland	47	74	62
19	Bulgaria	48	82	65
20	Denmark	41	63	58

Winter games, 1924–1998

		Gold	Silver	Bronze
1	Germany	96	89	80
2	Soviet Union[a]	87	63	67
3	Norway	83	87	69
4	United States	59	59	41
5	Austria	39	53	53
6	Sweden	39	28	25
7	Finland	38	49	48
8	Switzerland	29	31	32
9	Italy	27	27	23
10	Canada	25	25	29
11	Russia	21	14	7
12	Netherlands	19	23	19
13	France	18	17	26
14	South Korea	9	3	4
15	Japan	8	9	12
16	United Kingdom	7	4	13
17	Poland	1	1	2
18	Czech Republic	1	1	1
19	Bulgaria	1	0	0
20	China	0	10	4

a Includes unified team in 1992.

Drinking and smoking

Beer drinkers

Retail sales per head, litres

1	South Africa	110.0
2	Czech Republic	85.5
3	Australia	77.9
4	Germany	76.3
5	Austria	66.2
6	United States	62.2
7	Netherlands	57.9
7	Norway	57.9
9	Finland	55.2
10	Denmark	53.6
11	Sweden	52.5
12	Slovakia	51.7
13	Canada	49.8
14	Venezuela	48.9
15	United Kingdom	46.2
16	Hungary	45.5
17	New Zealand	45.4
18	Japan	41.5
19	Bulgaria	40.1
20	Poland	39.9
21	Colombia	39.0
22	Belgium	38.8
23	Brazil	36.6

Wine drinkers

Retail sales per head, litres

1	France	44.7
2	Argentina	32.1
3	Hungary	30.8
4	Switzerland	28.5
5	Denmark	26.0
6	Germany	21.3
7	Greece	20.0
8	New Zealand	19.5
	Romania	19.5
10	Portugal	17.9
11	Spain	17.8
12	Australia	17.2
13	Austria	16.9
14	Netherlands	16.0
15	Belgium	15.0
16	Slovakia	13.4
17	Chile	12.7
18	Sweden	11.9
19	Czech Republic	10.9
20	United Kingdom	10.2
21	South Africa	10.1
22	Japan	9.7
	Norway	9.7

Alcoholic drinks

$ per head

1	Finland	449.3
2	Denmark	414.8
3	Belgium	386.9
4	France	360.7
5	United Kingdom	341.5
6	Sweden	307.8
7	New Zealand	306.0
8	Ireland	259.6
9	United States	237.7
10	Canada	235.5
11	Austria	207.7
12	Australia	207.4
13	Netherlands	185.7
14	Japan	169.6
15	Germany	154.9
16	South Africa	127.7
17	Portugal	126.4
18	Venezuela	110.4
19	Italy	96.2
20	Mexico	92.1
21	Argentina	88.2
22	Norway	86.9
23	Hong Kong	84.8
24	Spain	84.0

Smokers

Av. ann. consumption of cigarettes per head per day

1	Greece	7.8
2	Poland	7.3
3	Hungary	7.1
4	Japan	7.0
5	Switzerland	6.6
6	South Korea	6.1
7	Czech Republic	5.9
8	Australia	5.8
	Bulgaria	5.8
	Serbia & Montenegro	5.8
	Spain	5.8
12	United States	5.7
13	Austria	5.1
14	Belarus	5.0
	Germany	5.0
16	Slovakia	4.9
17	Taiwan	4.7
18	Belgium	4.6
	Canada	4.6
	France	4.6
	Ireland	4.6
22	Israel	4.4
	Italy	4.4

Crime and punishment

Serious assault[a]

No. per 100,000 pop., 1999

1	Australia	708.5
2	Dominican Republic	682.4
3	South Africa	595.6
4	Namibia	533.6
5	Israel	491.8
6	Swaziland	471.7
7	Ghana	418.9
8	Lebanon	209.7
9	Zimbabwe	198.4
10	Tunisia	165.0
11	France	162.7
12	Uruguay	162.5
13	Barbados	161.9
14	Lesotho	156.9
15	Canada	140.2
16	Germany	139.6
17	Hong Kong	117.1
18	Rwanda	114.3
19	Turkey	112.0
20	Puerto Rico	101.8

Theft[a]

No. per 100,000 pop., 1999

1	Denmark	7,687.6
2	Australia	6,215.0
3	Dominican Republic	4,779.3
4	Norway	4,577.1
5	Canada	3,968.9
6	Germany	3,894.4
7	Switzerland	3,886.4
8	France	3,849.2
9	South Africa	3,407.2
10	Iceland	3,374.9
11	Luxembourg	3,079.9
12	Estonia	2,917.0
13	Austria	2,649.5
14	Finland	2,618.5
15	Hungary	2,591.0
16	Puerto Rico	2,214.3
17	Barbados	2,182.5
18	Swaziland	1,954.7
19	Zimbabwe	1,827.6
20	Slovenia	1,803.2

Prisoners

Total prison pop., latest available year

1	United States	1,931,859
2	China	1,427,407
3	Russia	923,765
4	India	381,147
5	Ukraine	219,955
6	Thailand	206,011
7	Brazil	194,074
8	South Africa	162,638
9	Rwanda	143,021
10	Mexico	139,707
11	Kazakhstan	82,945
12	Germany	79,493
13	Pakistan	74,485
14	Poland	70,544
15	England and Wales	64,631
16	South Korea	64,038
17	Belarus	58,879
18	Colombia	57,068
19	Japan	56,133
20	Vietnam	55,000
21	Italy	53,481
22	Indonesia	53,399

Per 100,000 pop., latest available year

1	United States	702
2	Russia	635
3	Belarus	577
4	Kazakhstan	494
5	Martinique	490
6	Bahamas	478
7	Bermuda	447
8	Kirgizstan	441
9	Suriname	437
10	Ukraine	436
11	South Africa	406
12	Puerto Rico	402
13	Botswana	401
14	Singapore	383
15	Netherlands Antilles	364
16	Latvia	357
17	Trinidad & Tobago	351
18	Thailand	336
19	Estonia	330
20	Azerbaijan	323
21	Panama	303
22	Cuba	297

a Crime statistics are based on offences recorded by the police. The number will therefore depend partly on the efficiency of police administration systems, the definition of offences, and the proportion of crimes reported, and therefore may not be strictly comparable.

Stars...

Space missions

Firsts and selected events

1957	Man-made satellite
	Dog in space, Laika
1961	Human in space, Yuri Gagarin
	Entire day in space, Gherman Titov
1963	Woman in space, Valentina Tereshkova
1964	Space crew, one pilot and two passengers
1965	Space walk, Alexei Leonov
	Computer guidance system
	Eight days in space achieved (needed to travel to moon and back)
1966	Docking between space craft and target vehicle
	Autopilot re-entry and landing
1968	Live television broadcast from space
	Moon orbit
1969	Astronaut transfer from one craft to another in space
	Moon landing
1971	Space station, Salyut
	Drive on the moon
1973	Space laboratory, Skylab
1978	Non-Amercian, non-Soviet, Vladimir Remek (Czechoslovakia)
1982	Space shuttle, Columbia (first craft to carry four crew members)
1983	Five crew mission
1984	Space walk, untethered
	Capture, repair and redeployment of satellite in space
	Seven crew mission
1986	Space shuttle explosion, Challenger
	Mir space station activated
1990	Hubble telescope deployed
2001	Dennis Tito, first paying space tourist

Astronauts

Longest time in space, hours

United States	
John Blaha	3,864
Norman Thagard	3,360
Andrew Thomas	3,268
David Wolf	3,216
Edward Gibson	2,017
William Pogue	2,017
Russia	
Musa Manarov	12,984
Sergi Krikalev	11,064
Yuri Ramanenko	10,344
Alexandr Volkov	9,384
Leonid Kizim	9,024
Other nations	
Jean-Loup Chrétien	784
Ulf Merbold	441
Pedro Duque	381
Claude Andre-Deshays	379
Jean-François Clervoy	262

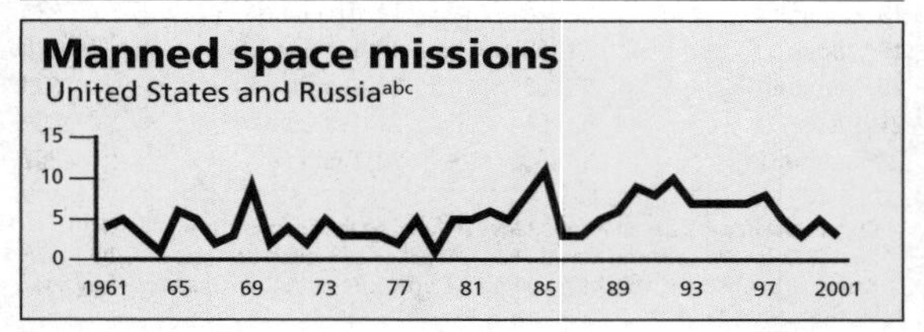

...and Wars

Defence spending

As % of GDP, 1998

1	Eritrea	44.4
2	Angola	16.5
3	Saudi Arabia	15.5
4	Qatar	15.4
5	Afghanistan	14.9
6	North Korea	14.3
7	Kuwait	11.1
8	Oman	10.9
9	Israel	8.9
10	Armenia	8.6
11	Bosnia	8.4
12	Congo-Brazzaville	7.8
13	Bahrain	7.7
	Jordan	7.7
15	Iraq	7.6
	Tajikistan	7.6
17	Ethiopia	7.1
18	Brunei	6.7
	Yemen	6.7
20	Algeria	6.6
21	Burundi	6.4
22	Iran	6.2
	Rwanda	6.2
	United Arab Emirates	6.2
25	Cyprus	6.1
	Zimbabwe	6.1
27	Pakistan	5.7
28	Liberia	5.6
	Singapore	5.6
	Syria	5.6
31	Suriname	5.5
	Turkey	5.5
33	China	5.4
34	Bhutan	5.3
35	Botswana	5.2
	Taiwan	5.2
37	Cambodia	5.1
	Russia	5.1
	Sri Lanka	5.1
40	Belarus	5.0
	Greece	5.0
	Morocco	5.0
	Myanmar	5.0

Armed forces

		'000	*% conscripts*
1	China	2,820.0	40
2	United States	1,371.5	
3	India	1,173.0	
4	North Korea	1,055.0	
5	Russia	1,004.1	33
6	South Korea	672.0	23
7	Turkey	639.0	87
8	Pakistan	587.0	
9	Iran	545.6	40
10	Vietnam	484.0	
11	Egypt	450.0	72
12	Iraq	429.0	
13	Afghanistan	400.0	
14	Taiwan	376.0	
15	Myanmar	343.8	
16	Germany	332.8	39
17	Ethiopia	325.5	
18	France	317.3	19
19	Syria	316.0	
20	Ukraine	311.4	
21	Indonesia	299.0	
22	Brazil	291.0	17
23	Italy	265.5	42
24	Japan	242.6	
25	Poland	240.7	47
26	Thailand	235.3	30
27	United Kingdom	212.4	
28	Romania	207.0	52
29	Eritrea	200.0	75
30	Morocco	196.3	51
31	Spain	186.2	28
32	Mexico	178.8	34
33	Israel	173.5	62
34	Greece	165.6	59
35	Colombia	144.0	52
36	Cambodia	139.0	
37	Bangladesh	137.0	
38	Algeria	122.0	61
39	Peru	115.0	56
	Sri Lanka	115.0	

a Previously Soviet Union. b United States only from 1994. c Up to April.

Environment

Top deforesters

Average annual rate, km² 1990–2000

Rank	Country	km²	Rank	Country	km²
1	Brazil	22,264	21	Ghana	1,200
2	Indonesia	13,124	22	Botswana	1,184
3	Sudan	9,589	23	Madagascar	1,174
4	Zambia	8,509	24	Nicaragua	1,172
5	Mexico	6,306	25	Papua New Guinea	1,129
6	Congo	5,324	26	Thailand	1,124
7	Myanmar	5,169	27	Mali	993
8	Nigeria	3,984	28	Kenya	931
9	Zimbabwe	3,199	29	Tanzania	913
10	Argentina	2,851		Uganda	913
11	Peru	2,688	31	Philippines	887
12	Côte d'Ivoire	2,649	32	Chad	817
13	Malaysia	2,377	33	Nepal	783
14	Cameroon	2,218	34	Namibia	734
15	Venezuela	2,175	35	Malawi	707
16	Colombia	1,905	36	Benin	699
17	Bolivia	1,611	37	Mozambique	637
18	Ecuador	1,372	38	Niger	617
19	Angola	1,242	39	Mongolia	600
20	Paraguay	1,230	40	Honduras	590

Top reafforesters

Average annual rate, km² 1990–2000

Rank	Country	km²	Rank	Country	km²
1	China	18,063	6	Spain	860
2	United States	3,880	7	France	616
3	Belarus	2,562	8	Portugal	570
4	Kazakhstan	2,390	9	Vietnam	516
5	Russia	1,353	10	Uruguay	501

Fastest forest depletion

% average annual decrease in forested area, 1990–2000

Rank	Country	%	Rank	Country	%
1	Burundi	9.0	20	Panama	1.6
2	Haiti	5.7		Sri Lanka	1.6
3	El Salvador	4.6	22	Jamaica	1.5
4	Rwanda	3.9		Zimbabwe	1.5
5	Niger	3.7	24	Myanmar	1.4
6	Togo	3.4		Philippines	1.4
7	Côte d'Ivoire	3.1		Sudan	1.4
8	Nicaragua	3.0	27	Ecuador	1.2
9	Sierra Leone	2.9		Indonesia	1.2
10	Mauritania	2.7		Malaysia	1.2
11	Nigeria	2.6	30	Mexico	1.1
12	Malawi	2.4		Pakistan	1.1
	Zambia	2.4	32	Honduras	1.0
14	Benin	2.3	33	Botswana	0.9
15	Uganda	2.0		Cameroon	0.9
16	Nepal	1.8		Guinea-Bissau	0.9
	Yemen	1.8		Madagascar	0.9
18	Ghana	1.7		Namibia	0.9
	Guatemala	1.7			

Most forested countries

% of total area covered with forest, 2000

1	Gabon	84.7	13	Malaysia	58.7
2	Guinea-Bissau	77.8	14	Indonesia	58.0
3	Finland	72.0	15	Venezuela	56.1
4	North Korea	68.2	16	Angola	56.0
5	Papua New Guinea	67.6	17	Slovenia	55.0
6	Sweden	65.9	18	Laos	54.4
7	Congo-Brazzaville	64.6	19	Cambodia	52.9
8	Japan	64.0	20	Myanmar	52.3
9	South Korea	63.3	21	Cameroon	51.3
10	Brazil	63.0	22	Peru	50.9
11	Congo	59.6	23	Trinidad & Tobago	50.5
12	Paraguay	58.8	24	Russia	50.4

Oil tanker spills

	Country affected	Oil spilled '000 tonnes	Name	Flag	Year
1	Trinidad & Tobago	276	Atlantic Express	Greece	1979
2	Italy	260	ABT Summer	Cyprus	1991
3	South Africa	256	Castello de Belvar	Spain	1983
4	France	228	Amoco Cadiz	Liberia	1978
5	Canada	140	Odyssey	Liberia	1988
6	United Kingdom	121	Torrey Canyon	Liberia	1967
7	Oman	120	Sea Star	South Korea	1972
8	Greece	102	Irenes Serenade	Greece	1980
9	Spain	101	Urquiola	Spain	1976
10	United States	99	Hawaiian Patriot	Liberia	1977
11	Turkey	95	Independenta	Romania	1979
12	United Kingdom	84	Braer	Liberia	1993

Industrial disasters, 1991–99[b]

	Location	Origin of accident	Deaths
1991	Thailand	explosives	171
	Livorno, Italy	oil explosion	140
1992	Kozlu, Turkey	gas explosion	270
1993	Shenzhen, China	fire (toy factory)	84
	Thailand	fire (toy factory)	189
1996	Dusseldorf, Germany	fire	16
	Lima, Peru	explosives	12
1997	Sichuan, China	explosives	21
	Columbus, USA	chemical fire	25
1998	Jilin, China	hotel fire	22
	Yaounde, Cameroon	train collision	200
	Mombasa, Kenya	school fire	24
	Rawalpindi, Pakistan	explosion	14
1999	Tambelan, Indonesia	ship sinking	313
	West Bengal, India	explosion (train)	286
	Nantucket Island, USA	air crash	217
2000	Kuwait	explosion (oil refinery)	403
	Nigeria	explosion and fire	312
	Netherlands	explosion (fireworks factory)	234

a 1992 b Not ranked due to difficulties in comparing the effects of each.

Environmental sustainability index[a]

Top 25, 100=perfect			Bottom 25, 100=perfect		
1	Finland	80.5	1	Haiti	24.7
2	Norway	78.2	2	Saudi Arabia	29.8
3	Canada	78.1	3	Burundi	30.1
4	Sweden	77.1	4	Ethiopia	31.2
5	Switzerland	74.6	5	Libya	31.3
6	New Zealand	71.3	6	Nigeria	31.8
7	Australia	70.7	7	Kuwait	31.9
8	Austria	67.8	8	Rwanda	33.5
9	Iceland	67.3	9	Vietnam	34.2
10	Denmark	67.0	10	Madagascar	35.4
11	United States	66.1	11	Philippines	35.7
12	Netherlands	66.0	12	Niger	36.5
13	France	65.8	13	Ukraine	36.8
14	Uruguay	64.6	14	Lebanon	37.5
15	Germany	64.2	15	China	37.6
16	United Kingdom	64.1	16	Sudan	37.7
17	Ireland	64.0	17	Syria	37.9
18	Slovakia	63.2	18	Iran	38.4
19	Argentina	62.5	19	Benin	38.6
20	Portugal	61.4		Burkina Faso	38.6
21	Hungary	61.0	21	Algeria	38.9
22	Japan	60.6	22	Togo	39.1
23	Lithuania	60.3	23	Macedonia	39.2
24	Slovenia	59.9	24	Bangladesh	39.5
25	Spain	59.5	25	Kirgizstan	39.6

Carbon dioxide emissions

Tonnes per head, 1997

1	United Arab Emirates	32.0	20	South Korea	9.9
2	Kuwait	28.2	21	Russia	9.8
3	Singapore	21.9	22	Japan	9.6
4	United States	20.1	23	Poland	9.2
5	Trinidad & Tobago	17.4	24	United Kingdom	8.9
6	Australia	17.2	25	Libya	8.4
7	Canada	16.6		New Zealand	8.4
8	Norway	15.6		Venezuela	8.4
9	Saudi Arabia	14.3	28	Greece	8.3
10	Estonia	13.1	29	Oman	8.2
11	Czech Republic	12.2	30	Kazakhstan	8.0
12	North Korea	11.4	31	South Africa	7.9
13	Finland	11.0	32	Austria	7.8
14	Denmark	10.9		Slovenia	7.8
15	Belgium	10.5	34	Italy	7.4
	Netherlands	10.5	35	Ukraine	7.3
17	Germany	10.4	36	Slovakia	7.1
	Israel	10.4	37	Turkmenistan	6.7
19	Ireland	10.2	38	Spain	6.6

a Based on 22 "core" indicators in five broad areas: environmental systems; reducing environmental stress, reducing human vulnerability, social and institutional capacity, global stewardship.

Water pollution

Emissions of organic pollutants[a], '000kg per day, latest available

1	China	8,491.9	**21**	Bangladesh	186.9
2	United States	2,577.0	**22**	Argentina	186.8
3	India	1,760.4	**23**	Turkey	186.3
4	Russia	1,531.5	**24**	Philippines	178.2
5	Japan	1,391.3	**25**	Australia	173.3
6	Germany	811.3	**26**	Malaysia	166.6
7	Brazil	690.9	**27**	Czech Republic	166.0
8	United Kingdom	611.7	**28**	Mexico	158.5
9	France	585.4	**29**	Hungary	140.9
10	Ukraine	519.0	**30**	Portugal	137.3
11	Poland	386.4	**31**	Switzerland	123.8
12	Italy	359.6	**32**	Netherlands	122.8
13	Thailand	355.8	**33**	Serbia & Montenegro	119.8
14	Spain	348.3	**34**	Pakistan	114.7
15	Indonesia	347.1	**35**	Belgium	113.5
16	Romania	333.2	**36**	Colombia	111.5
17	South Korea	317.9	**37**	Bulgaria	103.1
18	Canada	298.2	**38**	Algeria	103.0
19	South Africa	241.9	**39**	Iran	101.9
20	Egypt	225.8	**40**	Denmark	92.7

Municipal waste generated

'000 tonnes, latest available			*Kg per head, latest available*		
1	United States	190,204	**1**	United States	720
2	Japan	50,536	**2**	Norway	630
3	Russia	50,000	**3**	Switzerland	600
4	Germany	36,976	**4**	Denmark	560
5	Mexico	29,272		Iceland	560
6	France	28,800		Ireland	560
7	United Kingdom	28,000		Netherlands	560
8	Italy	26,605	**8**	Austria	510
9	Turkey	20,253	**9**	Hungary	500
10	South Korea	18,223	**10**	Canada	490
11	Spain	15,307	**11**	Belgium	480
12	Canada	14,740		France	480
13	Poland	12,183		United Kingdom	480
14	Netherlands	8,716	**14**	Germany	460
15	Hungary	5,000		Italy	460
16	Belgium	4,852		Luxembourg	460
17	Switzerland	4,277	**17**	Finland	410
18	Austria	4,110	**18**	Japan	400
19	Greece	3,900		South Korea	400
20	Portugal	3,800	**20**	Spain	390
21	Czech Republic	3,200	**21**	Portugal	380
	Sweden	3,200	**22**	Greece	370
23	Denmark	2,951	**23**	Sweden	360
24	Norway	2,721	**24**	Russia	340
25	Finland	2,100		Slovakia	340

a Industrial emissions.

Glass recycling

Recovery rates, %, 1997

1	Switzerland	91	11	Finland	62
2	Austria	88	12	Japan[a]	56
3	Netherlands	82	13	France	52
4	Germany	79	14	Portugal	44
5	Norway	76	15	Australia[b]	42
	Sweden	76	16	Slovakia	40
7	Belgium	75	17	Ireland	38
	Iceland[a]	75	18	Spain	37
9	Denmark	70	19	New Zealand[c]	36
10	South Korea	68	20	Italy	34

Paper recycling

Recovery rates, %, 1997

1	Germany	70		Denmark	50
2	Austria	69	12	Hungary[f]	49
3	New Zealand[d]	66	13	Norway	44
4	Switzerland	63	14	Spain	42
5	Netherlands	62	15	France	41
	Sweden	62		United States[f]	41
7	Finland[b]	57	17	Portugal	40
	South Korea	57		United Kingdom	40
9	Japan	54	19	Turkey	36
10	Australia[e]	50	20	Slovakia	34

Freshwater resources

Cubic metres per head, 1999

1	Congo-Brazzaville	291,000	11	Colombia	51,349
2	Papua New Guinea	170,258	12	Cambodia	40,505
3	Gabon	135,716	13	Central African Rep	39,833
4	Canada	91,567	14	Bolivia	38,830
5	Norway	88,117	15	Nicaragua	38,668
6	New Zealand	85,811	16	Venezuela	35,686
7	Peru	69,203	17	Ecuador	35,611
8	Chile	61,793	18	Sierra Leone	32,328
9	Laos	55,251	19	Brazil	32,256
10	Panama	52,437	20	Costa Rica	31,318

Least access to improved-water source

% of population, 2000

1	Ethiopia	24	11	Eritrea	46
2	Chad	27		Haiti	46
3	Sierra Leone	28	13	Madagascar	47
4	Cambodia	30	14	Guinea	48
5	Mauritania	37	15	Guinea-Bissau	49
6	Angola	38		Kenya	49
7	Oman	39	17	Uganda	50
8	Rwanda	41	18	Congo-Brazzaville	51
9	Papua New Guinea	42	19	Tanzania	54
10	Congo	45		Togo	54

a 1992 b 1995 c 1994 d 1993 e 1991 f 1996

Part II
COUNTRY PROFILES

ALGERIA

Area	2,381,741 sq km	Capital	Algiers
Arable as % of total land	3	Currency	Algerian dinar (AD)

People

Population	30.0m	Life expectancy: men	68.7 yrs
Pop. per sq km	13	women	71.8 yrs
Av. ann. growth		Adult literacy	61.6%
in pop. 1995–2000	1.82%	Fertility rate (per woman)	3.2
Pop. under 15	34.8%	Urban population	60.3%
Pop. over 65	6.0%		*per 1,000 pop.*
No. of men per 100 women	103	Crude birth rate	23.5
Human Development Index	68.3	Crude death rate	5.3

The economy

GDP	AD3,187bn	GDP per head	$1,600
GDP	$47.9bn	GDP per head in purchasing	
Av. ann. growth in real		power parity (USA=100)	15.2
GDP 1990–99	1.6%	Economic freedom index	3.20

Origins of GDP		**Components of GDP**	
	% of total		*% of total*
Agriculture	11	Private consumption	29.0
Industry, of which:	51	Public consumption	20.7
manufacturing	10	Investment	17.8
Services	38	Exports	43.0
		Imports	-14.0

Structure of employment[b]

	% of total		*% of labour force*
Agriculture	25	Unemployed 1997	28.0
Industry	26	Av. ann. rate 1990–97	24.5
Services	49		

Energy

	m TCE		
Total output	193.465	% output exported	71.3
Total consumption	49.029	% consumption imported	7.5
Consumption per head,			
kg coal equivalent	1,668		

Inflation and finance

Consumer price			*av. ann. increase 1994–99*
inflation 2000	0.1%	Narrow money (M1)	12.9%
Av. ann. inflation 1990–2000	16.3%	Broad money	14.9%
Money market rate, 2000	6.77%		

Exchange rates

	end 2000		*December 2000*
AD per $	77.94	Effective rates	1995 = 100
AD per SDR	98.17	– nominal	84.08
AD per euro	72.48	– real	104.84

Trade

Principal exports[a]		Principal imports[a]	
	$bn fob		*$bn cif*
Energy & products	9.7	Capital goods	3.2
		Food	2.6
Total including others	**12.3**	Total incl. others	**9.3**

Main export destinations		Main origins of imports	
	% of total		*% of total*
Italy	22.2	France	30.0
United States	14.8	Italy	8.9
France	11.2	Germany	7.0
Spain	10.6	Spain	5.9
Brazil	8.1	United States	5.4
Netherlands	5.2	Turkey	4.7

Balance of payments[c], reserves and debt, $bn

Visible exports fob	10.1	Overall balance[d]	1.2
Visible imports fob	-8.6	Change in reserves	-2.3
Trade balance	1.5	Level of reserves	
Invisibles inflows	1.1	end Dec.	6.1
Invisibles outflows	-4.6	No. months of import cover	5.2
Net transfers	1.1	Foreign debt	28.0
Current account balance	-0.9	– as % of GDP	61
– as % of GDP	-1.9	Debt service paid	5.3
Capital balance[d]	-2.3	Debt service ratio	38

Health and education

Health spending, % of GDP	3.6	Education spending, % of GDP	5.2
Doctors per 1,000 pop.	1.0	Enrolment, %: primary	108
Hospital beds per 1,000 pop.	2.1	secondary	63
Improved-water source access,		tertiary	13
% of pop.	94		

Society

No. of households	6.5m	Colour TVs per 100 households	67.9
Av. no. per household	4.6	Telephone lines per 100 pop.	5.2
Marriages per 1,000 pop.	5.5	Mobile telephone subscribers	
Divorces per 1,000 pop.	...	per 100 pop.	0.2
Cost of living, Dec. 1999		Computers per 100 pop.	0.6
New York = 100	...	Internet hosts per 100 pop.	...

a Estimate.
b 1996
c 1998
d 1997

ARGENTINA

Area	2,766,889 sq km	Capital	Buenos Aires
Arable as % of total land	9	Currency	Peso (P)

People

Population	36.6m	Life expectancy: men	70.6 yrs
Pop. per sq km	13	women	77.7 yrs
Av. ann. growth		Adult literacy	96.5%
in pop. 1995–2000	1.2%	Fertility rate (per woman)	2.6
Pop. under 15	27.7%	Urban population	89.9%
Pop. over 65	13.3%		*per 1,000 pop.*
No. of men per 100 women	96.3	Crude birth rate	19.0
Human Development Index	83.7	Crude death rate	7.8

The economy

GDP	P283bn	GDP per head	$7,740
GDP	$283bn	GDP per head in purchasing	
Av. ann. growth in real		power parity (USA=100)	37.4
GDP 1990–99	4.9%	Economic freedom index	2.25

Origins of GDP		**Components of GDP**	
	% of total		*% of total*
Agriculture	5.7	Private consumption[a]	81.3
Industry, of which:	27.7	Public consumption	...
manufacturing	17.1	Investment	20.2
Services	66.6	Exports	10.9
		Imports	-12.3

Structure of employment

	% of total		*% of labour force*
Agricultural	8	Unemployed 1998	12.8
Industry	20	Av. ann. rate 1990–98	11.7
Services	72		

Energy

	m TCE		
Total output	111.416	% output exported	26.6
Total consumption	78.784	% consumption imported	8.2
Consumption per head			
kg coal equivalent	2,209		

Inflation and finance

Consumer price			*av. ann. increase 1994–99*
inflation 2000	-0.9%	Narrow money (M1)	5.9%
Av. ann. inflation 1990–2000	14.9%	Broad money	10.8%
Money market rate, 2000	8.15%		

Exchange rates

	end 2000		*December 2000*
P per $	1.00	Effective rates	1995 = 100
P per SDR	1.37	– nominal	...
P per euro	0.93	– real	...

Trade

Principal exports		Principal imports	
	$bn fob		*$bn cif*
Agricultural products	8.2	Intermediate goods	8.4
Manufactures	7.0	Capital goods	6.7
Fuels	3.0	Consumer goods	4.5
Total incl. others	**23.3**	Total incl. others	**25.5**

Main export destinations		Main origins of imports	
	% of total		*% of total*
Brazil	24.4	Brazil	21.9
United States	11.3	United States	19.4
Chile	8.0	France	5.9
Netherlands	4.3	Germany	5.5
Spain	4.1	Italy	5.3

Balance of payments, reserves and debt, $bn

Visible exports fob	23.3	Overall balance	2.0
Visible imports fob	-24.1	Change in reserves	1.5
Trade balance	-0.8	Level of reserves	
Invisibles inflows	10.5	end Dec.	26.4
Invisibles outflows	-22.3	No. months of import cover	6.8
Net transfers	0.3	Foreign debt	147.9
Current account balance	-12.3	– as % of GDP	54
– as % of GDP	-4.3	Debt service paid	25.7
Capital balance	14.7	Debt service ratio	76

Health and education

Health spending, % of GDP	10.3	Education spending, % of GDP	3.5
Doctors per 1,000 pop.	2.7	Enrolment, %: primary	111
Hospital beds per 1,000 pop.	3.3	secondary	73
Improved-water source access,		tertiary	42
% of pop.	79		

Society

No. of households	13.2m	Colour TVs per 100 households	88.4
Av. no. per household	2.7	Telephone lines per 100 pop.	21.5
Marriages per 1,000 pop.	3.8	Mobile telephone subscribers	
Divorces per 1,000 pop.	...	per 100 pop.	12.1
Cost of living, Dec. 1999		Computers per 100 pop.	5.1
New York = 100	92	Internet hosts per 100 pop.	7.4

a Including public consumption.

AUSTRALIA

Area	7,682,300 sq km	Capital	Canberra
Arable as % of total land	7	Currency	Australian dollar (A$)

People

Population	19m	Life expectancy: men	76.4 yrs
Pop. per sq km	2	women	82.0 yrs
Av. ann. growth		Adult literacy	99.0%
in pop. 1995–2000	1.1%	Fertility rate (per woman)	1.8
Pop. under 15	20.5%	Urban population	84.7%
Pop. over 65	16.3%		*per 1,000 pop.*
No. of men per 100 women	98.7	Crude birth rate	12.7
Human Development Index	92.9	Crude death rate	7.4

The economy

GDP	A$611bn	GDP per head	$21,270
GDP	$404bn	GDP per head in purchasing	
Av. ann. growth in real		power parity (USA=100)	74.7
GDP 1990–99	4.1%	Economic freedom index	1.90

Origins of GDP		**Components of GDP**	
	% of total		*% of total*
Agriculture & mining	8.0	Private consumption	58.6
Industry, of which:	22.0	Public consumption	18.0
manufacturing	15.7	Investment	24.4
Services	70.0	Exports	19.9
		Imports	-20.9

Structure of employment

	% of total		*% of labour force*
Agriculture	5	Unemployed 1999	7.2
Industry	22	Av. ann. rate 1990–99	8.9
Services	73		

Energy

	m TCE		
Total output	286.662	% output exported	57.8
Total consumption	199.344	% consumption imported	23.0
Consumption per head,			
kg coal equivalent	7,873		

Inflation and finance

Consumer price			*av. ann. increase 1994–99*
inflation 2000	4.5%	Narrow money (M1)	9.8%
Av. ann. inflation 1990–2000	2.2%	Broad money	9.3%
Treasury bill rate, 2000	5.98%		

Exchange rates

	end 2000		*December 2000*
A$ per $	1.81	Effective rates	1995 = 100
A$ per SDR	2.35	– nominal	90.3
A$ per euro	1.68	– real	93.1

Trade

Principal exports		Principal imports	
	$bn fob		*$bn cif*
Ores & minerals	11.6	Machinery	17.5
Coal & oil	9.0	Consumer goods	13.9
Machinery	7.0	Transport equipment	11.8
Cereals	3.2	Energy & products	3.7
Gold	3.1	Chemicals	2.1
Total incl. others	**55.9**	Total incl. others	**65.7**

Main export destinations		Main origins of imports	
	% of total		*% of total*
Japan	19.3	EU15	23.9
EU15	13.5	United States	21.4
Asean[a]	12.1	Japan	13.9
United States	9.3	Asean[a]	12.7

Balance of payments, reserves and aid, $bn

Visible exports fob	56.1	Capital balance	27.5
Visible imports fob	-65.8	Overall balance	6.7
Trade balance	-9.8	Change in reserves	6.6
Invisibles inflows	24.1	Level of reserves	
Invisibles outflows	-37.5	end Dec.	22.0
Net transfers	-0.0	No. months of import cover	2.5
Current account balance	-23.2	Aid given	0.98
– as % of GDP	-5.7	– as % of GDP	0.25

Health and education

Health spending, % of GDP	8.5	Education spending, % of GDP	5.4
Doctors per 1,000 pop.	2.5	Enrolment, %: primary	101
Hospital beds per 1,000 pop.	8.5	secondary[b]	153
Improved-water source access,		tertiary	80
% of pop.	100		

Society

No. of households	7.1m	Colour TVs per 100 households	91.2
Av. no. per household	2.6	Telephone lines per 100 pop.	52.4
Marriages per 1,000 pop.	6.9	Mobile telephone subscribers	
Divorces per 1,000 pop.	2.7	per 100 pop.	44.6
Cost of living, Dec. 1999		Computers per 100 pop.	46.5
New York = 100	75	Internet hosts per 100 pop.	85.1

a Brunei, Indonesia, Laos, Malaysia, Myanmar, Philippines, Singapore, Thailand, Vietnam.
b Includes training for unemployed.

AUSTRIA

Area	83,855 sq km	Capital	Vienna
Arable as % of total land	17	Currency	Schilling (ASch)

People

Population	8.1m	Life expectancy: men	75.4 yrs
Pop. per sq km	98	women	81.5 yrs
Av. ann. growth		Adult literacy	99.0%
in pop. 1995–2000	0.08%	Fertility rate (per woman)	1.4
Pop. under 15	16.6%	Urban population	64.7%
Pop. over 65	20.7%		*per 1,000 pop.*
No. of men per 100 women	95	Crude birth rate	8.3
Human Development Index	90.8	Crude death rate	9.9

The economy

GDP	ASch2,712bn	GDP per head	$25,740
GDP	$208bn	GDP per head in purchasing	
Av. ann. growth in real		power parity (USA=100)	77.1
GDP 1990–99	1.9%	Economic freedom index	2.05

Origins of GDP		**Components of GDP**	
	% of total		*% of total*
Agriculture	2.2	Private consumption	55.6
Industry, of which:	30.4	Public consumption	19.5
manufacturing	...	Investment	24.7
Services	67.4	Exports	46.6
		Imports	-45.9

Structure of employment[a]

	% of total		*% of labour force*
Agriculture	6	Unemployed 1999	3.8
Industry	31	Av. ann. rate 1990–99	3.8
Services	63		

Energy

	m TCE		
Total output	8.300	% output exported	35.8
Total consumption	35.697	% consumption imported	86.0
Consumption per head,			
kg coal equivalent	4,408		

Inflation and finance

Consumer price		*av. ann. increase 1994–99*	
inflation 2000	2.4%	Euro area:	
Av. ann. inflation 1990–2000	2.3%	Narrow money (M1)	7.9%
Deposit rate, 2000	3.11%	Broad money	5.9%

Exchange rates

	end 2000		*July 2000*
ASch per $	14.90	Effective rates	1995 = 100
ASch per SDR	19.37	– nominal	93.6
ASch per euro	13.76	– real	83.6

Trade

Principal exports		Principal imports	
	$bn fob		*$bn cif*
Machinery & transport equipment	27.5	Machinery & transport equipment	27.6
Semi-manufactured goods	15.2	Semi-manufactured products	11.6
Consumer goods	8.8	Consumer goods	11.5
Chemicals	6.0	Chemicals	6.9
Food, drink & tobacco	3.1	Food, drink & tobacco	4.0
Raw materials	2.3	Fuel	2.8
Total incl. others	**63.7**	Total incl. others	**67.3**

Main export destinations		Main origins of imports	
	% of total		*% of total*
Germany	34.8	Germany	41.7
Italy	8.4	Italy	7.6
Switzerland	6.1	United States	5.4
Hungary	5.0	France	5.0
EU15	62.6	EU15	68.4

Balance of payments, reserves and aid, $bn

Visible exports fob	64.4	Capital balance	2.7
Visible imports fob	-68.1	Overall balance	-2.2
Trade balance	-3.6	Change in reserves	-2.3
Invisibles inflows	40.7	Level of reserves	
Invisibles outflows	-40.7	end Dec.	18.9
Net transfers	-2.0	No. months of import cover	2.1
Current account balance	-5.7	Aid given	0.53
– as % of GDP	-2.8	– as % of GDP	0.25

Health and education

Health spending, % of GDP	8.3	Education spending, % of GDP	5.4
Doctors per 1,000 pop.	3.0	Enrolment, %: primary	100
Hospital beds per 1,000 pop.	8.9	secondary	103
Improved-water source access,		tertiary	48
% of pop.	100		

Society

No. of households	3.4m	Colour TVs per 100 households	97.2
Av. no. per household	2.4	Telephone lines per 100 pop.	48.1
Marriages per 1,000 pop.	4.8	Mobile telephone subscribers	
Divorces per 1,000 pop.	2.1	per 100 pop.	78.6
Cost of living, Dec. 1999		Computers per 100 pop.	27.7
New York = 100	84	Internet hosts per 100 pop.	62.3

a 1997

BANGLADESH

Area	143,998 sq km	Capital	Dhaka
Arable as % of total land	61	Currency	Taka (Tk)

People

Population	127.7m	Life expectancy: men	60.6 yrs
Pop. per sq km	981	women	60.8 yrs
Av. ann. growth		Adult literacy	38.9%
in pop. 1995–2000	2.12%	Fertility rate (per woman)	3.8
Pop. under 15	38.7%	Urban population	24.5%
Pop. over 65	4.9%		*per 1,000 pop.*
No. of men per 100 women	106	Crude birth rate	29.9
Human Development Index	46.1	Crude death rate	8.7

The economy

GDP[a]	Tk1,898bn	GDP per head	$360
GDP	$46.0bn	GDP per head in purchasing	
Av. ann. growth in real		power parity (USA=100)	4.8
GDP 1990–99	4.7%	Economic freedom index	3.80

Origins of GDP		**Components of GDP[b]**	
	% of total		*% of total*
Agriculture	25	Private consumption	79.5
Industry, of which:	24	Public consumption	14.4
manufacturing	15	Investment	12.4
Services	50	Exports	17.7
		Imports	-24.8

Structure of employment[b]

	% of total		*% of labour force*
Agriculture	63	Unemployed 1996[b]	2.5
Industry	10	Av. ann. rate 1990–96	...
Services	27		

Energy

	m TCE		
Total output	9.884	% output exported	0.0
Total consumption	13.701	% consumption imported	34.2
Consumption per head,			
kg coal equivalent	112		

Inflation and finance

Consumer price			*av. ann. increase 1994–99*
inflation 1999	6.2%	Narrow money (M1)	9.8%
Av. ann. inflation 1990–99	4.9%	Broad money	11.9%
Deposit rate, 2000	8.51%		

Exchange rates

	end 2000		*December 2000*
Tk per $	54.00	Effective rates	1995 = 100
Tk per SDR	70.36	– nominal	...
Tk per euro	50.22	– real	...

Trade

Principal exports[b]		Principal imports[b]	
	$bn fob		*$bn cif*
Clothing	2.7	Textiles	1.7
Fish & fish products	0.3	Machinery & transport equipment	0.9
Jute goods	0.2	Cereal & dairy products	0.9
Leather	0.2	Iron & steel	0.3
		Fuels	0.3
Total incl. others	**3.7**	Total incl. others	**7.6**

Main export destinations		Main origins of imports	
	% of total		*% of total*
United States	32.3	India	13.5
Germany	10.4	Singapore	7.9
United Kingdom	8.3	China	7.2
France	5.7	Japan	6.0
Italy	4.8	Hong Kong	5.5

Balance of payments, reserves and debt, $bn

Visible exports fob	5.5	Overall balance	-0.2
Visible imports fob	-7.4	Change in reserves	-0.3
Trade balance	-2.0	Level of reserves end Dec.	1.6
Invisibles inflows	0.9	No. months of import cover	2.2
Invisibles outflows	-1.7	Foreign debt	17.5
Net transfers	2.5	– as % of GDP	37
Current account balance	-0.3	Debt service paid	0.8
– as % of GDP	-0.6	Debt service ratio	10
Capital balance	-0.2		

Health and education

Health spending, % of GDP	3.6	Education spending, % of GDP	2.2
Doctors per 1,000 pop.	0.2	Enrolment, %: primary	...
Hospital beds per 1,000 pop.	0.3	secondary	...
Improved-water source access, % of pop.	97	tertiary	6

Society

No. of households	22.9m	Colour TVs per 100 households	0.6
Av. no. per household	5.5	Telephone lines per 100 pop.	0.3
Marriages per 1,000 pop.[c]	9.7	Mobile telephone subscribers per 100 pop.	0.1
Divorces per 1,000 pop.	...	Computers per 100 pop.	0.1
Cost of living, Dec. 1999 New York = 100	57	Internet hosts per 100 pop.	...

a Fiscal year ending June 30 2000.
b Fiscal year ending June 30 1999.
b Fiscal year ending June 30 1996.
c 1997

BELGIUM

Area	30,520 sq km	Capital	Brussels
Arable as % of total land	25	Currency	Belgian franc (BFr)

People

Population	10.2m	Life expectancy: men	75.7 yrs
Pop. per sq km	312	women	81.9 yrs
Av. ann. growth		Adult literacy	99.0%
in pop. 1995–2000	0.2%	Fertility rate (per woman)	1.6
Pop. under 15	17.3%	Urban population	97.3%
Pop. over 65	22.1%		*per 1,000 pop.*
No. of men per 100 women	96.0	Crude birth rate	9.6
Human Development Index	92.5	Crude death rate	10.0

The economy

GDP	BFr9,440bn	GDP per head	$24,380
GDP	$248bn	GDP per head in purchasing	
Av. ann. growth in real		power parity (USA=100)	80.6
GDP 1990–99	1.7%	Economic freedom index	2.10

Origins of GDP		**Components of GDP**	
	% of total		*% of total*
Agriculture	1.4	Private consumption	53.6
Industry, of which:	26.3	Public consumption	21.4
manufacturing	21.7	Investment	21.2
Services	72.3	Exports	76.5
		Imports	-72.8

Structure of employment

	% of total		*% of labour force*
Agriculture	2	Unemployed 1999	8.6
Industry	26	Av. ann. rate 1990–99	8.5
Services	72		

Energy

	m TCE		
Total output	17.098	% output exported[a]	172.2
Total consumption	72.826	% consumption imported[a]	136.1
Consumption per head,			
kg coal equivalent	7,191		

Inflation and finance

Consumer price			*av. ann. increase 1994–99*
inflation 2000	2.5%	Euro area:	
Av. ann. inflation 1990–2000	2.1%	Narrow money (M1)	7.9%
Treasury bill rate, 2000	4.02%	Broad money	5.9%

Exchange rates

	end 2000		*July 2000*
BFr per $	43.68	Effective rates	1995 = 100
BFr per SDR	56.78	– nominal	90.5
BFr per euro	40.34	– real	88.8

Trade

Principal exports	$bn fob	Principal imports	$bn cif
Chemicals	26.9	Machinery & electrical products	29.6
Machinery & electrical goods	26.8	Chemicals	21.4
Vehicles	25.7	Vehicles	20.8
Metals & products	14.9	Metals & products	11.8
Total incl. others	**176.3**	Total incl. others	**160.9**

Main export destinations	% of total	Main origins of imports	% of total
Germany	17.8	Germany	17.7
France	17.6	Netherlands	16.8
Netherlands	12.5	France	13.5
United Kingdom	10.1	United Kingdom	8.6
EU15	75.8	EU15	70.6

Balance of payments[b], reserves and aid, $bn

Visible exports fob	154.1	Capital balance	-13.3
Visible imports fob	-146.8	Overall balance	-1.9
Trade balance	7.3	Change in reserves	-2.1
Invisibles inflows	106.9	Level of reserves end Dec.	13.3
Invisibles outflows	-97.9	No. months of import cover	0.7
Net transfers	-4.6	Aid given	0.76
Current account balance	11.7	– as % of GDP	0.31
– as % of GDP	4.7		

Health and education

Health spending, % of GDP	8.9	Education spending, % of GDP	3.1
Doctors per 1,000 pop.	3.4	Enrolment, %: primary	103
Hospital beds per 1,000 pop.	7.2	secondary[c]	146
Improved-water source access, % of pop.	...	tertiary	57

Society

No. of households	4.2m	Colour TVs per 100 households	98.5
Av. no. per household	2.4	Telephone lines per 100 pop.	49.9
Marriages per 1,000 pop.	3.8	Mobile telephone subscribers per 100 pop.	54.9
Divorces per 1,000 pop.	2.7	Computers per 100 pop.	34.5
Cost of living, Dec. 1999 New York = 100	74	Internet hosts per 100 pop.	40.8

a Energy trade data are distorted by transitory and oil refining activities.
b Including Luxembourg.
c Includes training for unemployed.

BRAZIL

Area	8,511,965 sq km	Capital	Brasilia
Arable as % of total land	6	Currency	Real (R)

People

Population	168.0m	Life expectancy: men	64.7 yrs
Pop. per sq km	20	women	72.6 yrs
Av. ann. growth		Adult literacy	84.0%
in pop. 1995–2000	1.3%	Fertility rate (per woman)	2.2
Pop. under 15	28.8%	Urban population	81.3%
Pop. over 65	7.8%		*per 1,000 pop.*
No. of men per 100 women	97.6	Crude birth rate	19.1
Human Development Index	74.7	Crude death rate	7.0

The economy

GDP	R961bn	GDP per head	$4,470
GDP	$752bn	GDP per head in purchasing	
Av. ann. growth in real		power parity (USA=100)	21.4
GDP 1990–99	3.0%	Economic freedom index	3.25

Origins of GDP		**Components of GDP**	
	% of total		*% of total*
Agriculture	8.7	Private consumption	61.8
Industry, of which:	33.9	Public consumption	18.9
manufacturing	21.5	Investment	20.4
Services	57.4	Exports	10.6
		Imports	-11.7

Structure of employment

	% of total		*% of labour force*
Agriculture	26	Unemployed 1998	9.0
Industry	23	Av. ann. rate 1995–98	7.8
Services	51		

Energy

	m TCE		
Total output	108.831	% output exported	2.6
Total consumption	165.189	% consumption imported	45.3
Consumption per head,			
kg coal equivalent	1,009		

Inflation and finance

Consumer price			*av. ann. increase 1994–99*
inflation 2000	7.1%	Narrow money (M1)	22.5%
Av. ann. inflation 1990–2000	199.9%	Broad money (M4)	25.8%
Money market rate, 2000	17.59%		

Exchange rates

	end 2000		*December 2000*
R per $	1.96	Effective rates	1995 = 100
R per SDR	2.55	– Nominal	...
R per euro	1.82	– Real	...

Trade

Principal exports		Principal imports	
	$bn fob		*$bn fob*
Transport equipment	6.6	Machines & electrical equipment	16.5
Metal goods	5.1	Chemical products	9.0
Soyabeans etc.	3.8	Fuels & lubricants	4.8
Chemical products	3.5	Transport equipment & parts	4.7
Iron ore	2.9	Total incl. others	**49.2**
Total incl. others	**48.0**		

Main export destinations		Main origins of imports	
	% of total		*% of total*
United States	22.6	United States	24.1
Argentina	11.2	Argentina	11.8
Netherlands	5.4	Germany	9.6
Germany	5.3	Japan	5.2

Balance of payments, reserves and debt, $bn

Visible exports fob	48.0	Overall balance	-16.8
Visible imports fob	-49.2	Change in reserves	-8.2
Trade balance	-1.2	Level of reserves end Dec.	35.7
Invisibles inflows	8.7	No. months of import cover	5.0
Invisibles outflows	-37.2	Foreign debt	244.7
Net transfers	1.7	– as % of GDP	34
Current account balance	-25.1	Debt service paid	67.5
– as % of GDP	-3.3	Debt service ratio	111
Capital balance	7.6		

Health and education

Health spending, % of GDP	6.6	Education spending, % of GDP	5.1
Doctors per 1,000 pop.	1.3	Enrolment, %: primary	125
Hospital beds per 1,000 pop.	3.1	secondary	62
Improved-water source access, % of pop.	87	tertiary	15

Society

No. of households	40.2m	Colour TVs per 100 households	85.4
Av. no. per household	4.1	Telephone lines per 100 pop.	14.9
Marriages per 1,000 pop.	4.6	Mobile telephone subscribers per 100 pop.	9.0
Divorces per 1,000 pop.	0.8	Computers per 100 pop.	4.4
Cost of living, Dec. 1999 New York = 100	67	Internet hosts per 100 pop.	5.2

BULGARIA

Area	110,994 sq km	Capital	Sofia
Arable as % of total land	39	Currency	Lev (BGL)

People

Population	8.2m	Life expectancy: men	67.1 yrs
Pop. per sq km	74	women	74.8 yrs
Av. ann. growth		Adult literacy	98.2%
in pop. 1995–2000	-1.12%	Fertility rate (per woman)	1.1
Pop. under 15	15.7%	Urban population	69.6%
Pop. over 65	21.7%		*per 1,000 pop.*
No. of men per 100 women	94.6	Crude birth rate	7.8
Human Development Index	77.2	Crude death rate	15.1

The economy

GDP	BGL23bn	GDP per head	$1,510
GDP	$12.4bn	GDP per head in purchasing	
Av. ann. growth in real		power parity (USA=100)	15.9
GDP 1990–99	-2.7%	Economic freedom index	3.30

Origins of GDP		**Components of GDP**	
	% of total		*% of total*
Agriculture	17.3	Private consumption	82.3
Industry, of which:	26.8	Public consumption	8.4
manufacturing	16.6	Investment	19.0
Services	55.9	Exports	44.1
		Imports	-51.9

Structure of employment[a]

	% of total		*% of labour force*
Agriculture	14	Unemployed 1998	14.4
Industry	50	Av. ann. rate 1990–98	14.3
Services	36		

Energy

	m TCE		
Total output	13.937	% output exported	20.5
Total consumption	27.770	% consumption imported	67.8
Consumption per head,			
kg coal equivalent	3,309		

Inflation and finance

Consumer price			*av. ann change 1994–99*
inflation 2000	10.4%	Narrow money (M1)	109%
Av. ann. inflation 1990–2000	108.8%	Broad money	76%
Money market rate 2000	3.02%		

Exchange rates

	end 2000		*December 2000*
BGL per $	2.10	Effective rates	1995 = 100
BGL per SDR	2.74	– Nominal	5.93
BGL per euro	1.95	– Real	124.59

Trade

Principal exports		Principal imports	
	$bn fob		*$bn fob*
Textiles	0.9	Machinery & transport equip.	1.7
Base metals	0.6	Mineral products & fuels	1.4
Machinery & transport equipment	0.6	Textiles	0.8
Chemicals	0.5	Chemicals	0.7
Minerals & fuels	0.4	Base metals	0.3
Total incl. others	**4.0**	Total incl. others	**5.5**

Main export destinations		Main origins of imports	
	% of total		*% of total*
Italy	13.9	Russia	20.2
Germany	9.8	Germany	14.8
Greece	8.5	Italy	8.4
Turkey	7.3	Greece	5.6
Russia	4.8	France	5.2
EU15	51.9	EU15	48.1

Balance of payments, reserves and debt, $bn

Visible exports fob	4.0	Overall balance	0.1
Visible imports fob	-5.1	Change in reserves	0.3
Trade balance	-1.1	Level of reserves end Dec.	3.4
Invisibles inflows	2.1	No. months of import cover	5.8
Invisibles outflows	-2.0	Foreign debt	9.9
Net transfers	0.3	– as % of GDP	81
Current account balance	-0.7	Debt service paid	1.2
– as % of GDP	-5.5	Debt service ratio	19
Capital balance	0.8		

Health and education

Health spending, % of GDP	4.7	Education spending, % of GDP	3.2
Doctors per 1,000 pop.	3.5	Enrolment, %: primary	99
Hospital beds per 1,000 pop.	10.6	secondary	77
Improved-water source access, % of pop.	100	tertiary	41

Society

No. of households	3.0m	Colour TVs per 100 households	58.8
Av. no. per household	2.9	Telephone lines per 100 pop.	35.4
Marriages per 1,000 pop.	4.1	Mobile telephone subscribers per 100 pop.	4.2
Divorces per 1,000 pop.	1.4	Computers per 100 pop.	2.7
Cost of living, Dec. 1999 New York = 100	...	Internet hosts per 100 pop.	2.1

a 1990

CAMEROON

Area	475,442 sq km	Capital	Yaoundé
Arable as % of total land	13	Currency	CFA franc (CFAfr)

People

Population	14.7m	Life expectancy: men	49.3 yrs
Pop. per sq km	31	women	50.6 yrs
Av. ann. growth		Adult literacy	71.4%
in pop. 1995–2000	2.28%	Fertility rate (per woman)	5.1
Pop. under 15	43.1%	Urban population	48.9%
Pop. over 65	5.6%		*per 1,000 pop.*
No. of men per 100 women	98.9	Crude birth rate	36.3
Human Development Index	52.8	Crude death rate	14.6

The economy

GDP[a]	CFAfr5,744bn	GDP per head	$630
GDP	$9.2bn	GDP per head in purchasing	
Av. ann. growth in real		power parity (USA=100)	4.7
GDP 1990–99	1.3%	Economic freedom index	3.20

Origins of GDP[a]		**Components of GDP[a]**	
	% of total		*% of total*
Agriculture	43.5	Private consumption	70.1
Industry, of which:	20.2	Public consumption	7.5
manufacturing	...	Investment	20.5
Services	36.6	Exports	24.7
		Imports	-22.5

Structure of employment[b]

	% of total		*% of labour force*
Agriculture	70	Unemployed 1999	...
Industry	9	Av. ann. rate 1990–99	...
Services	21		

Energy

	m TCE		
Total output	8.317	% output exported	86.1
Total consumption	1.962	% consumption imported	7.1
Consumption per head,			
kg coal equivalent	141		

Inflation and finance

Consumer price			*av. ann. change 1994–99*
inflation 1999	5.3%	Narrow money (M1)	8.3%
Av. ann. inflation 1990–99	5.8%	Broad money	4.1%
Deposit rate, 2000	5.00%		

Exchange rates

	end 2000		*December 2000*
CFAfr per $	704.95	Effective rates	1995 = 100
CFAfr per SDR	918.49	– nominal	95.4
CFAfr per euro	655.60	– real	

Trade

Principal exports[a]		**Principal imports**[a]	
	$bn fob		*$bn fob*
Crude oil	1.0	Capital goods	0.2
Cocoa	0.1	Food	0.2
Coffee	0.1		
Total incl. others	**1.6**	Total incl. others	**1.4**

Main export destinations		**Main origins of imports**	
	% of total		*% of total*
France	22.0	France	35.0
Spain	13.9	Germany	5.7
Italy	12.3	Italy	3.7

Balance of payments[c], reserves and debt, $bn

Visible exports fob	1.7	Overall balance	0.0
Visible imports fob	-1.1	Change in reserves	0.00
Trade balance	0.6	Level of reserves	
Invisibles inflows	0.3	end Dec.	0.00
Invisibles outflows	-0.9	No. months of import cover	0.02
Net transfers	0.1	Foreign debt	9.4
Current account balance	0.1	– as % of GDP	108
– as % of GDP	1.0	Debt service paid	0.5
Capital balance	0.1	Debt service ratio	24

Health and education

Health spending, % of GDP	5.0	Education spending, % of GDP	2.9
Doctors per 1,000 pop.	0.1	Enrolment, %: primary	85
Hospital beds per 1,000 pop.	2.6	secondary	27
Improved-water source access,		tertiary	4
% of pop.	62		

Society

No. of households	3.9m	Colour TVs per 100 households	3.2
Av. no. per household	3.7	Telephone lines per 100 pop.[d]	0.6
Marriages per 1,000 pop.	...	Mobile telephone subscribers	
Divorces per 1,000 pop.	...	per 100 pop.	...
Cost of living, Dec. 1999		Computers per 100 pop.	0.3
New York = 100	62	Internet hosts per 100 pop.	...

a Fiscal year ending June 30 1999.
b 1990
c 1995

CANADA

Area[a]	9,970,610 sq km	Capital	Ottawa
Arable as % of total land	5	Currency	Canadian dollar (C$)

People

Population	30.6m	Life expectancy: men	76.2 yrs
Pop. per sq km	3	women	81.8 yrs
Av. ann. growth		Adult literacy	99.0%
in pop. 1995–2000	0.93%	Fertility rate (per woman)	1.6
Pop. under 15	19.1%	Urban population	77.1%
Pop. over 65	16.7%		*per 1,000 pop.*
No. of men per 100 women	98.0	Crude birth rate	10.8
Human Development Index	93.5	Crude death rate	7.7

The economy

GDP	C$958bn	GDP per head	$20,750
GDP	$635bn	GDP per head in purchasing	
Av. ann. growth in real		power parity (USA=100)	79.7
GDP 1990–99	2.7%	Economic freedom index	2.05

Origins of GDP		**Components of GDP**	
	% of total		*% of total*
Agriculture	2.5	Private consumption	58.3
Industry, of which:	30.3	Public consumption	18.9
manufacturing & mining	21.4	Investment	19.9
Services	67.2	Exports	43.2
		Imports	-40.3

Structure of employment

	% of total		*% of labour force*
Agriculture	4	Unemployed 1999	7.6
Industry	23	Av. ann. rate 1990–99	9.6
Services	73		

Energy

	m TCE		
Total output	521.712	% output exported	47.9
Total consumption	338.656	% consumption imported	23.0
Consumption per head,			
kg coal equivalent	11,191		

Inflation and finance

Consumer price			*av. ann. increase 1994–99*
inflation 2000	2.7%	Narrow money (M1)	9.8%
Av. ann. inflation 1990–2000	2.0%	Broad money	5.4%
Money market rate, 2000	5.80%		

Exchange rates

	end 2000		*December 2000*
C$ per $	1.50	Effective rates	1995 = 100
C$ per SDR	1.95	– nominal	90.1
C$ per euro	1.40	– real	

Trade

Principal exports		Principal imports	
	$bn fob		*$bn fob*
Motor vehicles & parts	64.1	Machinery & industrial equipment	72.6
Machinery & industrial equipment	57.7	Motor vehicles & parts	50.9
Industrial supplies	38.5	Industrial supplies	41.7
Forest products	26.2	Consumer goods	24.8
Energy products	19.9	Agric. products	11.8
Agric. products & foodstuffs	17.2	Energy products	7.2
Total incl. others	**174.9**	Total incl. others	**219.3**

Main export destinations		Main origins of imports	
	% of total		*% of total*
United States	85.8	United States	76.3
Japan	2.6	Japan	3.2
United Kingdom	1.5	United Kingdom	2.4
EU15	5.1	EU15	8.8

Balance of payments, reserves and aid, $bn

Visible exports fob	242.8	Capital balance	1.6
Visible imports fob	-220.1	Overall balance	5.9
Trade balance	22.8	Change in reserves	4.6
Invisibles inflows	56.1	Level of reserves end Dec.	28.7
Invisibles outflows	-81.8	No. months of import cover	1.1
Net transfers	0.7	Aid given	1.70
Current account balance	-2.3	– as % of GDP	0.28
– as % of GDP	-0.4		

Health and education

Health spending, % of GDP	9.2	Education spending, % of GDP	6.9
Doctors per 1,000 pop.	2.1	Enrolment, %: primary	102
Hospital beds per 1,000 pop.	4.2	secondary	105
Improved-water source access, % of pop.	100	tertiary	90

Society

No. of households	11.7m	Colour TVs per 100 households	98.7
Av. no. per household	2.6	Telephone lines per 100 pop.	65.5
Marriages per 1,000 pop.	4.9	Mobile telephone subscribers per 100 pop.	22.6
Divorces per 1,000 pop.	2.2	Computers per 100 pop.	39.0
Cost of living, Dec. 1999 New York = 100	76	Internet hosts per 100 pop.	77.2

a Including freshwater.

CHILE

Area	756,945 sq km	Capital	Santiago
Arable as % of total land	3	Currency	Chilean peso (Ps)

People

Population	15.0m	Life expectancy: men	73 yrs
Pop. per sq km	20	women	79 yrs
Av. ann. growth		Adult literacy	95.2%
in pop. 1995–2000	1.36%	Fertility rate (per woman)	2.4
Pop. under 15	28.5%	Urban population	84.0%
Pop. over 65	10.2%		*per 1,000 pop.*
No. of men per 100 women	98.1	Crude birth rate	18.1
Human Development Index	82.6	Crude death rate	5.7

The economy

GDP	34,423bn pesos	GDP per head	$4,490
GDP	$67.5bn	GDP per head in purchasing	
Av. ann. growth in real		power parity (USA=100)	26.4
GDP 1990–99	7.2%	Economic freedom index	2.00

Origins of GDP		**Components of GDP**	
	% of total		*% of total*
Agriculture	8.7	Private consumption	67.8
Industry, of which:	37.8	Public consumption	8.0
manufacturing	17.5	Investment	26.3
Services	53.4	Exports	42.2
		Imports	-44.4

Structure of employment

	% of total		*% of labour force*
Agriculture	14	Unemployed 1998	7.2
Industry	24	Av. ann. rate 1990–98	5.4
Services	62		

Energy

	m TCE		
Total output	7.037	% output exported	3.8
Total consumption	27.614	% consumption imported	77.8
Consumption per head,			
kg coal equivalent	1,888		

Inflation and finance

Consumer price		*av. ann. increase 1994–99*	
inflation 2000	4.0%	Narrow money (M1)	14.5%
Av. ann. inflation 1990–2000	9.4%	Broad money	17.0%
Money market rate, 2000	10.09%		

Exchange rates

	end 2000		*December 2000*
Ps per $	572.7	Effective rates	1995 = 100
Ps per SDR	746.2	– nominal	89.8
Ps per Ecu	532.6	– real	103.0

Trade

Principal exports	$bn fob	Principal imports	$bn cif
Industrial goods	7.2	Intermediate goods	9.0
Copper	5.9	Capital goods	3.3
Agricultural goods	1.5	Consumer goods	2.8
Total incl. others	**15.6**	Total incl. others	**15.1**

Main export destinations	% of total	Main origins of imports	% of total
United States	18.6	United States	20.8
Japan	14.6	Argentina	13.9
United Kingdom	6.9	Brazil	6.7
Argentina	4.7	Japan	4.4
Brazil	4.5	Germany	4.3
Italy	4.1	Mexico	4.0

Balance of payments, reserves and debt, $bn

Visible exports fob	15.6	Overall balance	-0.8
Visible imports fob	-14.0	Change in reserves	-1.3
Trade balance	1.7	Level of reserves	
Invisibles inflows	4.9	end Dec.	14.8
Invisibles outflows	-7.1	No. months of import cover	8.4
Net transfers	0.5	Foreign debt	37.8
Current account balance	-0.1	– as % of GDP	56
– as % of GDP	-0.1	Debt service paid	5.2
Capital balance	-0.8	Debt service ratio	25

Health and education

Health spending, % of GDP	5.9	Education spending, % of GDP	3.6
Doctors per 1,000 pop.	1.1	Enrolment, %: primary	101
Hospital beds per 1,000 pop.	2.7	secondary	75
Improved-water source access,		tertiary	31
% of pop.	94		

Society

No. of households	3.4m	Colour TVs per 100 households	58.5
Av. no. per household	4.4	Telephone lines per 100 pop.	20.7
Marriages per 1,000 pop.	5.3	Mobile telephone subscribers	
Divorces per 1,000 pop.	0.6	per 100 pop.	15.1
Cost of living, Dec. 1999		Computers per 100 pop.	8.6
New York = 100	66	Internet hosts per 100 pop.	5.0

CHINA

Area	9,560,900 sq km	Capital	Beijing
Arable as % of total land	13	Currency	Yuan

People

Population	1,249.6m	Life expectancy: men	69.1 yrs
Pop. per sq km	134	women	73.5 yrs
Av. ann. growth		Adult literacy	82.9%
in pop. 1995–2000	0.90%	Fertility rate (per woman)	1.8
Pop. under 15	24.8%	Urban population	32.1%
Pop. over 65	10.1%		*per 1,000 pop.*
No. of men per 100 women	105.9	Crude birth rate	14.3
Human Development Index	70.6	Crude death rate	7.0

The economy

GDP	Yuan8,205bn	GDP per head	$790
GDP	$989bn	GDP per head in purchasing	
Av. ann. growth in real		power parity (USA=100)	11.1
GDP 1990–99	10.7%	Economic freedom index	3.55

Origins of GDP	*% of total*	**Components of GDP**	*% of total*
Agriculture	17.6	Private consumption	47.1
Industry, of which:	49.3	Public consumption	12.7
manufacturing	38.0	Investment	35.4
Services	33.0	Exports	21.8
		Imports	-19.0

Structure of employment

	% of total		*% of labour force*
Agriculture	50	Unemployed 1999	3.1
Industry	23	Av. ann. rate 1990–99	2.8
Services	27		

Energy

	m TCE		
Total output	1,271.209	% output exported	5.8
Total consumption	1,208.832	% consumption imported	7.5
Consumption per head,			
kg coal equivalent	989		

Inflation and finance

Consumer price			*av. ann. increase 1994–99*
inflation 2000	0.3%	Narrow money (M1)	19.0%
Av. ann. inflation 1991–2000	7.2%	Broad money	20.4%
Deposit rate, 2000	3.24%		

Exchange rates

	end 2000		*December 2000*
Yuan per $	8.28	Effective rates	1995 = 100
Yuan per SDR	10.78	– nominal	119.4
Yuan per euro	7.70	– real	109.3

Trade

Principal exports		Principal imports	
	$bn fob		*$bn cif*
Machinery & transport equipment	58.8	Machinery & transport equipment	69.5
Textiles & clothing	41.3	Chemicals	24.0
Footwear & accessories	10.3	Textiles	11.1
Chemicals	10.0	Fuels	8.9
Energy	4.6	Iron & steel	7.2
Total incl. others	**195.2**	Total incl. others	**165.8**

Main export destinations		Main origins of imports	
	% of total		*% of total*
United States	21.5	Japan	20.4
Hong Kong	18.9	Taiwan	11.8
Japan	16.6	United States	11.8
Germany	4.0	South Korea	10.4
South Korea	4.0	Germany	5.0
Netherlands	2.8	Hong Kong	4.2
United Kingdom	2.5	Russia	2.5
Singapore	2.3	Singapore	2.5

Balance of payments, reserves and debt, $bn

Visible exports fob	194.7	Overall balance	8.7
Visible imports fob	-158.5	Change in reserves	8.6
Trade balance	36.2	Level of reserves end Dec.	161.4
Invisibles inflows	34.3	No. months of import cover	8.9
Invisibles outflows	-59.8	Foreign debt	154.2
Net transfers	4.9	– as % of GDP	16
Current account balance	15.7	Debt service paid	20.7
– as % of GDP	1.6	Debt service ratio	9
Capital balance	7.6		

Health and education

Health spending, % of GDP	4.5	Education spending, % of GDP	2.3
Doctors per 1,000 pop.	2.0	Enrolment, %: primary	123
Hospital beds per 1,000 pop.	2.9	secondary	70
Improved-water source access, % of pop.	75	tertiary	6

Society

No. of households	340.3m	Colour TVs per 100 households	44.4
Av. no. per household	3.7	Telephone lines per 100 pop.	8.6
Marriages per 1,000 pop.	6.7	Mobile telephone subscribers per 100 pop.	6.7
Divorces per 1,000 pop.	0.9	Computers per 100 pop.	1.6
Cost of living, Dec. 1999 New York = 100	94	Internet hosts per 100 pop.	0.1

COLOMBIA

Area	1,141,748 sq km	Capital	Bogota
Arable as % of total land	2	Currency	Colombian peso (peso)

People

Population	41.4m	Life expectancy: men	69.2 yrs
Pop. per sq km	36	women	75.3 yrs
Av. ann. growth		Adult literacy	90.9%
in pop. 1995–2000	1.77%	Fertility rate (per woman)	2.8
Pop. under 15	32.8%	Urban population	73.9%
Pop. over 65	6.9%		*per 1,000 pop.*
No. of men per 100 women	97.7	Crude birth rate	22.2
Human Development Index	76.4	Crude death rate	6.4

The economy

GDP	152,185bn pesos	GDP per head	$2,090
GDP	$86.6bn	GDP per head in purchasing	
Av. ann. growth in real		power parity (USA=100)	17.5
GDP 1990–99	3.3%	Economic freedom index	2.95

Origins of GDP		**Components of GDP**	
	% of total		*% of total*
Agriculture	12.1	Private consumption	64.7
Industry, of which:	18.7	Public consumption	24.1
manufacturing	16.6	Investment	12.6
Services	69.2	Exports	18.1
		Imports	-19.5

Structure of employment[a]

	% of total		*% of labour force*
Agriculture	23	Unemployed 1999	20.1
Industry	19	Av. ann. rate 1990–99	11.3
Services	58		

Energy

	m TCE		
Total output	89.368	% output exported	62.6
Total consumption	31.702	% consumption imported	6.3
Consumption per head,			
kg coal equivalent	792		

Inflation and finance

Consumer price			*av. ann. increase 1994–99*
inflation 2000	9.5%	Narrow money (M1)	14.9%
Av. ann. inflation 1990–2000	20.3%	Broad money	19.6%
Money market rate, 2000	10.9%		

Exchange rates

	end 2000		*December 2000*
Peso per $	2,187	Effective rates	1995 = 100
Peso per SDR	2,849	– nominal	54.2
Peso per euro	2,034	– real	96.1

Trade

Principal exports		Principal imports	
	$bn fob		*$bn cif*
Petroleum & products	3.8	Industrial supplies	5.0
Coffee	1.3	Capital goods	3.7
Coal	0.8	Consumer goods	2.0
Nickel	0.1		
Total incl. others	**10.9**	Total	**14.6**

Main export destinations		Main origins of imports	
	% of total		*% of total*
United States	48.5	United States	38.3
Venezuela	7.9	Venezuela	8.7
Germany	4.2	Japan	5.3
Peru	3.1	Germany	4.9

Balance of payments, reserves and debt, $bn

Visible exports fob	12.0	Overall balance	-0.3
Visible imports fob	-10.3	Change in reserves	-0.7
Trade balance	1.8	Level of reserves	
Invisibles inflows	2.6	end Dec.	8.2
Invisibles outflows	-5.3	No. months of import cover	6.3
Net transfers	0.8	Foreign debt	34.5
Current account balance	-0.1	– as % of GDP	41
– as % of GDP	-0.1	Debt service paid	6.6
Capital balance	-0.1	Debt service ratio	44

Health and education

Health spending, % of GDP	9.3	Education spending, % of GDP	4.1
Doctors per 1,000 pop.	1.1	Enrolment, %: primary	113
Hospital beds per 1,000 pop.	1.5	secondary	67
Improved-water source access,		tertiary	17
% of pop.	91		

Society

No. of households	8.7m	Colour TVs per 100 households	84.5
Av. no. per household	4.7	Telephone lines per 100 pop.	16.0
Marriages per 1,000 pop.	...	Mobile telephone subscribers	
Divorces per 1,000 pop.	0.2	per 100 pop.	7.5
Cost of living, Dec. 1999		Computers per 100 pop.	3.4
New York = 100	56	Internet hosts per 100 pop.	1.1

a Main cities.

CÔTE D'IVOIRE

Area	322,463 sq km	Capital	Abidjan/Yamoussoukro
Arable as % of total land	9	Currency	CFA franc (CFAfr)

People

Population	14.7m	Life expectancy: men	47.7 yrs
Pop. per sq km	45.6	women	48.1 yrs
Av. ann. growth		Adult literacy	42.6%
in pop. 1995–2000	2.14%	Fertility rate (per woman)	5.1
Pop. under 15	42.1%	Urban population	46.4%
Pop. over 65	5.0%		*per 1,000 pop.*
No. of men per 100 women	105	Crude birth rate	35.2
Human Development Index	42.0	Crude death rate	15.3

The economy

GDP	CFAfr6,900bn	GDP per head	$760
GDP	$11.2bn	GDP per head in purchasing	
Av. ann. growth in real		power parity (USA=100)	4.8
GDP 1990–99	3.7%	Economic freedom index	3.00

Origins of GDP		**Components of GDP**	
	% of total		*% of total*
Agriculture	26	Private consumption	61.8
Industry, of which:	26	Public consumption	13.4
manufacturing	21	Investment	15.1
Services	48	Exports	40.3
		Imports	-30.4

Structure of employment[a]

	% of total		*% of labour force*
Agriculture	60	Unemployed 1998	...
Industry	10	Av. ann. rate 1990–98	...
Services	30		

Energy

	m TCE		
Total output	2.026	% output exported	19.9
Total consumption	3.376	% consumption imported	143.7
Consumption per head,			
kg coal equivalent	240		

Inflation and finance

Consumer price			*av. ann. change 1994–99*
inflation 2000	2.4%	Narrow money (M1)	8.4%
Av. ann. inflation 1990–2000	6.2%	Broad money	6.7%
Money market rate, 2000	4.95%		

Exchange rates

	end 2000		*December 2000*
CFAfr per $	705.0	Effective rates	1995 = 100
CFAfr per SDR	918.5	– nominal	94.5
CFAfr per euro	656.0	– real	

Trade

Principal exports		Principal imports	
	$bn fob		*$bn cif*
Cocoa beans & products	1.4	Raw materials & semi-processed goods	0.9
Petroleum products	0.5	Capital goods	0.8
Coffee & products	0.3	Consumer goods	0.6
Timber	0.2	Fuel	0.6
Total incl. others	**4.3**	Total incl. others	**2.8**

Main export destinations		Main origins of imports	
	% of total		*% of total*
France	15.2	France	26.2
United States	8.1	Nigeria	9.7
Netherlands	7.0	China	6.8
Germany	6.5	Italy	5.0
Italy	6.3	Germany	4.0

Balance of payments[b], reserves and debt, $bn

Visible exports fob	4.6	Overall balance	-0.6
Visible imports fob	-2.7	Change in reserves	-0.2
Trade balance	1.9	Level of reserves end Dec.	0.6
Invisibles inflows	0.7	No. months of import cover	1.6
Invisibles outflows	-2.3	Foreign debt	13.1
Net transfers	-0.5	– as % of GDP	126
Current account balance	-0.3	Debt service paid	1.4
– as % of GDP	-3.0	Debt service ratio	26
Capital balance	-0.5		

Health and education

Health spending, % of GDP	3.8	Education spending, % of GDP	5.0
Doctors per 1,000 pop.	0.1	Enrolment, %: primary	71
Hospital beds per 1,000 pop.	0.8	secondary	25
Improved-water source access, % of pop.	77	tertiary	5

Society

No. of households	3.1m	Colour TVs per 100 households	38.7
Av. no. per household	4.6	Telephone lines per 100 pop.	1.8
Marriages per 1,000 pop.	...	Mobile telephone subscribers per 100 pop.	1.8
Divorces per 1,000 pop.	...	Computers per 100 pop.	0.6
Cost of living, Dec. 1999 New York = 100	77	Internet hosts per 100 pop.	0.1

a 1990
b 1998

CZECH REPUBLIC

Area	78,864 sq km	Capital	Prague
Arable as % of total land	40	Currency	Koruna (Kc)

People

Population	10.2m	Life expectancy: men	72.1 yrs
Pop. per sq km	129	women	78.7 yrs
Av. ann. growth		Adult literacy	99.0%
in pop. 1995–2000	-0.11	Fertility rate (per woman)	1.1
Pop. under 15	16.4%	Urban population	74.7%
Pop. over 65	18.4%		*per 1,000 pop.*
No. of men per 100 women	94.9	Crude birth rate	8.7
Human Development Index	84.3	Crude death rate	10.8

The economy

GDP	Kcs1,833bn	GDP per head	$5,170
GDP	$53.1bn	GDP per head in purchasing	
Av. ann. growth in real		power parity (USA=100)	40.2
GDP 1990–99	0.8%	Economic freedom index	2.20

Origins of GDP		**Components of GDP**	
	% of total		*% of total*
Agriculture	3.7	Private consumption	53.4
Industry, of which:	41.8	Public consumption	19.7
manufacturing	...	Investment	28.5
Services	54.5	Exports	63.6
		Imports	-65.2

Structure of employment

	% of total		*% of labour force*
Agriculture	6	Unemployed 1999	9.0
Industry	42	Av. ann. rate 1993–99	5.4
Services	52		

Energy

	m TCE		
Total output	43.378	% output exported	26.3
Total consumption	56.959	% consumption imported	49.0
Consumption per head, kg coal equivalent	5,529		

Inflation and finance

Consumer price			*av. ann. increase 1994–99*
inflation 2000	3.9%	Narrow money (M1)	2.1%
Av. ann. inflation 1990–2000	13.3%	Broad money	8.2%
Refinancing rate, 2000	7.50%		

Exchange rates

	end 2000		*December 2000*
Kc per $	37.81	Effective rates	1995 = 100
Kc per SDR	49.28	– nominal	105.3
Kc per euro	35.16	– real	119.2

Trade

Principal exports	$bn fob	Principal imports	$bn fob
Machinery & transport equipment	11.6	Machinery & transport equipment	11.7
Semi-manufactures	6.8	Semi-manufactures	5.8
Chemicals	1.9	Chemicals	3.5
Raw materials & fuels	1.8	Raw materials & fuels	2.8
Total incl. others	**26.3**	Total incl. others	**28.1**

Main export destinations	% of total	Main origins of imports	% of total
Germany	43.0	Germany	37.5
Slovakia	8.4	Slovakia	6.7
Austria	6.6	Austria	6.2
Poland	5.6	Italy	5.9
France	4.0	France	5.4

Balance of payments, reserves and debt, $bn

Visible exports fob	26.3	Overall balance	1.6
Visible imports fob	-28.2	Change in reserves	0.3
Trade balance	-1.9	Level of reserves end Dec.	12.9
Invisibles inflows	8.6	No. months of import cover	4.3
Invisibles outflows	-8.2	Foreign debt	22.5
Net transfers	0.5	– as % of GDP	43
Current account balance	-1.0	Debt service paid	3.6
– as % of GDP	-1.9	Debt service ratio	10
Capital balance	2.5		

Health and education

Health spending, % of GDP	7.2	Education spending, % of GDP	5.1
Doctors per 1,000 pop.	3.0	Enrolment, %: primary	104
Hospital beds per 1,000 pop.	8.7	secondary	99
Improved-water source access, % of pop.	...	tertiary	24

Society

No. of households	3.5m	Colour TVs per 100 households	87.1
Av. no. per household	3.0	Telephone lines per 100 pop.	37.1
Marriages per 1,000 pop.	4.5	Mobile telephone subscribers per 100 pop.	19.0
Divorces per 1,000 pop.	3.1	Computers per 100 pop.	12.2
Cost of living, Dec. 1999 New York = 100	52	Internet hosts per 100 pop.	15.0

DENMARK

Area	43,075 sq km	Capital	Copenhagen
Arable as % of total land	56	Currency	Danish krone (DKr)

People

Population	5.3m	Life expectancy: men	74.2 yrs
Pop. per sq km	123	women	79.1 yrs
Av. ann. growth		Adult literacy	99.0%
in pop. 1995–2000	0.3	Fertility rate (per woman)	1.7
Pop. under 15	18.3%	Urban population	85.3%
Pop. over 65	20.0%		*per 1,000 pop.*
No. of men per 100 women	97.8	Crude birth rate	11.0
Human Development Index	91.1	Crude death rate	11.3

The economy

GDP	DKr1,222bn	GDP per head	$32,780
GDP	$174bn	GDP per head in purchasing	
Av. ann. growth in real		power parity (USA=100)	80.2
GDP 1990–99	2.4%	Economic freedom index	2.05

Origins of GDP		**Components of GDP**	
	% of total		*% of total*
Agriculture	2.9	Private consumption	50.5
Industry, of which:	22.7	Public consumption	25.7
manufacturing	16.8	Investment	19.6
Services	74.4	Exports	36.9
		Imports	-32.7

Structure of employment

	% of total		*% of labour force*
Agriculture	4	Unemployed 1998	5.5
Industry	27	Av. ann. rate 1990–98	7.8
Services	69		

Energy

	m TCE		
Total output	26.484	% output exported	82.4
Total consumption	24.457	% consumption imported	101.5
Consumption per head,			
kg coal equivalent	4,653		

Inflation and finance

Consumer price			*av. ann. increase 1994–99*
inflation 2000	2.9%	Narrow money (M1)	7.0%
Av. ann. inflation 1990–2000	2.1%	Broad money	4.7%
Money market rate, 2000	4.98%		

Exchange rates

	end 2000		*July 2000*
DKr per $	8.02	Effective rates	1995 = 100
DKr per SDR	10.45	– nominal	92.2
DKr per euro	7.46	– real	96.6

Trade

Principal exports		Principal imports	
	$bn fob		*$bn cif*
Manufactured goods	37.1	Intermediate goods	20.1
Agric. products	5.3	Consumer goods	12.6
Energy & products	2.1	Capital goods	5.8
Ships	0.9	Transport equipment	3.5
Total incl. others	**49.7**	Total incl. others	**44.7**

Main export destinations		Main origins of imports	
	% of total		*% of total*
Germany	20.0	Germany	21.8
Sweden	11.5	Sweden	12.3
United Kingdom	9.6	United Kingdom	8.0
Norway	5.9	Netherlands	8.0
United States	5.5	France	5.9
France	5.3	Italy	4.8
EU15	66.2	EU15	72.1

Balance of payments, reserves and aid, $bn

Visible exports fob	50.2	Capital balance	6.5
Visible imports fob	-43.3	Overall balance	9.4
Trade balance	6.9	Change in reserves	7.0
Invisibles inflows	26.4	Level of reserves	
Invisibles outflows	-26.7	end Dec.	22.9
Net transfers	-2.7	No. months of import cover	3.9
Current account balance	3.9	Aid given	1.73
– as % of GDP	1.5	– as % of GDP	0.99

Health and education

Health spending, % of GDP	8.3	Education spending, % of GDP	8.1
Doctors per 1,000 pop.	2.9	Enrolment, %: primary	102
Hospital beds per 1,000 pop.	4.6	secondary	121
Improved-water source access,		tertiary	45
% of pop.	100		

Society

No. of households	2.3m	Colour TVs per 100 households	92.0
Av. no. per household	2.3	Telephone lines per 100 pop.	63.8
Marriages per 1,000 pop.	9.1	Mobile telephone subscribers	
Divorces per 1,000 pop.	2.5	per 100 pop.	61.4
Cost of living, Dec. 1999		Computers per 100 pop.	43.2
New York = 100	85	Internet hosts per 100 pop.	81.9

EGYPT

Area	1,000,250 sq km	Capital	Cairo
Arable as % of total land	3	Currency	Egyptian pound (£E)

People

Population	62.4m	Life expectancy: men	66.7 yrs
Pop. per sq km	62	women	69.9 yrs
Av. ann. growth		Adult literacy	52.7%
in pop. 1995–2000	1.82%	Fertility rate (per woman)	3.4
Pop. under 15	35.4%	Urban population	45.2%
Pop. over 65	6.3%		*per 1,000 pop.*
No. of men per 100 women	102.9	Crude birth rate	23.2
Human Development Index	62.3	Crude death rate	6.1

The economy

GDP[a]	£E302bn	GDP per head	$1,430
GDP	$89.1bn	GDP per head in purchasing	
Av. ann. growth in real		power parity (USA=100)	10.8
GDP 1990–99	4.4%	Economic freedom index	3.60

Origins of GDP[a]		**Components of GDP[a]**	
	% of total		*% of total*
Agriculture	17.4	Private consumption	74.2
Industry, of which:	31.5	Public consumption	10.1
manufacturing	20.0	Investment	21.3
Services	51.1	Exports	16.0
		Imports	-24.4

Structure of employment[b]

	% of total		*% of labour force*
Agriculture	34	Unemployed 1998	8.2
Industry	22	Av. ann. rate 1990–98	9.6
Services	44		

Energy

	m TCE		
Total output	84.826	% output exported	34.0
Total consumption	53.243	% consumption imported	5.9
Consumption per head,			
kg coal equivalent	823		

Inflation and finance

Consumer price			*av. ann. increase 1994–99*
inflation 2000	2.7%	Narrow money (M1)	9.1%
Av. ann. inflation 1990–2000	9.0%	Broad money	7.8%
Treasury bill rate, 2000	9.1%		

Exchange rates

	end 2000		*December 2000*
£E per $	3.69	Effective rates	1995 = 100
£E per SDR	4.81	– nominal	...
£E per euro	3.43	– real	...

Trade

Principal exports[a]		Principal imports[a]	
	$bn fob		*$bn fob*
Petroleum & products	1.0	Machinery & transport equipment	4.0
Cotton yarn & textiles	0.6	Agric. products & foodstuffs	1.8
Industrial goods	0.3	Chemicals & rubber	1.1
Other agric. products	0.3	Petroleum & products	1.1
Raw cotton	0.2	Wood, paper & textiles	1.1
Total incl. others	**4.4**	Total incl. others	**17.0**

Main export destinations		Main origins of imports	
	% of total		*% of total*
United States	12.3	United States	14.4
EU15	35.0	EU15	35.9

Balance of payments, reserves and debt, $bn

Visible exports fob	5.2	Overall balance	-4.6
Visible imports fob	-15.2	Change in reserves	-3.6
Trade balance	-9.9	Level of reserves end Dec.	15.2
Invisibles inflows	11.3	No. months of import cover	8.0
Invisibles outflows	-7.5	Foreign debt	30.4
Net transfers	4.5	– as % of GDP	34
Current account balance	-1.6	Debt service paid	1.7
– as % of GDP	-1.8	Debt service ratio	9
Capital balance	-1.4		

Health and education

Health spending, % of GDP	3.8	Education spending, % of GDP	4.8
Doctors per 1,000 pop.	1.6	Enrolment, %: primary	101
Hospital beds per 1,000 pop.	2.1	secondary	78
Improved-water source access, % of pop.	95	tertiary	23

Society

No. of households	15.0m	Colour TVs per 100 households	44.5
Av. no. per household	4.4	Telephone lines per 100 pop.	8.1
Marriages per 1,000 pop.	9.9	Mobile telephone subscribers per 100 pop.	2.1
Divorces per 1,000 pop.	1.6	Computers per 100 pop.	1.2
Cost of living, Dec. 1999 New York = 100	81	Internet hosts per 100 pop.	0.1

a Year ending June 30, 1999.
b 1995
c Year ending June 30, 1999.

EURO AREA[a]

Area	2,365 sq km	Capital	–
Arable as % of total land	25.6	Currency	Euro (€)

People

Population	293.3m	Life expectancy: men[b]	74.5 yrs
Pop. per sq km	124	women[b]	81.2 yrs
Av. ann. growth		Adult literacy	98.3%
in pop. 1995–2000	0.22%	Fertility rate (per woman)	1.4
Pop. under 15	16.5%	Urban population	77.6%
Pop. over 65	16.3%		*per 1,000 pop.*
No. of men per 100 women	95	Crude birth rate	9.2
Human Development Index	90.9	Crude death rate[c]	9.7

The economy

GDP	€6,124bn	GDP per head	$22,280
GDP	$6,535bn	GDP per head in purchasing	
Av. ann. growth in real		power parity (USA=100)	69.5
GDP 1990–99	1.8%	Economic freedom index	2.25

Origins of GDP		**Components of GDP**	
	% of total		*% of total*
Agriculture	2	Private consumption	56.7
Industry, of which:	27	Public consumption	20.1
manufacturing	...	Investment	21.4
Services	71	Exports	33.3
		Imports	-31.5

Structure of employment

	% of total		*% of labour force*
Agriculture	4.8	Unemployed 1999	10.0
Industry	30.5	Av. ann. rate 1991–99	10.5
Services	64.7		

Energy

	m TCE		
Total output	592.5	% output exported	...
Total consumption	1,470.5	% consumption imported	...
Consumption per head,			
kg coal equivalent	5,154		

Inflation and finance

Consumer price			*av. ann. increase 1994–99*
inflation 2000	2.3%	Narrow money (M1)	7.9%
Av. ann. inflation 1990–2000	...	Broad money	5.9%
Interbank rate, 2000	4.39%		

Exchange rates

	end 2000		*July 2000*
€ per $	1.07	Effective rates	1995 = 100
€ per SDR	1.40	– nominal	80.0
		– real	71.7

Trade

Principal exports[d]		Principal imports[d]	
	$bn fob		*$bn fob*
Machinery & transport equip.	373.9	Machinery & transport equip.	325.1
Manufactures	353.8	Manufactures	324.8
Food, drink & tobacco	46.4	Fuels	82.8
Fuels	17.6	Food, drink & tobacco	53.4
Raw materials	16.3	Raw materials	42.9
Total	**808.0**	Total	**829.0**

Main export destinations		Main origins of imports	
	% of total		*% of total*
Germany	12.8	Germany	13.4
France	10.4	France	9.2
United Kingdom	9.5	United Kingdom	8.1
United States	8.0	United States	7.7
Italy	6.3	Netherlands	6.4
EU15	64.8	EU15	61.2
EU11	51.1	EU11	49.7

Balance of payments, reserves and debt, $bn

Visible exports fob	866.8	Capital balance	23.3
Visible imports fob	-778.1	Overall balance	-11.7
Trade balance	88.7	Change in reserves	-11.3
Invisibles inflows	484.2	Level of reserves	
Invisibles outflows	-1,047.7	end Dec.	374.0
Net transfers	-47.6	No. months of import cover	3.4
Current account balance	-6.1	Aid given	19.80
– as % of gdp	-0.1	– as % of GDP	0.31

Health and education

Health spending, % of GDP[e]	8.9	Education spending, % of GDP	
Doctors per 1,000 pop.	4.0	Enrolment[b], %: primary	104
Hospital beds per 1,000 pop.	6.7	secondary	108
Improved-water source access,		tertiary	49
% of pop.	...		

Society

No. of households	150.9m	Colour TVs per 100 households	95.6
Av. no. per household	1.94	Telephone lines per 100 pop.	52.2
Marriages per 1,000 pop.	5.1	Mobile telephone subscribers	
Divorces per 1,000 pop.	1.7	per 100 pop.	31.8
Cost of living, Dec. 1999		Computers per 100 pop.	27.3
New York = 100	...	Internet hosts per 100 pop.	30.6

a Data refer to EU11; Greece joined on January 1, 2001. Where necessary, population-weighted averages have been calculated.
b 1997
c 2001
d EU15 data (trade with non-EU15 countries).
e 1998

FINLAND

Area	338,145 sq km	Capital	Helsinki
Arable as % of total land	7	Currency	Markka (Fmk)

People

Population	5.1m	Life expectancy: men	74.4 yrs
Pop. per sq km	17	women	81.5 yrs
Av. ann. growth		Adult literacy	99.0%
in pop. 1995–2000	0.25%	Fertility rate (per woman)	1.7
Pop. under 15	18.0%	Urban population	67.3%
Pop. over 65	19.9%		*per 1,000 pop.*
No. of men per 100 women	95.2	Crude birth rate	9.7
Human Development Index	91.7	Crude death rate	9.8

The economy

GDP	Fmk722bn	GDP per head	$25,090
GDP	$130bn	GDP per head in purchasing	
Av. ann. growth in real		power parity (USA=100)	70.8
GDP 1990–99	2.4%	Economic freedom index	2.15

Origins of GDP		**Components of GDP**	
	% of total		*% of total*
Agriculture	3.5	Private consumption	50.0
Industry, of which:	31.1	Public consumption	20.8
manufacturing & mining	24.9	Investment	18.3
Services	65.4	Exports	42.7
		Imports	-31.8

Structure of employment

	% of total		*% of labour force*
Agriculture	7	Unemployed 1999	10.1
Industry	27	Av. ann. rate 1990–99	11.7
Services	66		

Energy

	m TCE		
Total output	13.033	% output exported[a]	42.6
Total consumption	37.993	% consumption imported[a]	81.3
Consumption per head,			
kg coal equivalent	7,390		

Inflation and finance

Consumer price			*av. ann. increase 1994–99*
inflation 2000	3.4%	Euro area:	
Av. ann. inflation 1990–2000	1.9%	Narrow money (M1)	7.9%
Money market rate, 1999	2.97%	Broad money	5.9%

Exchange rates

	end 2000		*July 2000*
Fmk per $	6.44	Effective rates	1995 = 100
Fmk per SDR	8.37	– nominal	88.4
Fmk per euro	5.95	– real	83.0

Trade

Principal exports	$bn fob	Principal imports	$bn cif
Electrical & optical equipment	11.1	Intermediate goods	12.3
Metals, machinery & transport equipment	10.0	Capital goods	7.8
Paper & products	9.2	Consumer goods	7.3
Wood & products	2.5	Energy & products	2.7
Total incl. others	**41.8**	Total incl. others	**31.6**

Main export destinations	% of total	Main origins of imports	% of total
Germany	13.1	Germany	15.3
Sweden	9.9	Sweden	11.2
United Kingdom	9.1	United States	7.9
United States	7.9	Russia	7.2
France	5.3	United Kingdom	6.6
Netherlands	4.3	Japan	6.2

Balance of payments, reserves and aid, $bn

Visible exports fob	42.0	Capital balance	-5.0
Visible imports fob	-30.3	Overall balance	-0.1
Trade balance	11.7	Change in reserves	-1.1
Invisibles inflows	11.7	Level of reserves end Dec.	8.7
Invisibles outflows	-15.2	No. months of import cover	2.3
Net transfers	-1.0	Aid given	0.42
Current account balance	7.1	– as % of GDP	0.33
– as % of GDP	5.5		

Health and education

Health spending, % of GDP	6.9	Education spending, % of GDP	7.5
Doctors per 1,000 pop.	3.0	Enrolment, %: primary	99
Hospital beds per 1,000 pop.	7.8	secondary	118
Improved-water source access, % of pop.	100	tertiary	74

Society

No. of households	2.2m	Colour TVs per 100 households	97.0
Av. no. per household	2.3	Telephone lines per 100 pop.	55.2
Marriages per 1,000 pop.	5.0	Mobile telephone subscribers per 100 pop.	72.6
Divorces per 1,000 pop.	2.6	Computers per 100 pop.	39.6
Cost of living, Dec. 1999 New York = 100	79	Internet hosts per 100 pop.	149.4

a Energy trade data are distorted by transitory and oil refinery activities.

FRANCE

Area	543,965 sq km	Capital	Paris
Arable as % of total land	33	Currency	Franc (FFr)

People

Population	60.8m	Life expectancy: men	75.2 yrs
Pop. per sq km	112	women	82.8 yrs
Av. ann. growth		Adult literacy	99.0%
in pop. 1995–2000	0.37%	Fertility rate (per woman)	1.7
Pop. under 15	18.7%	Urban population	75.0%
Pop. over 65	20.5%		*per 1,000 pop.*
No. of men per 100 women	95.1	Crude birth rate	12.2
Human Development Index	91.7	Crude death rate	9.4

The economy

GDP	FFr8,825bn	GDP per head	$23,560
GDP	$1,432bn	GDP per head in purchasing	
Av. ann. growth in real		power parity (USA=100)	72.1
GDP 1990–99	1.5%	Economic freedom index	2.50

Origins of GDP		**Components of GDP**	
	% of total		*% of total*
Agriculture	3.3	Private consumption	54.9
Industry, of which:	25.1	Public consumption	23.7
manufacturing	...	Investment	18.9
Services	71.6	Exports	26.1
		Imports	-23.7

Structure of employment

	% of total		*% of labour force*
Agriculture	5	Unemployed 1999	11.9
Industry	26	Av. ann. rate 1990–99	11.2
Services	69		

Energy

	m TCE		
Total output	168.387	% output exported	20.1
Total consumption	322.193	% consumption imported	65.2
Consumption per head,			
kg coal equivalent	5,507		

Inflation and finance

Consumer price			*av. ann. increase 1994–99*
inflation 2000	1.7%	Euro area:	
Av. ann. inflation 1990–2000	1.7%	Narrow money (M1)	7.9%
Treasury bill rate, 2000	4.23%	Broad money	5.9%

Exchange rates

	end 2000		*July 2000*
FFr per $	7.10	Effective rates	1995 = 100
FFr per SDR	9.23	– nominal	93.1
FFr per euro	6.56	– real	85.2

Trade

Principal exports		Principal imports	
	$bn fob		*$bn cif*
Intermediate goods	94.7	Intermediate goods	94.5
Capital equipment	73.6	Capital equipment	66.7
Consumer goods	40.5	Consumer goods	44.4
Motor vehicles & other transport equipment	40.3	Motor vehicles & other transport equipment	31.6
Food & drink	28.3	Food & drink	30.2
Total incl. others	**296.7**	Total incl. others	**287.5**

Main export destinations		Main origins of imports	
	% of total		*% of total*
Germany	15.8	Germany	17.2
United Kingdom	10.3	Italy	9.6
Spain	9.4	United States	8.8
Italy	9.1	United Kingdom	8.4
United States	7.8	Belgium & Luxembourg	7.3
EU15	64.3	EU15	63.0

Balance of payments, reserves and aid, $bn

Visible exports fob	298.2	Capital balance	-39.7
Visible imports fob	-278.8	Overall balance	-1.5
Trade balance	19.4	Change in reserves	-1.0
Invisibles inflows	151.7	Level of reserves end Dec.	67.9
Invisibles outflows	-121.5	No. months of import cover	2.0
Net transfers	-13.0	Aid given[a]	5.64
Current account balance	36.6	– as % of GDP	0.40
– as % of GDP	2.6		

Health and education

Health spending, % of GDP	9.6	Education spending, % of GDP	6.0
Doctors per 1,000 pop.	3.0	Enrolment, %: primary	105
Hospital beds per 1,000 pop.	8.5	secondary	111
Improved-water source access, % of pop.	...	tertiary	51

Society

No. of households	24.0m	Colour TVs per 100 households	95.8
Av. no. per household	2.5	Telephone lines per 100 pop.	58.0
Marriages per 1,000 pop.	4.9	Mobile telephone subscribers per 100 pop.	49.4
Divorces per 1,000 pop.	2.0	Computers per 100 pop.	30.5
Cost of living, Dec. 1999 New York = 100	88	Internet hosts per 100 pop.	20.2

a Including aid to French overseas territories.

GERMANY

Area	357,868 sq km	Capital	Berlin
Arable as % of total land	34	Currency	Deutschemark (DM)

People

Population	82.0m	Life expectancy: men	75.0 yrs
Pop. per sq km	235	women	81.1 yrs
Av. ann. growth		Adult literacy	99.0%
in pop. 1995–2000	0.09%	Fertility rate (per woman)	1.3
Pop. under 15	15.5%	Urban population	87.5%
Pop. over 65	23.2%		*per 1,000 pop.*
No. of men per 100 women	96.0	Crude birth rate	8.1
Human Development Index	91.1	Crude death rate	10.8

The economy

GDP	DM3,877bn	GDP per head	$25,750
GDP	$2,112bn	GDP per head in purchasing	
Av. ann. growth in real		power parity (USA=100)	73.7
GDP 1990–99	1.3%	Economic freedom index	2.10

Origins of GDP		**Components of GDP**	
	% of total		*% of total*
Agriculture	1.2	Private consumption	57.8
Industry, of which:	30.3	Public consumption	19.0
manufacturing	...	Investment	21.6
Services	68.5	Exports	28.8
		Imports	-27.2

Structure of employment

	% of total		*% of labour force*
Agriculture	3	Unemployed 1999	8.8
Industry	37	Av. ann. rate 1991–99	9.1
Services	60		

Energy

	m TCE		
Total output	194.955	% output exported	15.8
Total consumption	467.105	% consumption imported	69.9
Consumption per head,			
kg coal equivalent	5,692		

Inflation and finance

Consumer price			*av. ann. increase 1994–99*
inflation 2000	2.0%	Euro area:	
Av. ann. inflation 1990–2000	2.4%	Narrow money (M1)	7.9%
Money market rate, 2000	4.11%	Broad money	5.9%

Exchange rates

	end 2000		*July 2000*
DM per $	2.12	Effective rates	1995 = 100
DM per SDR	2.76	– nominal	88.0
DM per euro	1.96	– real	81.1

Trade

Principal exports	$bn fob	Principal imports	$bn fob
Machinery	160.4	Machinery	115.2
Road vehicles	96.2	Road vehicles	45.6
Chemicals	69.7	Food, drink & tobacco	33.4
Metals & manufactures	37.2	Chemicals	41.5
Scientific instruments	19.4	Metals & manufactures	19.7
Total incl. others	**543.0**	Total incl. others	**471.0**

Main export destinations	% of total	Main origins of imports	% of total
France	11.4	France	10.3
United States	10.1	United States	8.2
United Kingdom	8.4	Netherlands	7.9
Italy	7.4	Italy	7.3
Netherlands	6.5	United Kingdom	6.9
Japan	2.1	Japan	4.8
EU15	52.9	EU15	52.5

Balance of payments, reserves and aid, $bn

Visible exports fob	543.0	Capital balance	-34.0
Visible imports fob	-471.0	Overall balance	-14.1
Trade balance	72.0	Change in reserves	-16.2
Invisibles inflows	169.0	Level of reserves	
Invisibles outflows	-233.0	end Dec.	93.4
Net transfers	-27.3	No. months of import cover	1.6
Current account balance	-19.3	Aid given	5.52
– as % of GDP	-0.9	– as % of GDP	0.27

Health and education

Health spending, % of GDP	10.6	Education spending, % of GDP	4.8
Doctors per 1,000 pop.	3.5	Enrolment, %: primary	104
Hospital beds per 1,000 pop.	9.3	secondary	104
Improved-water source access,		tertiary	47
% of pop.	...		

Society

No. of households	36.0m	Colour TVs per 100 households	96.9
Av. no. per household	2.3	Telephone lines per 100 pop.	60.1
Marriages per 1,000 pop.	5.4	Mobile telephone subscribers	
Divorces per 1,000 pop.	2.4	per 100 pop.	57.9
Cost of living, Dec. 1999		Computers per 100 pop.	33.6
New York = 100	75	Internet hosts per 100 pop.	26.4

GREECE

Area	131,957 sq km	Capital	Athens
Arable as % of total land	22	Currency	Drachma (Dr)

People

Population	10.5m	Life expectancy: men	75.9 yrs
Pop. per sq km	80	women	81.2 yrs
Av. ann. growth		Adult literacy	96.6%
in pop. 1995–2000	0.30%	Fertility rate (per woman)	1.3
Pop. under 15	15.1%	Urban population	60.1%
Pop. over 65	23.4%		*per 1,000 pop.*
No. of men per 100 women	96.9	Crude birth rate	8.8
Human Development Index	87.5	Crude death rate	10.4

The economy

GDP	Dr38,147bn	GDP per head	$11,870
GDP	$125bn	GDP per head in purchasing	
Av. ann. growth in real		power parity (USA=100)	49.5
GDP 1990–99	2.2%	Economic freedom index	2.70

Origins of GDP	*% of total*	**Components of GDP**	*% of total*
Agriculture	8.7	Private consumption	70.1
Industry, of which:	23.6	Public consumption	14.6
manufacturing	...	Investment	22.7
Services	67.7	Exports	17.8
		Imports	-25.2

Structure of employment

	% of total		*% of labour force*
Agriculture	20	Unemployed 1998	10.8
Industry	23	Av. ann. rate 1990–98	9.3
Services	57		

Energy

	m TCE		
Total output	13.080	% output exported[a]	30.2
Total consumption	36.743	% consumption imported[a]	88.0
Consumption per head,			
kg coal equivalent	3,476		

Inflation and finance

Consumer price		*av. ann. increase 1994–99*	
inflation 2000	3.1%	Narrow money (M1)	16.3%
Av. ann. inflation 1990–2000	9.2%	Broad money	11.9%
Treasury bill rate, 2000	6.20%		

Exchange rates

	end 2000		*July 2000*
Dr per $	365.6	Effective rates	1995 = 100
Dr per SDR	476.4	– nominal	85.1
Dr per euro	340.0	– real	101.2

Trade

Principal exports	$bn fob	Principal imports	$bn cif
Food & beverages	1.5	Machinery	5.1
Petroleum products	0.9	Transport equipment	4.2
Chemicals	0.8	Chemicals	3.3
Textiles	0.7	Fuels	1.4
Non-ferrous metals	0.6	Iron & steel	1.0
Total incl. others	**9.8**	Total incl. others	**25.4**

Main export destinations	% of total	Main origins of imports	% of total
Germany	15.9	Italy	15.6
Italy	13.5	Germany	15.0
United Kingdom	6.4	France	9.2
United States	5.7	Netherlands	6.4
EU15	51.6	EU15	66.2

Balance of payments[b], reserves and debt, $bn

Visible exports fob	5.6	Overall balance	-4.5
Visible imports fob	-21.0	Change in reserves	0.9
Trade balance	-15.4	Level of reserves	
Invisibles inflows	10.5	end Dec.	19.4
Invisibles outflows	-7.5	No. months of import cover	7.1
Net transfers	7.5	Aid given	0.19
Current account balance	-4.9	– as % of GDP	0.16
– as % of GDP	-4.0		
Capital balance	0.1		

Health and education

Health spending, % of GDP	8.3	Education spending, % of GDP	3.1
Doctors per 1,000 pop.	4.0	Enrolment, %: primary	93
Hospital beds per 1,000 pop.	5.0	secondary	95
Improved-water source access,		tertiary	47
% of pop.	...		

Society

No. of households	3.6m	Colour TVs per 100 households	90.8
Av. no. per household	2.9	Telephone lines per 100 pop.	52.8
Marriages per 1,000 pop.	5.5	Mobile telephone subscribers	
Divorces per 1,000 pop.	0.9	per 100 pop.	55.9
Cost of living, Dec. 1999		Computers per 100 pop.	7.1
New York = 100	...	Internet hosts per 100 pop.	14.1

a Energy trade figures are distorted by transitory and oil refining activities.
b 1997

HONG KONG

Area	1,075 sq km	Capital	Victoria
Arable as % of total land	5	Currency	Hong Kong dollar (HK$)

People

Population	6.9m	Life expectancy[a]: men	77.3 yrs
Pop. per sq km	6,628	women	82.8 yrs
Av. ann. growth		Adult literacy	92.4%
in pop. 1995–2000	1.99%	Fertility rate (per woman)	1.1
Pop. under 15	16.3%	Urban population	100.0%
Pop. over 65	14.3%		*per 1,000 pop.*
No. of men per 100 women	104	Crude birth rate	9.5
Human Development Index	87.2	Crude death rate[a]	5.9

The economy

GDP	HK$1,231bn	GDP per head	$23,110
GDP	$159bn	GDP per head in purchasing	
Av. ann. growth in real		power parity (USA=100)	70.7
GDP 1990–99	3.9%	Economic freedom index	1.30

Origins of GDP		**Components of GDP**	
	% of total		*% of total*
Agriculture	0.1	Private consumption	60.2
Industry, of which:	14.5	Public consumption	9.8
manufacturing	5.7	Investment	25.4
Services	85.4	Exports	132.0
		Imports	-127.4

Structure of employment

	% of total		*% of labour force*
Agriculture	0	Unemployed 1999	6.3
Industry	17	Av. ann. rate 1990–99	2.8
Services	83		

Energy

	m TCE		
Total output	nil	% output exported	nil
Total consumption	10.161	% consumption imported	320.0
Consumption per head,			
kg coal equivalent	1,561		

Inflation and finance

Consumer price			*av. ann. increase 1994–99*
inflation 2000	-3.6%	Narrow money (M1)	4.1%
Av. ann. inflation 1990–2000	5.2%	Broad money	10.2%
Money market rate, 2000	7.13%		

Exchange rates

	end 2000		*December 2000*
HK$ per $	7.80	Effective rates	1995 = 100
HK$ per SDR	10.16	– nominal	...
HK$ per euro	8.39	– real	...

Trade

Principal exports[b]		Principal imports	
	$bn fob		$bn cif
Clothing	9.5	Consumer goods	65.2
Electrical machinery		Raw materials & semi-	
& apparatus	3.1	manufactured products	60.5
Textiles	1.2	Capital goods	42.0
Office machinery	0.8	Agric. products & foodstuffs	7.3
		Fuels	3.5
Total incl. others	**21.9**	Total incl. others	**178.6**

Main export destinations[c]		Main origins of imports	
	% of total		% of total
China	33.4	China	43.6
United States	23.8	Japan	11.7
Japan	5.4	Taiwan	7.2
United Kingdom	4.1	United States	7.1

Balance of payments, reserves and debt, $bn

Visible exports fob	174.7	Overall balance	9.5
Visible imports cif	-177.9	Change in reserves	6.6
Trade balance	-3.2	Level of reserves	
Services inflows	94.4	end Dec.	96.3
Services outflows	-69.2	No. months of import cover	4.7
Net transfers	-1.5	Foreign debt	54.2
Current account balance	10.5	– as % of GDP	34.2
– as % of GDP	6.6	Debt service paid	4.8
Capital balance	-1.3	Debt service ratio	2.9

Health and education

Health spending, % of GDP	5.0	Education spending, % of GDP	2.9
Doctors per 1,000 pop.	1.3	Enrolment, %: primary	94
Hospital beds per 1,000 pop.	...	secondary	73
Improved-water source access,		tertiary	23
% of pop.	...		

Society

No. of households	2.1m	Colour TVs per 100 households	99.2
Av. no. per household	3.2	Telephone lines per 100 pop.	57.6
Marriages per 1,000 pop.	4.4	Mobile telephone subscribers	
Divorces per 1,000 pop.	1.7	per 100 pop.	63.6
Cost of living, Dec. 1999		Computers per 100 pop.	34.7
New York = 100	117	Internet hosts per 100 pop.	33.3

a 1995–2000.
b Domestic.
c Including re-exports.
Note: Hong Kong became a Special Administrative Region of China from July 1 1997.

HUNGARY

Area	93,030 sq km	Capital	Budapest
Arable as % of total land	52	Currency	Forint (Ft)

People

Population	10.1m	Life expectancy: men	67.8 yrs
Pop. per sq km	108	women	76.1 yrs
Av. ann. growth		Adult literacy	99.0%
in pop. 1995–2000	-0.49%	Fertility rate (per woman)	1.4
Pop. under 15	16.9%	Urban population	64.0%
Pop. over 65	19.7%		*per 1,000 pop.*
No. of men per 100 women	91.5	Crude birth rate	8.8
Human Development Index	81.7	Crude death rate	13.5

The economy

GDP	Ft11,498bn	GDP per head	$4,810
GDP	$48.4bn	GDP per head in purchasing	
Av. ann. growth in real		power parity (USA=100)	34.6
GDP 1990–99	1.0%	Economic freedom index	2.55

Origins of GDP[a]		**Components of GDP**	
	% of total		*% of total*
Agriculture	5.7	Private consumption	63.7
Industry, of which:	33.7	Public consumption	10.0
manufacturing	...	Investment	28.8
Services	60.6	Exports	52.8
		Imports	-55.3

Structure of employment

	% of total		*% of labour force*
Agriculture	7	Unemployed 1999	7.0
Industry	33	Av. ann. rate 1990–99	8.6
Services	60		

Energy

	m TCE		
Total output	19.016	% output exported	15.6
Total consumption	35.656	% consumption imported	64.8
Consumption per head,			
kg coal equivalent	3,511		

Inflation and finance

Consumer price			*av. ann. increase 1994–99*
inflation 2000	9.7%	Narrow money (M1)	16.9%
Av. ann. inflation 1990–2000	20.1%	Broad money	23.5%
Treasury bill rate, 2000	10.7%		

Exchange rates

	end 2000		*December 2000*
Ft per $	284.7	Effective rates	1995 = 100
Ft per SDR	371.0	– nominal	61.8
Ft per euro	264.8	– real	111.1

Trade

Principal exports		Principal imports	
	$bn fob		*$bn cif*
Machinery & transport equipment	14.3	Machinery & transport equipment	14.1
Other manufactures	7.7	Other manufactures	10.8
Food & beverages	2.0	Fuels	1.7
Raw materials	0.6	Food & food products	0.8
Total incl. others	**25.0**	Total incl. others	**28.0**

Main export destinations		Main origins of imports	
	% of total		*% of total*
Germany	38.4	Germany	32.7
Austria	9.6	Austria	10.0
Italy	5.9	Italy	8.6
United States	5.2	Russia	6.6

Balance of payments, reserves and debt, $bn

Visible exports fob	21.8	Overall balance	2.3
Visible imports fob	-24.0	Change in reserves	1.6
Trade balance	-2.2	Level of reserves end Dec.	11.0
Invisibles inflows	6.4	No. months of import cover	4.3
Invisibles outflows	-6.7	Foreign debt	29.0
Net transfers	0.3	– as % of GDP	62
Current account balance	-2.1	Debt service paid	7.5
– as % of GDP	-4.3	Debt service ratio	27
Capital balance	4.7		

Health and education

Health spending, % of GDP	6.4	Education spending, % of GDP	4.6
Doctors per 1,000 pop.	3.5	Enrolment, %: primary	103
Hospital beds per 1,000 pop.	8.3	secondary	98
Improved-water source access, % of pop.	99	tertiary	25

Society

No. of households	3.9m	Colour TVs per 100 households	85.2
Av. no. per household	2.6	Telephone lines per 100 pop.	37.1
Marriages per 1,000 pop.	4.7	Mobile telephone subscribers per 100 pop.	16.2
Divorces per 1,000 pop.	2.6	Computers per 100 pop.	8.5
Cost of living, Dec. 1999 New York = 100	46	Internet hosts per 100 pop.	15.8

a 1998

INDIA

Area	3,287,263 sq km	Capital	New Delhi
Arable as % of total land	54	Currency	Indian rupee (Rs)

People

Population	997.5m	Life expectancy: men	63.6 yrs
Pop. per sq km	336	women	64.6 yrs
Av. ann. growth		Adult literacy	53.5%
in pop. 1995–2000	1.69%	Fertility rate (per woman)	3.3
Pop. under 15	33.5%	Urban population	28.4%
Pop. over 65	7.6%		*per 1,000 pop.*
No. of men per 100 women	106	Crude birth rate	23.7
Human Development Index	56.3	Crude death rate	8.4

The economy

GDP[a]	Rs19,570bn	GDP per head	$450
GDP	$447bn	GDP per head in purchasing	
Av. ann. growth in real		power parity (USA=100)	7.0
GDP 1990–99	6.0%	Economic freedom index	3.85

Origins of GDP[b]		**Components of GDP[b]**	
	% of total		*% of total*
Agriculture	26.8	Private consumption	64.0
Industry, of which:	26.5	Public consumption	11.9
manufacturing	17.5	Investment	24.2
Services	46.6	Exports	12.3
		Imports	-13.4

Structure of employment[b]

	% of total		*% of labour force*
Agriculture	60	Unemployed 1998	...
Industry	18	Av. ann. rate 1990–98	...
Services	22		

Energy

	m TCE		
Total output	344.781	% output exported	0.4
Total consumption	406.498	% consumption imported	22.6
Consumption per head,			
kg coal equivalent	421		

Inflation and finance

Consumer price			*av. ann. increase 1994–99*
inflation 2000	4.0%	Narrow money (M1)	13.3%
Av. ann. inflation 1990–2000	9.0%	Broad money	16.5%
Bank rate, 2000	8.00%		

Exchange rates

	end 2000		*December 2000*
Rs per $	46.75	Effective rates	1995 = 100
Rs per SDR	60.91	– nominal	...
Rs per euro	43.48	– real	...

Trade

Principal exports[b]		Principal imports[b]	
	$bn fob		*$bn cif*
Textiles	8.5	Capital goods	6.9
Gems & jewellery	5.9	Crude oil & products	6.4
Engineering goods	4.4	Gems	3.8
Chemicals	3.4	Iron & steel	1.2
Total incl. others	**34.0**	Total incl. others	**41.0**

Main export destinations		Main origins of imports	
	% of total		*% of total*
United States	22.3	United States	8.9
Germany	5.3	Belgium & Luxembourg	7.9
United Kingdom	5.6	Japan	5.9
Japan	5.2	United Kingdom	5.7
Hong Kong	5.1	Saudi Arabia	5.6
United Arab Emirates	4.4	Germany	4.8

Balance of payments, reserves and debt, $bn

Visible exports fob	37.5	Overall balance	6.7
Visible imports fob	-45.6	Change in reserves	5.4
Trade balance	-8.0	Level of reserves	
Invisibles inflows	16.4	end Dec.	36.0
Invisibles outflows	-23.0	No. months of import cover	6.3
Net transfers	11.9	Foreign debt	94.4
Current account balance	-2.8	– as % of GDP	21
– as % of GDP	-0.6	Debt service paid	10.1
Capital balance	9.2	Debt service ratio	15

Health and education

Health spending, % of GDP	5.4	Education spending, % of GDP	3.2
Doctors per 1,000 pop.	0.4	Enrolment, %: primary	100
Hospital beds per 1,000 pop.	0.8	secondary	49
Improved-water source access,		tertiary	7
% of pop.	88		

Society

No. of households	194.6m	Colour TVs per 100 households	28.3
Av. no. per household	5.1	Telephone lines per 100 pop.	2.7
Marriages per 1,000 pop.	...	Mobile telephone subscribers	
Divorces per 1,000 pop.	...	per 100 pop.	0.2
Cost of living, Dec. 1999		Computers per 100 pop.	0.5
New York = 100	40	Internet hosts per 100 pop.	...

a Year ending March 31, 2000.
b Year ending March 31, 1999.
b 1998

INDONESIA

Area[a]	1,904,443 sq km	Capital	Jakarta
Arable as % of total land	10	Currency	Rupiah (Rp)

People

Population	207.0m	Life expectancy: men	65.3 yrs
Pop. per sq km	109	women	69.3 yrs
Av. ann. growth		Adult literacy	85.0%
in pop. 1995–2000	1.41%	Fertility rate (per woman)	2.6
Pop. under 15	30.8%	Urban population	40.0%
Pop. over 65	7.6%		*per 1,000 pop.*
No. of men per 100 women	101	Crude birth rate	20.0
Human Development Index	67.0	Crude death rate	7.1

The economy

GDP	Rp1,291trn	GDP per head	$690
GDP	$143bn	GDP per head in purchasing	
Av. ann. growth in real		power parity (USA=100)	8.3
GDP 1990–99	4.7%	Economic freedom index	3.55

Origins of GDP		**Components of GDP**	
	% of total		*% of total*
Agriculture	19.5	Private consumption	72.5
Industry, of which:	42.1	Public consumption	6.5
manufacturing	25.4	Investment	13.0
Services	38.4	Exports	34.9
		Imports	-26.9

Structure of employment

	% of total		*% of total*
Agriculture	43	Unemployed 1998	5.5
Industry	17	Av. ann. rate 1996–98	4.7
Services	40		

Energy

	m TCE		
Total output	305.729	% output exported	50.8
Total consumption	129.755	% consumption imported	21.1
Consumption per head,			
kg coal equivalent	638		

Inflation and finance

Consumer price			*av. ann. increase 1994–99*
inflation 2000	3.7%	Narrow money (M1)	22.5%
Av. ann. inflation 1990–2000	13.5%	Broad money	30.1%
Money market rate, 2000	10.32%		

Exchange rates

	end 2000		*December 2000*
Rp per $	8,780	Effective rates	1995 = 100
Rp per SDR	11,340	– nominal	...
Rp per euro	8,165	– real	...

Trade

Principal exports	*$bn fob*	Principal imports	*$bn cif*
Petroleum & products	5.4	Raw materials	10.4
Natural gas	4.4	Machinery & transport equipment	6.4
Garments	3.8	Fuels	3.7
Plywood	2.3	Food, drink & tobacco	3.4
Total incl. others	**48.7**	Total incl. others	**24.0**

Main export destinations	*% of total*	Main origins of imports	*% of total*
Japan	21.4	Japan	12.1
United States	14.2	United States	11.8
Singapore	10.1	Singapore	10.5
South Korea	6.8	Australia	6.1
Netherlands	3.2	Germany	5.8
Australia	3.1	South Korea	5.5

Balance of payments, reserves and debt, $bn

Visible exports fob	51.2	Overall balance	2.0
Visible imports fob	-30.6	Change in reserves	3.7
Trade balance	20.6	Level of reserves end Dec.	27.3
Invisibles inflows	6.5	No. months of import cover	6.1
Invisibles outflows	-23.2	Foreign debt	150.0
Net transfers	1.9	– as % of GDP	113
Current account balance	5.8	Debt service paid	17.8
– as % of GDP	4.1	Debt service ratio	30
Capital balance	-5.9		

Health and education

Health spending, % of GDP	1.6	Education spending, % of GDP	1.4
Doctors per 1,000 pop.	0.2	Enrolment, %: primary	113
Hospital beds per 1,000 pop.	0.7	secondary	56
Improved-water source access, % of pop.	76	tertiary	11

Society

No. of households	48.2m	Colour TVs per 100 households	44.0
Av. no. per household	4.3	Telephone lines per 100 pop.	3.1
Marriages per 1,000 pop.	...	Mobile telephone subscribers per 100 pop.	1.7
Divorces per 1,000 pop.	...	Computers per 100 pop.	1.0
Cost of living, Dec. 1999 New York = 100	61	Internet hosts per 100 pop.	0.1

a Excludes East Timor, 14,874 sq km.

IRAN

Area	1,648,000 sq km	Capital	Tehran
Arable as % of total land	10	Currency	Rial (IR)

People

Population	63.0m	Life expectancy: men	68.8 yrs
Pop. per sq km	38	women	70.8 yrs
Av. ann. growth		Adult literacy	73.3%
in pop. 1995–2000	1.69%	Fertility rate (per woman)	3.2
Pop. under 15	37.4%	Urban population	61.0%
Pop. over 65	5.2%		*per 1,000 pop.*
No. of men per 100 women	105	Crude birth rate	22.0
Human Development Index	70.9	Crude death rate	5.0

The economy

GDP[a]	IR418,169bn	GDP per head	$1,760
GDP	$111bn	GDP per head in purchasing	
Av. ann. growth in real		power parity (USA=100)	17.3
GDP 1990–99	3.6%	Economic freedom index	4.70

Origins of GDP		**Components of GDP[b]**	
	% of total		*% of total*
Agriculture	21	Private consumption	63.5
Industry, of which:	31	Public consumption	13.5
manufacturing	17	Investment	18.1
Services	48	Exports	20.3
		Imports	-15.4

Structure of employment[c]

	% of total		*% of labour force*
Agriculture	39	Unemployed 1998	...
Industry	23	Av. ann. rate 1990–98	...
Services	38		

Energy

	m TCE		
Total output	333.630	% output exported	57.2
Total consumption	139.793	% consumption imported	7.8
Consumption per head,			
kg coal equivalent	2,163		

Inflation and finance

Consumer price		*av. ann. increase 1994–99*	
inflation 2000	14.5%	Narrow money (M1)	25.9%
Av. ann. inflation 1990–2000	24.2%	Broad money	25.5%

Exchange rates

	end 2000		*December 2000*
IR per $	2,263	Effective rates	1995 = 100
IR per SDR	2,948	– nominal	151.0
IR per euro	2,105	– real	306.8

Trade

Principal exports[d]		Principal imports[e]	
	$bn fob		*$bn cif*
Oil & gas	15.1	Raw materials &	
Carpets	0.9	intermediate goods	7.4
Fruit	0.5	Capital goods	4.4
		Consumer goods	1.8
Total incl. others	**18.4**	Total incl. others	**14.8**

Main export destinations		Main origins of imports	
	% of total		*% of total*
Japan	20.5	Germany	11.0
Italy	7.0	Italy	8.3
United Arab Emirates	5.9	China	6.1
France	4.7	Japan	5.3
China	4.1	United Arab Emirates	5.0

Balance of payments[b], reserves and debt, $bn

Visible exports fob	13.0	Overall balance	-1.6
Visible imports fob	-13.6	Change in reserves	...
Trade balance	-0.6	Level of reserves	
Invisibles inflows	1.5	end Dec.	...
Invisibles outflows	-3.3	No. months of import cover	...
Net transfers	0.5	Foreign debt	10.4
Current account balance	-1.9	– as % of GDP	9
– as % of GDP	-1.9	Debt service paid	4.6
Capital balance	3.1	Debt service ratio	23

Health and education

Health spending, % of GDP	4.2	Education spending, % of GDP	4.0
Doctors per 1,000 pop.	0.8	Enrolment, %: primary	98
Hospital beds per 1,000 pop.	1.6	secondary	77
Improved-water source access,		tertiary	18
% of pop.	95		

Society

No. of households	12.8m	Colour TVs per 100 households	15.7
Av. no. per household	5.1	Telephone lines per 100 pop.	12.5
Marriages per 1,000 pop.[f]	7.8	Mobile telephone subscribers	
Divorces per 1,000 pop.	0.5	per 100 pop.	0.7
Cost of living, Dec. 1999		Computers per 100 pop.	5.2
New York = 100	...	Internet hosts per 100 pop.	...

a Iranian year ending March 20, 2000.
b Iranian year ending March 20, 1999.
c 1990
d Iranian year ending March 20, 1996, estimated.
e 1998
f 1996

IRAQ

Area	438,317 sq km	Capital	Baghdad
Arable as % of total land	12	Currency	Iraqi dinar (ID)

People

Population	22.8m	Life expectancy: men	63.5 yrs
Pop. per sq km	52	women	66.5 yrs
Av. ann. growth in pop. 1995–2000	2.70%	Adult literacy	58.0%
		Fertility rate (per woman)	5.2
Pop. under 15	41.6%	Urban population	76.0%
Pop. over 65	4.6%		*per 1,000 pop.*
No. of men per 100 women	103.5	Crude birth rate	33.9
Human Development Index	58.3	Crude death rate	7.0

The economy

GDP[a]	ID62bn	GDP per head[a]	$850
GDP[a]	$19.3bn	GDP per head in purchasing power parity (USA=100)[a]	2.7
Av. ann. growth in real GDP 1985–95	-9.3%	Economic freedom index	4.90

Origins of GDP[a]		**Components of GDP[a]**	
	% of total		*% of total*
Agriculture	6.1	Private consumption	72.3
Industry, of which:	13.1	Public consumption	13.9
manufacturing	...	Investment	15.5
Services	80.8	Exports	1.3
		Imports	-3.0

Structure of employment[b]

	% of total		*% of labour force*
Agriculture	16	Unemployed 1998	...
Industry	18	Av. ann. rate 1990–98	...
Services	66		

Energy

	m TCE		
Total output	88.132	% output exported	54.8
Total consumption	36.256	% consumption imported	nil
Consumption per head, kg coal equivalent	1,712		

Inflation and finance

			av. ann. increase 1994–99
Consumer price inflation 2000	...	Narrow money (M1)	...
Av. ann. inflation 1990–2000	...	Broad money	...

Exchange rates

	end 2000		*December 2000*
ID per $	0.31	Effective rates	1995 = 100
ID per SDR	0.41	– nominal	161.7
ID per euro	0.29	– real	...

Trade

Principal exports[c]		Principal imports[d]	
	$bn fob		*$bn cif*
Crude oil	11.1	Civilian goods	3.7
		Military goods	0.9
Total incl. others	**11.6**	Total incl. others	**4.6**

Main export destinations[c]		Main origins of imports[c]	
	% of total		*% of total*
United States	56.4	France	19.2
Netherlands	12.3	Australia	18.0
Japan	9.4	China	12.5
France	7.6	Germany	8.4

Balance of payments[ce], reserves and debt, $bn

Visible exports fob	12.0	Overall balance	...
Visible imports fob	-7.7	Change in reserves	...
Trade balance	4.3	Level of reserves	
Invisibles inflows	...	end Dec.	...
Invisibles outflows	...	No. months of import cover	...
Net transfers	...	Foreign debt	...
Current account balance	0.03	– as % of GDP	...
– as % of GDP	0.2	Debt service	...
Capital balance	...	Debt service ratio	...

Health and education

Health spending, % of GDP	5.6	Education spending, % of GDP	...
Doctors per 1,000 pop.	0.6	Enrolment, %: primary	85
Hospital beds per 1,000 pop.	1.5	secondary	42
Improved-water source access,		tertiary	11
% of pop.	85		

Society

No. of households	4.1m	Colour TVs per 100 households	8.3
Av. no. per household	5.3	Telephone lines per 100 pop.	3.0
Marriages per 1,000 pop.	...	Mobile telephone subscribers	
Divorces per 1,000 pop.	...	per 100 pop.	...
Cost of living, Dec. 1999		Computers per 100 pop.	...
New York = 100	...	Internet hosts per 100 pop.	...

a Estimated.
a 1993
b 1990
c Trade and balance of payments data for Iraq are estimates based on limited and inconsistent information.
d 1997
e 1999, estimated.

IRELAND

Area	70,282 sq km	Capital	Dublin
Arable as % of total land	20	Currency	Punt (I£)

People

Population	3.7m	Life expectancy: men	74.4 yrs
Pop. per sq km	53	women	79.6 yrs
Av. ann. growth		Adult literacy	99.0%
in pop. 1995–2000	1.05%	Fertility rate (per woman)	1.9
Pop. under 15	21.6%	Urban population	59.0%
Pop. over 65	15.2%		*per 1,000 pop.*
No. of men per 100 women	98.6	Crude birth rate	15.2
Human Development Index	90.7	Crude death rate	8.2

The economy

GDP	I£69.1bn	GDP per head	$25,060
GDP	$93.4bn	GDP per head in purchasing	
Av. ann. growth in real		power parity (USA=100)	70.4
GDP 1990–99	6.9%	Economic freedom index	1.65

Origins of GDP[a]		**Components of GDP**	
	% of total		*% of total*
Agriculture	5	Private consumption	50.3
Industry, of which:	39	Public consumption	12.7
manufacturing	...	Investment	23.3
Services	56	Exports	87.6
		Imports	-73.8

Structure of employment

	% of total		*% of labour force*
Agriculture	10	Unemployed 1999	5.7
Industry	28	Av. ann. rate 1990–99	12.1
Services	62		

Energy

	m TCE		
Total output	4.230	% output exported	42.5
Total consumption	17.172	% consumption imported	90.6
Consumption per head,			
kg coal equivalent	4,694		

Inflation and finance

Consumer price			*av. ann. increase 1994–99*
inflation 2000	5.6%	Euro area:	
Av. ann. inflation 1990–2000	2.5%	Narrow money (M1)	7.9%
Money market rate, 2000	4.84%	Broad money	5.9%

Exchange rates

	end 2000		*July 2000*
I£ per $	0.85	Effective rates	1995 = 100
I£ per SDR	1.11	– nominal	89.2
I£ per euro	0.79	– real	...

Trade

Principal exports[a]		Principal imports[a]	
	$bn fob		*$bn cif*
Machinery & transport equipment	23.5	Machinery & transport equipment	22.5
Chemicals	20.3	Chemicals	4.9
Manufactured goods	7.5	Manufactured goods	4.9
Agric. products & foodstuffs	5.7		
Total incl. others	**71.1**	Total incl. others	**46.9**

Main export destinations[a]		Main origins of imports[a]	
	% of total		*% of total*
United Kingdom	22.2	United Kingdom	33.6
Germany	14.6	United States	16.1
United States	13.7	Japan	7.1
France	8.3	Germany	6.2
Netherlands	6.4	Singapore	5.0
Belgium & Luxembourg	5.5	France	3.9

Balance of payments, reserves and aid, $bn

Visible exports fob	67.0	Capital balance	-1.1
Visible imports fob	-42.8	Overall balance	-2.0
Trade balance	24.2	Change in reserves	-2.1
Invisibles inflows	39.7	Level of reserves end Dec.	5.3
Invisibles outflows	-64.5	No. months of import cover	0.6
Net transfers	1.3	Aid given	0.25
Current account balance	0.6	– as % of GDP	0.29
– as % of GDP	0.6		

Health and education

Health spending, % of GDP	6.1	Education spending, % of GDP	6.0
Doctors per 1,000 pop.	2.2	Enrolment, %: primary	105
Hospital beds per 1,000 pop.	3.7	secondary	118
Improved-water source access, % of pop.	...	tertiary	41

Society

No. of households	0.9m	Colour TVs per 100 households	99.1
Av. no. per household	4.3	Telephone lines per 100 pop.	47.8
Marriages per 1,000 pop.	2.2	Mobile telephone subscribers per 100 pop.	44.7
Divorces per 1,000 pop.	...	Computers per 100 pop.	36.5
Cost of living, Dec. 1999 New York = 100	71	Internet hosts per 100 pop.	23.7

a 1998

ISRAEL

Area	20,770 sq km	Capital	Jerusalem
Arable as % of total land	17	Currency	New Shekel (NIS)

People

Population	6.1m	Life expectancy: men	77.1 yrs
Pop. per sq km	296	women	81.0 yrs
Av. ann. growth		Adult literacy	95.4%
in pop. 1995–2000	2.43%	Fertility rate (per woman)	2.9
Pop. under 15	28.3%	Urban population	91.2%
Pop. over 65	13.2%		*per 1,000 pop.*
No. of men per 100 women	97	Crude birth rate	19.7
Human Development Index	88.3	Crude death rate	6.0

The economy

GDP	NIS417bn	GDP per head	$16,550
GDP	$101bn	GDP per head in purchasing	
Av. ann. growth in real		power parity (USA=100)	56.6
GDP 1990–99	5.2%	Economic freedom index	2.75

Origins of GDP		**Components of GDP**	
	% of total		*% of total*
Agriculture	3.9	Private consumption	59.1
Industry, of which:	36.6	Public consumption	28.8
manufacturing	...	Investment	17.8
Services	59.5	Exports	40.0
		Imports	-47.0

Structure of employment

	% of total		*% of labour force*
Agriculture	3	Unemployed 1999	8.9
Industry	21	Av. ann. rate 1990–99	8.8
Services	76		

Energy

	m TCE		
Total output	0.176	% output exported[b]	1,984.1
Total consumption	32.498	% consumption imported[b]	125.4
Consumption per head,			
kg coal equivalent	3,839		

Inflation and finance

Consumer price			*av. ann. increase 1994–99*
inflation 2000	1.1%	Narrow money (M1)	15.8%
Av. ann. inflation 1990–2000	9.5%	Broad money	19.3%
Deposit rate, 2000	8.6%		

Exchange rates

	end 2000		*December 2000*
NIS per $	4.04	Effective rates	1995 = 100
NIS per SDR	5.27	– nominal	94.02
NIS per euro	3.76	– real	114.39

Trade

Principal exports		Principal imports	
	$bn fob		*$bn cif*
Industrial goods	16.5	Raw materials	13.0
Diamonds	5.5	Diamonds	5.5
Agricultural goods	0.8	Investment goods	5.4
		Consumer goods	4.0
		Fuel	2.1
Total incl. others	**22.8**	Total incl. others	**30.6**

Main export destinations		Main origins of imports	
	% of total		*% of total*
United States	35.5	United States	20.3
United Kingdom	5.5	Belgium & Luxembourg	11.3
Belgium & Luxembourg	5.4	Germany	8.1
Germany	4.5	United Kingdom	7.5
Hong Kong	4.1	Switzerland	5.6
Netherlands	3.8	Italy	5.3

Balance of payments, reserves and debt, $bn

Visible exports fob	25.6	Overall balance	0.3
Visible imports fob	-30.0	Change in reserves	-0.1
Trade balance	-4.4	Level of reserves	
Invisibles inflows	13.8	end Dec.	22.6
Invisibles outflows	-17.6	No. months of import cover	5.7
Net transfers	6.8	Foreign debt	36.4
Current account balance	-1.9	– as % of GDP	36.1
– as % of GDP	-1.9	Debt service	7.4
Capital balance	3.5	Debt service ratio	17.6

Health and education

Health spending, % of GDP	9.5	Education spending, % of GDP	7.6
Doctors per 1,000 pop.	4.6	Enrolment, %: primary	98
Hospital beds per 1,000 pop.	6.0	secondary	88
Improved-water source access,		tertiary	44
% of pop.	...		

Society

No. of households	1.5m	Colour TVs per 100 households	94.4
Av. no. per household	4.0	Telephone lines per 100 pop.	55.8
Marriages per 1,000 pop.	4.7	Mobile telephone subscribers	
Divorces per 1,000 pop.	2.0	per 100 pop.	47.2
Cost of living, Dec. 1999		Computers per 100 pop.	25.4
New York = 100	99	Internet hosts per 100 pop.	29.6

b Energy trade data are distorted by transitory and oil refining activities.

ITALY

Area	301,245 sq km	Capital	Rome
Arable as % of total land	28	Currency	Lira (L)

People

Population	57.6m	Life expectancy: men	75.5 yrs
Pop. per sq km	196	women	81.9 yrs
Av. ann. growth		Adult literacy	98.3%
in pop. 1995–2000	0.08%	Fertility rate (per woman)	1.2
Pop. under 15	14.3%	Urban population	67.0%
Pop. over 65	24.1%		*per 1,000 pop.*
No. of men per 100 women	94.3	Crude birth rate	8.5
Human Development Index	90.3	Crude death rate	10.9

The economy

GDP	L2,128trn	GDP per head	$20,310
GDP	$1,171bn	GDP per head in purchasing	
Av. ann. growth in real		power parity (USA=100)	68.9
GDP 1990–99	1.4%	Economic freedom index	2.30

Origins of GDP		**Components of GDP**	
	% of total		*% of total*
Agriculture	2.6	Private consumption	59.6
Industry, of which:	31.0	Public consumption	18.6
manufacturing	...	Investment	19.8
Services	66.4	Exports	25.5
		Imports	-23.5

Structure of employment

	% of total		*% of labour force*
Agriculture	7	Unemployed 1999	11.4
Industry	32	Av. ann. rate 1990–99	11.1
Services	61		

Energy

	m TCE		
Total output	44.120	% output exported	63.8
Total consumption	238.059	% consumption imported	93.7
Consumption per head,			
kg coal equivalent	4,147		

Inflation and finance

Consumer price			*av. ann. increase 1994–99*
inflation 2000	2.5%	Euro area:	
Av. ann. inflation 1990–2000	3.7%	Narrow money (M1)	7.9%
Money market rate, 2000	4.39%	Broad money	5.9%

Exchange rates

	end 2000		*July 2000*
L per $	2,097	Effective rates	1995 = 100
L per SDR	2,726	– nominal	104.7
L per euro	1,936	– real	110.9

Trade

Principal exports		Principal imports	
	$bn fob		*$bn cif*
Engineering products	88.1	Engineering products	72.2
Textiles & clothing	35.8	Transport equipment	32.8
Transport equipment	26.5	Chemicals	29.5
Chemicals	20.5	Food, drink & tobacco	16.2
Food, drink & tobacco	12.6	Textiles & clothing	15.5
Total incl. others	**229.7**	Total incl. others	**215.9**

Main export destinations		Main origins of imports	
	% of total		*% of total*
Germany	16.7	Germany	19.2
France	13.0	France	12.6
United States	9.5	Netherlands	6.3
United Kingdom	7.1	United Kingdom	6.1
Spain	6.0	United States	5.0
EU15	57.2	EU15	60.6

Balance of payments, reserves and aid, $bn

Visible exports fob	230.8	Capital balance	-15.0
Visible imports fob	-210.4	Overall balance	-8.1
Trade balance	20.4	Change in reserves	-8.1
Invisibles inflows	107.4	Level of reserves	
Invisibles outflows	-116.1	end Dec.	45.3
Net transfers	-5.4	No. months of import cover	1.7
Current account balance	6.3	Aid given	1.81
– as % of GDP	0.5	– as % of GDP	0.16

Health and education

Health spending, % of GDP	8.2	Education spending, % of GDP	4.9
Doctors per 1,000 pop.	5.9	Enrolment, %: primary	101
Hospital beds per 1,000 pop.	6.5	secondary	95
Improved-water source access,		tertiary	47
% of pop.	...		

Society

No. of households	22.9m	Colour TVs per 100 households	95.4
Av. no. per household	2.5	Telephone lines per 100 pop.	46.2
Marriages per 1,000 pop.	4.7	Mobile telephone subscribers	
Divorces per 1,000 pop.	0.7	per 100 pop.	73.7
Cost of living, Dec. 1999		Computers per 100 pop.	20.9
New York = 100	66	Internet hosts per 100 pop.	28.3

JAPAN

Area	377,727 sq km	Capital	Tokyo
Arable as % of total land	12	Currency	Yen (¥)

People

Population	126.5m	Life expectancy: men	77.8 yrs
Pop. per sq km	336	women	85.0 yrs
Av. ann. growth		Adult literacy	99.0%
in pop. 1995–2000	0.26%	Fertility rate (per woman)	1.4
Pop. under 15	14.7%	Urban population	78.8%
Pop. over 65	23.2%		*per 1,000 pop.*
No. of men per 100 women	96.1	Crude birth rate	9.2
Human Development Index	92.4	Crude death rate	8.3

The economy

GDP	¥495trn	GDP per head	$34,340
GDP	$4,347bn	GDP per head in purchasing	
Av. ann. growth in real		power parity (USA=100)	78.9
GDP 1990–99	1.3%	Economic freedom index	2.05

Origins of GDP		**Components of GDP**	
	% of total		*% of total*
Agriculture	1.5	Private consumption	56.3
Industry, of which:	32.1	Public consumption	16.1
manufacturing	21.6	Investment	26.1
Services	66.4	Exports	10.0
		Imports	-8.4

Structure of employment

	% of total		*% of labour force*
Agriculture	5	Unemployed 1999	4.7
Industry	33	Av. ann. rate 1990–99	3.1
Services	62		

Energy

	m TCE		
Total output	143.395	% output exported[a]	9.3
Total consumption	653.997	% consumption imported[a]	87.9
Consumption per head,			
kg coal equivalent	5,189		

Inflation and finance

Consumer price			*av. ann. increase 1994–99*
inflation 2000	-0.7%	Narrow money (M1)	9.6%
Av. ann. inflation 1990–2000	0.8%	Broad money	3.1%
Money market rate, 2000	0.11%		

Exchange rates

	end 2000		*July 2000*
¥ per $	114.9	Effective rates	1995 = 100
¥ per SDR	149.7	– nominal	98.7
¥ per euro	106.9	– real	85.6

Trade

Principal exports		Principal imports	
	$bn fob		*$bn cif*
Electrical machinery	101.5	Machinery & equipment	96.8
Transport equipment	94.8	Mineral fuels	49.4
Non-electrical machinery	89.0	Food	44.1
Chemicals	30.7	Chemicals	23.0
Metals	23.8	Textiles	20.8
Total incl. others	**419.2**	Total incl. others	**311.3**

Main export destinations		Main origins of imports	
	% of total		*% of total*
United States	30.7	United States	21.7
Taiwan	6.9	China	13.8
China	5.6	South Korea	5.2
South Korea	5.5	Australia	4.1
Hong Kong	5.3	Taiwan	4.1

Balance of payments, reserves and aid, $bn

Visible exports fob	403.7	Capital balance	-47.6
Visible imports fob	-280.4	Overall balance	76.3
Trade balance	123.3	Change in reserves	71.5
Invisibles inflows	249.3	Level of reserves	
Invisibles outflows	-253.6	end Dec.	293.9
Net transfers	-12.1	No. months of import cover	6.6
Current account balance	106.9	Aid given	15.32
– as % of GDP	2.5	– as % of GDP	0.35

Health and education

Health spending, % of GDP	7.6	Education spending, % of GDP	3.6
Doctors per 1,000 pop.	1.9	Enrolment, %: primary	101
Hospital beds per 1,000 pop.	16.5	secondary	103
Improved-water source access, % of pop.	97	tertiary	43

Society

No. of households	41.5m	Colour TVs per 100 households	99.2
Av. no. per household	3.0	Telephone lines per 100 pop.	55.8
Marriages per 1,000 pop.	6.2	Mobile telephone subscribers per 100 pop.	44.9
Divorces per 1,000 pop.	1.8	Computers per 100 pop.	31.5
Cost of living, Dec. 1999 New York = 100	160	Internet hosts per 100 pop.	36.7

a Energy trade data are distorted by transitory and oil refining activities.

KENYA

Area	582,646 sq km	Capital	Nairobi
Arable as % of total land	7	Currency	Kenyan shilling (KSh)

People

Population	29.4m	Life expectancy: men	48.7 yrs
Pop. per sq km	50	women	49.9 yrs
Av. ann. growth		Adult literacy	79.3%
in pop. 1995–2000	2.32%	Fertility rate (per woman)	4.6%
Pop. under 15	43.5%	Urban population	32.0%
Pop. over 65	4.2%		*per 1,000 pop.*
No. of men per 100 women	99	Crude birth rate	34.1
Human Development Index	50.8	Crude death rate	13.7

The economy

GDP	KSh749bn	GDP per head	$360
GDP	$10.6bn	GDP per head in purchasing	
Av. ann. growth in real		power parity (USA=100)	3.2
GDP 1990–99	2.2%	Economic freedom index	3.15

Origins of GDP		**Components of GDP**	
	% of total		*% of total*
Agriculture	24.5	Private consumption	71.6
Industry, of which:	...	Public consumption	16.9
manufacturing	13.2	Investment	15.2
Other	62.3	Exports	25.0
		Imports	-28.7

Structure of employment[a]

	% of total		*% of labour force*
Agriculture	80	Unemployed 1998	...
Industry	7	Av. ann. rate 1990–98	...
Services	13		

Energy

	m TCE		
Total output	0.897	% output exported[b]	106.7
Total consumption	3.551	% consumption imported[b]	113.2
Consumption per head,			
kg coal equivalent	125		

Inflation and finance

Consumer price		*av. ann. increase 1994–99*	
inflation 2000	5.8%	Narrow money (M1)	10.4%
Av. ann. inflation 1990–2000	15.2%	Broad money	15.1%
Treasury bill rate, 2000	12.05%		

Exchange rates

	end 2000		*December 2000*
KSh per $	78.0	Effective rates	1995 = 100
KSh per SDR	101.8	– nominal	...
KSh per euro	72.5	– real	...

Trade

Principal exports		Principal imports	
	$m fob		*$m cif*
Tea	431	Petroleum & products	488
Horticultural products	178	Industrial machinery	426
Coffee	165	Motor vehicles & chassis	215
Petroleum products	80	Iron & steel	100
Total incl. others	**1,748**	Total incl. others	**2,831**

Main export destinations		Main origins of imports	
	% of total		*% of total*
Uganda	18.3	United Kingdom	11.9
United Kingdom	14.7	Japan	7.8
Tanzania	11.8	United Arab Emirates	7.5
Pakistan	7.9	United States	6.8

Balance of payments, reserves and debt, $bn

Visible exports fob	1.7	Overall balance	0.1
Visible imports fob	-2.6	Change in reserves	0.01
Trade balance	-0.8	Level of reserves	
Invisibles inflows	0.9	end Dec.	0.8
Invisibles outflows	-0.8	No. months of import cover	2.8
Net transfers	0.7	Foreign debt	6.6
Current account balance	0.0	– as % of GDP	63
– as % of GDP	0.1	Debt service paid	0.7
Capital balance	0.2	Debt service ratio	27

Health and education

Health spending, % of GDP	7.8	Education spending, % of GDP	6.5
Doctors per 1,000 pop.	0.1	Enrolment, %: primary	85
Hospital beds per 1,000 pop.	1.6	secondary	24
Improved-water source access,		tertiary	2
% of pop.	49		

Society

No. of households	5.9m	Colour TVs per 100 households	2.1
Av. no. per household	4.9	Telephone lines per 100 pop.	1.0
Marriages per 1,000 pop.	...	Mobile telephone subscribers	
Divorces per 1,000 pop.	...	per 100 pop.	0.1
Cost of living, Dec. 1999		Computers per 100 pop.	0.4
New York = 100	58	Internet hosts per 100 pop.	0.1

a 1990
b Energy trade data are distorted by transitory and oil refining activities.

MALAYSIA

Area	332,665 sq km	Capital	Kuala Lumpur
Arable as % of total land	6	Currency	Malaysian dollar/ringgit (M$)

People

Population	22.7m	Life expectancy: men	70.6 yrs
Pop. per sq km	68	women	75.5 yrs
Av. ann. growth		Adult literacy	85.7%
in pop. 1995–2000	2.09%	Fertility rate (per woman)	3.2
Pop. under 15	34.1%	Urban population	57.4%
Pop. over 65	6.6%		*per 1,000 pop.*
No. of men per 100 women	102.8	Crude birth rate	22.3
Human Development Index	77.2	Crude death rate	4.7

The economy

GDP	M$300bn	GDP per head	$3,480
GDP	$79.0bn	GDP per head in purchasing	
Av. ann. growth in real		power parity (USA=100)	23.9
GDP 1990–99	7.3%	Economic freedom index	3.00

Origins of GDP		**Components of GDP**	
	% of total		*% of total*
Agriculture	9.3	Private consumption	43.7
Industry, of which:	44.3	Public consumption	12.4
manufacturing	30.0	Investment	27.2
Services	46.4	Exports	110.2
		Imports	-93.4

Structure of employment

	% of total		*% of labour force*
Agriculture	26	Unemployed 1999	3.4
Industry	29	Av. ann. rate 1990–99	3.3
Services	45		

Energy

	m TCE		
Total output	103.297	% output exported	53.2
Total consumption	60.332	% consumption imported	31.3
Consumption per head,			
kg coal equivalent	2,875		

Inflation and finance

Consumer price			*av. ann. increase 1994–99*
inflation 2000	1.6%	Narrow money (M1)	6.1%
Av. ann. inflation 1990–2000	3.7%	Broad money	15.2%
Money market rate, 2000	2.66%		

Exchange rates

	end 2000		*December 2000*
M$ per $	3.80	Effective rates	1995 = 100
M$ per SDR	4.95	– nominal	82.1
M$ per euro	3.53	– real	87.7

Trade

Principal exports		Principal imports	
	$bn fob		*$bn cif*
Electronics & electrical machinery	51.3	Manufacturing supplies	24.5
Petroleum & LNG	4.1	Machinery	4.7
Palm oil	3.8	Transport equipment	3.5
Chemicals & products	2.9	Metal products	2.8
Textiles, clothing & footwear	2.5	Food	1.8
		Consumer durables	1.3
Total incl. others	**84.5**	Total incl. others	**60.1**

Main export destinations		Main origins of imports	
	% of total		*% of total*
United States	21.9	Japan	20.8
Singapore	16.5	United States	17.4
Japan	11.6	Singapore	14.0
Taiwan	4.5	Taiwan	5.3
Hong Kong	4.2	South Korea	5.2
EU15	15.7	EU15	11.6

Balance of payments, reserves and debt, $bn

Visible exports fob	84.1	Overall balance	4.7
Visible imports fob	-61.4	Change in reserves	4.7
Trade balance	22.6	Level of reserves end Dec.	30.9
Invisibles inflows	13.9	No. months of import cover	4.4
Invisibles outflows	-22.2	Foreign debt	45.9
Net transfers	-1.7	as % of GDP	62
Current account balance	12.6	Debt service paid	4.7
– as % of GDP	15.9	Debt service ratio	5
Capital balance	-6.6		

Health and education

Health spending, % of GDP	2.5	Education spending, % of GDP	4.9
Doctors per 1,000 pop.	0.5	Enrolment, %: primary	101
Hospital beds per 1,000 pop.	2.0	secondary	64
Improved-water source access, % of pop.	...	tertiary	11

Society

No. of households	4.4m	Colour TVs per 100 households	90.3
Av. no. per household	4.9	Telephone lines per 100 pop.	21.1
Marriages per 1,000 pop.	...	Mobile telephone subscribers per 100 pop.	15.5
Divorces per 1,000 pop.	...	Computers per 100 pop.	10.5
Cost of living, Dec. 1999 New York = 100	60	Internet hosts per 100 pop.	3.0

MEXICO

Area	1,972,545 sq km	Capital	Mexico City
Arable as % of total land	13	Currency	Mexican peso (PS)

People

Population	97.4m	Life expectancy: men	70.4 yrs
Pop. per sq km	49	women	76.4 yrs
Av. ann. growth		Adult literacy	90.1%
in pop. 1995–2000	1.63%	Fertility rate (per woman)	2.7
Pop. under 15	33.1%	Urban population	74.4%
Pop. over 65	6.9%		*per 1,000 pop.*
No. of men per 100 women	98.0	Crude birth rate	22.1
Human Development Index	78.4	Crude death rate	5.1

The economy

GDP	4,584bn pesos	GDP per head	$4,970
GDP	$484bn	GDP per head in purchasing	
Av. ann. growth in real		power parity (USA=100)	25.3
GDP 1990–99	2.7%	Economic freedom index	2.95

Origins of GDP		**Components of GDP**	
	% of total		*% of total*
Agriculture	5.8	Private consumption	68.1
Industry, of which:	28.8	Public consumption	9.9
manufacturing	21.5	Investment	22.1
Services	68.2	Exports	32.7
		Imports	-32.8

Structure of employment

	% of total		*% of labour force*
Agriculture	23	Unemployed 1999	1.7
Industry	23	Av. ann. rate 1991–99	3.0
Services	54		

Energy

	m TCE		
Total output	314.393	% output exported	42.9
Total consumption	184.496	% consumption imported	11.7
Consumption per head,			
kg coal equivalent	1,957		

Inflation and finance

Consumer price			*av. ann. increase 1994–99*
inflation 2000	9.5%	Narrow money (M1)	22.2%
Av. ann. inflation 1990–2000	18.4%	Broad money	24.2%
Money market rate, 2000	16.96%		

Exchange rates

	end 2000		*December 2000*
PS per $	9.57	Effective rates	1995 = 100
PS per SDR	12.47	– nominal	...
PS per euro	8.90	– real	...

Trade

Principal exports		Principal imports	
	$bn fob		*$bn cif*
Manufactured products	122.1	Intermediate goods	109.4
Crude oil & products	9.9	Capital goods	20.5
Agricultural products	3.9	Consumer goods	12.2
Total incl. others	**136.4**	Total	**142.1**

Main export destinations		Main origins of imports	
	% of total		*% of total*
United States	83.2	United States	74.8
Canada	5.2	Japan	3.9
Japan	1.3	Germany	3.8
Spain	1.1	France	1.6

Balance of payments, reserves and debt, $bn

Visible exports fob	136.4	Overall balance	4.3
Visible imports fob	-142.0	Change in reserves	-0.04
Trade balance	-5.6	Level of reserves	
Invisibles inflows	16.6	end Dec.	31.8
Invisibles outflows	-31.5	No. months of import cover	2.2
Net transfers	6.3	Foreign debt	167.0
Current account balance	-14.2	– as % of GDP	35
– as % of gdp	-2.9	Debt service paid	40.0
Capital balance	19.3	Debt service ratio	25

Health and education

Health spending, % of GDP	4.7	Education spending, % of GDP	4.9
Doctors per 1,000 pop.	1.6	Enrolment, %: primary	114
Hospital beds per 1,000 pop.	1.1	secondary	64
Improved-water source access,		tertiary	16
% of pop.	86		

Society

No. of households	21.1m	Colour TVs per 100 households	88.5
Av. no. per household	4.6	Telephone lines per 100 pop.	12.5
Marriages per 1,000 pop.	7.0	Mobile telephone subscribers	
Divorces per 1,000 pop.	0.5	per 100 pop.	12.3
Cost of living, Dec. 1999		Computers per 100 pop.	5.1
New York = 100	87	Internet hosts per 100 pop.	5.7

MOROCCO

Area	446,550 sq km	Capital	Rabat
Arable as % of total land	20	Currency	Dirham (Dh)

People

Population	28.2m	Life expectancy: men	66.8 yrs
Pop. per sq km	63	women	70.5 yrs
Av. ann. growth		Adult literacy	45.9%
in pop. 1995–2000	1.87%	Fertility rate (per woman)	3.4
Pop. under 15	34.7%	Urban population	55.0%
Pop. over 65	6.4%		*per 1,000 pop.*
No. of men per 100 women	100.2	Crude birth rate	24.7
Human Development Index	58.9	Crude death rate	6.0

The economy

GDP	Dh343bn	GDP per head	$1,240
GDP	$35.0bn	GDP per head in purchasing	
Av. ann. growth in real		power parity (USA=100)	10.4
GDP 1990–99	2.3%	Economic freedom index	2.70

Origins of GDP		**Components of GDP**	
	% of total		*% of total*
Agriculture	13.0	Private consumption	65.4
Industry, of which:	26.0	Public consumption	19.3
manufacturing	18.1	Investment	24.3
Services	61.0	Exports	24.4
		Imports	-29.0

Structure of employment[a]

	% of total		*% of labour force*
Agriculture	5	Unemployed 1996	17.8
Industry	41	Av. ann. rate 1995–96	20.0
Services	54		

Energy

	m TCE		
Total output	0.687	% output exported	nil
Total consumption	12.434	% consumption imported	106.6
Consumption per head,			
kg coal equivalent	462		

Inflation and finance

Consumer price			*av. ann. increase 1994–99*
inflation 2000	1.9%	Narrow money (M1)	9.4%
Av. ann. inflation 1990–2000	3.9%	Broad money	9.2%
Money market rate, 2000	5.41%		

Exchange rates

	end 2000		*December 2000*
Dh per $	10.62	Effective rates	1995 = 100
Dh per SDR	13.84	– nominal	109.7
Dh per euro	9.88	– real	109.3

Trade

Principal exports	$bn fob	Principal imports	$bn cif
Finished goods	2.9	Machinery & equipment	2.8
Food, drink & tobacco	1.4	Consumer goods	2.5
Semi-finished goods	1.4	Semi-finished goods	2.2
Mineral ores	0.6	Energy & fuels	1.3
Energy & fuels	0.2	Food, drink & tobacco	1.2
Total incl. others	**7.4**	Total incl. others	**10.8**

Main export destinations	% of total	Main origins of imports	% of total
France	39.2	France	29.1
Spain	15.2	Spain	11.3
United States	8.8	Germany	6.5
Italy	8.7	Saudi Arabia	6.5
India	7.8	United States	5.8

Balance of payments, reserves and debt, $bn

Visible exports fob	7.5	Overall balance	-0.1
Visible imports fob	-10.0	Change in reserves	1.3
Trade balance	-2.4	Level of reserves	
Invisibles inflows	3.3	end Dec.	5.9
Invisibles outflows	-3.2	No. months of import cover	5.4
Net transfers	2.1	Foreign debt	19.0
Current account balance	-0.2	– as % of GDP	56
– as % of GDP	-0.5	Debt service paid	3.1
Capital balance	-0.0	Debt service ratio	24

Health and education

Health spending, % of GDP	4.4	Education spending, % of GDP	5.0
Doctors per 1,000 pop.	0.4	Enrolment, %: primary	86
Hospital beds per 1,000 pop.	1.0	secondary	39
Improved-water source access,		tertiary	11
% of pop.	82		

Society

No. of households	6.3m	Colour TVs per 100 households	41.9
Av. no. per household	4.4	Telephone lines per 100 pop.	5.3
Marriages per 1,000 pop.	...	Mobile telephone subscribers	
Divorces per 1,000 pop.	...	per 100 pop.	1.3
Cost of living, Dec. 1999		Computers per 100 pop.	1.1
New York = 100	64	Internet hosts per 100 pop.	...

a Urban areas, 1997.

NETHERLANDS

Area[a]	41,526 sq km	Capital	Amsterdam
Arable as % of total land	27	Currency	Guilder (Fl)

People

Population	15.8m	Life expectancy: men	75.6 yrs
Pop. per sq km	466	women	81.0 yrs
Av. ann. growth		Adult literacy	99.0%
in pop. 1995–2000	0.52%	Fertility rate (per woman)	1.5
Pop. under 15	18.3%	Urban population	89.4%
Pop. over 65	18.3%		*per 1,000 pop.*
No. of men per 100 women	98.1	Crude birth rate	10.5
Human Development Index	92.5	Crude death rate	9.0

The economy

GDP	Fl824bn	GDP per head	$24,910
GDP	$394bn	GDP per head in purchasing	
Av. ann. growth in real		power parity (USA=100)	76.5
GDP 1990–99	2.7%	Economic freedom index	1.85

Origins of GDP		**Components of GDP**	
	% of total		*% of total*
Agriculture	3.4	Private consumption	49.9
Industry, of which:	26.4	Public consumption	22.8
manufacturing	...	Investment	22.3
Services	70.1	Exports	60.8
		Imports	-55.9

Structure of employment

	% of total		*% of labour force*
Agriculture	4	Unemployed 1999	6.8
Industry	22	Av. ann. rate 1990–99	7.9
Services	74		

Energy

	m TCE		
Total output	101.264	% output exported[b]	118.2
Total consumption	118.483	% consumption imported[b]	127.6
Consumption per head,			
kg coal equivalent	7,588		

Inflation and finance

Consumer price		*av. ann. increase 1994–99*	
inflation 2000	2.6%	Euro area:	
Av. ann. inflation 1990–2000	2.3%	Narrow money (M1)	7.9%
Deposit rate, 2000	2.89%	Broad money	5.9%

Exchange rates

	end 2000		*July 2000*
Fl per $	2.39	Effective rates	1995 = 100
Fl per SDR	3.11	– nominal	89.5
Fl per euro	2.20	– real	83.8

Trade

Principal exports		Principal imports	
	$bn fob		*$bn cif*
Machinery & transport equipment	68.0	Machinery & transport equipment	76.5
Food, drink & tobacco	31.9	Chemicals	20.9
Chemicals	30.7	Food, drink & tobacco	19.0
Fuels	11.8	Fuels	12.9
		Raw materials	7.4
Total incl. others	**200.7**	Total incl. others	**190.2**

Main export destinations		Main origins of imports	
	% of total		*% of total*
Germany	25.9	Germany	19.5
Belgium & Luxembourg	12.3	Belgium & Luxembourg	10.1
France	10.7	United Kingdom	9.7
United Kingdom	10.7	United States	9.5
Italy	6.0	France	6.5
EU15	78.1	EU15	59.0

Balance of payments, reserves and aid, $bn

Visible exports fob	197.4	Capital balance	-19.8
Visible imports fob	-179.4	Overall balance	-4.6
Trade balance	17.9	Change in reserves	-4.1
Invisibles inflows	99.8	Level of reserves end Dec.	19.3
Invisibles outflows	-93.9	No. months of import cover	0.9
Net transfers	-6.2	Aid given	3.13
Current account balance	17.6	– as % of GDP	0.81
– as % of GDP	4.4		

Health and education

Health spending, % of GDP	8.6	Education spending, % of GDP	5.1
Doctors per 1,000 pop.	2.6	Enrolment, %: primary	108
Hospital beds per 1,000 pop.	11.3	secondary[c]	132
Improved-water source access, % of pop.	100	tertiary	47

Society

No. of households	6.7m	Colour TVs per 100 households	98.2
Av. no. per household	2.3	Telephone lines per 100 pop.	60.7
Marriages per 1,000 pop.	5.4	Mobile telephone subscribers per 100 pop.	67.1
Divorces per 1,000 pop.	2.0	Computers per 100 pop.	39.5
Cost of living, Dec. 1999 New York = 100	76	Internet hosts per 100 pop.	82.9

a Includes water.
b Energy trade data are distorted due to transitory and oil refining activities.
c Includes training for unemployed.

NEW ZEALAND

Area	270,534 sq km	Capital	Wellington
Arable as % of total land	6	Currency	New Zealand dollar (NZ$)

People

Population	3.8m	Life expectancy: men	75.3 yrs
Pop. per sq km	14	women	80.7 yrs
Av. ann. growth		Adult literacy	99.0%
in pop. 1995–2000	0.94%	Fertility rate (per woman)	2.0
Pop. under 15	23.0%	Urban population	87.0%
Pop. over 65	15.6%		*per 1,000 pop.*
No. of men per 100 women	97.2	Crude birth rate	13.7
Human Development Index	90.3	Crude death rate	7.7

The economy

GDP	NZ$106bn	GDP per head	$14,300
GDP	$54.7bn	GDP per head in purchasing	
Av. ann. growth in real		power parity (USA=100)	55.2
GDP 1990–99	3.1%	Economic freedom index	1.70

Origins of GDP		**Components of GDP**	
	% of total		*% of total*
Agriculture	8.3	Private consumption	64.9
Industry, of which:	23.1	Public consumption	15.9
manufacturing	...	Investment	20.3
Services	68.6	Exports	31.0
		Imports	-32.0

Structure of employment

	% of total		*% of labour force*
Agriculture	9	Unemployed 1999	6.8
Industry	23	Av. ann. rate 1990–99	7.9
Services	68		

Energy

	m TCE		
Total output	19.408	% output exported	18.9
Total consumption	22.243	% consumption imported	33.0
Consumption per head,			
kg coal equivalent	5,914		

Inflation and finance

Consumer price		*av. ann. increase 1994–99*	
inflation 2000	2.6%	Narrow money (M1)	6.3%
Av. ann. inflation 1990–2000	1.8%	Broad money	7.8%
Treasury bill rate, 2000	6.39%		

Exchange rates

	end 2000		*December 2000*
NZ$ per $	2.27	Effective rates	1995 = 100
NZ$ per SDR	2.96	– nominal	81.7
NZ$ per euro	2.11	– real	80.9

Trade

Principal exports	$bn fob	Principal imports	$bn cif
Dairy produce	2.4	Vehicles & aircraft	2.2
Meat	1.6	Machinery	1.8
Forest products	1.4	Electrical machinery	1.4
Fruit & vegetables	0.8	Mineral fuels	0.8
Fish	0.5		
Total incl. others	**12.5**	Total incl. others	**14.3**

Main export destinations	% of total	Main origins of imports	% of total
Australia	21.7	Australia	24.5
United States	13.6	United States	16.8
Japan	12.6	Japan	12.1
United Kingdom	6.6	United Kingdom	4.1

Balance of payments, reserves and aid, $bn

Visible exports fob	12.6	Capital balance	1.8
Visible imports fob	-13.0	Overall balance	0.2
Trade balance	-0.4	Change in reserves	0.3
Invisibles inflows	5.2	Level of reserves	
Invisibles outflows	-8.6	end Dec.	4.5
Net transfers	0.2	No. months of import cover	2.5
Current account balance	-3.6	Aid given	0.13
– as % of GDP	-7.9	– as % of GDP	0.25

Health and education

Health spending, % of GDP	8.1	Education spending, % of GDP	7.3
Doctors per 1,000 pop.	2.3	Enrolment, %: primary	101
Hospital beds per 1,000 pop.	6.2	secondary	113
Improved-water source access, % of pop.	...	tertiary	63

Society

No. of households	1.3m	Colour TVs per 100 households	96.8
Av. no. per household	3.0	Telephone lines per 100 pop.	49.6
Marriages per 1,000 pop.	5.1	Mobile telephone subscribers	
Divorces per 1,000 pop.	3.2	per 100 pop.	36.6
Cost of living, Dec. 1999		Computers per 100 pop.	36.0
New York = 100	59	Internet hosts per 100 pop.	90.3

NIGERIA

Area	923,768 sq km	Capital	Abuja
Arable as % of total land	31	Currency	Naira (N)

People

Population	123.9m	Life expectancy: men	52.0 yrs
Pop. per sq km	134	women	52.2 yrs
Av. ann. growth		Adult literacy	59.5%
in pop. 1995–2000	2.74%	Fertility rate (per woman)	5.9
Pop. under 15	45.1%	Urban population	43.0%
Pop. over 65	4.8%		*per 1,000 pop.*
No. of men per 100 women	102	Crude birth rate	39.4
Human Development Index	43.9	Crude death rate	13.3

The economy

GDP	N3,236bn	GDP per head	$280
GDP	$35.0bn	GDP per head in purchasing	
Av. ann. growth in real		power parity (USA=100)	2.4
GDP 1990–99	2.4%	Economic freedom index	3.35

Origins of GDP[a]		**Components of GDP**[a]	
	% of total		*% of total*
Agriculture	37.4	Private consumption	77.5
Industry, of which:	17.3	Public consumption	10.7
manufacturing	5.9	Investment	20.0
Services	45.3	Exports	23.3
		Imports	-31.7

Structure of employment[b]

	% of total		*% of labour force*
Agriculture	43	Unemployed 1998	...
Industry	7	Av. ann. rate 1990–98	...
Services	50		

Energy

	m TCE		
Total output	141.922	% output exported	89.4
Total consumption	17.243	% consumption imported	18.4
Consumption per head,			
kg coal equivalent	166		

Inflation and finance

Consumer price		*av. ann. increase 1994–99*	
inflation 2000	6.9%	Narrow money (M1)	17.9%
Av. ann. inflation 1990–2000	28.5%	Broad money	21.5%

Exchange rates

	end 2000		*December 2000*
N per $	109.6	Effective rates	1995 = 100
N per SDR	142.7	– nominal	49.1
N per euro	101.9	– real	84.5

Trade

Principal exports[c]		Principal imports[c]	
	$bn fob		*$bn cif*
Petroleum	14.5	Manufactured goods	3.0
Cocoa beans & products	0.1	Machinery & transport equipment	2.4
		Chemicals	2.3
		Agric products & foodstuffs	1.2
Total incl. others	**16.0**	Total incl. others	**10.3**

Main export destinations		Main origins of imports	
	% of total		*% of total*
United States	37.5	United States	11.2
India	8.9	Germany	10.1
Spain	6.1	United Kingdom	9.7
France	4.9	France	8.6

Balance of payments, reserves[d] and debt, $bn

Visible exports fob	12.9	Overall balance	-3.5
Visible imports fob	-8.6	Change in reserves	2.6
Trade balance	4.3	Level of reserves end Dec.	4.3
Invisibles inflows	1.2		
Invisibles outflows	-6.3	No. months of import cover	4.6
Net transfers	1.3	Foreign debt	29.4
Current account balance	0.5	– as % of GDP	93
– as % of GDP	1.4	Debt service paid	0.9
Capital balance	-4.1	Debt service ratio	6

Health and education

Health spending, % of GDP	2.8	Education spending, % of GDP	0.7
Doctors per 1,000 pop.	0.2	Enrolment, %: primary	98
Hospital beds per 1,000 pop.	1.7	secondary	33
Improved-water source access, % of pop.	57	tertiary	4

Society

No. of households	23.9m	Colour TVs per 100 households	45.1
Av. no. per household	4.5	Telephone lines per 100 pop.	0.4
Marriages per 1,000 pop.	...	Mobile telephone subscribers per 100 pop.	...
Divorces per 1,000 pop.	...		
Cost of living, Dec. 1999 New York = 100	82	Computers per 100 pop.	0.6
		Internet hosts per 100 pop.	...

a 1998
b 1990
c 1997
d 1996

NORWAY

Area	323,878 sq km	Capital	Oslo
Arable as % of total land	3	Currency	Norwegian krone (Nkr)

People

Population	4.5m	Life expectancy: men	76.0 yrs
Pop. per sq km	15	women	81.9 yrs
Av. ann. growth		Adult literacy	99.0%
in pop. 1995–2000	0.50%	Fertility rate (per woman)	1.8
Pop. under 15	19.8%	Urban population	75.5%
Pop. over 65	19.6%		*per 1,000 pop.*
No. of men per 100 women	98.3	Crude birth rate	11.4
Human Development Index	93.4	Crude death rate	10.0

The economy

GDP	Nkr1,193bn	GDP per head	$34,340
GDP	$153bn	GDP per head in purchasing	
Av. ann. growth in real		power parity (USA=100)	88.2
GDP 1990–99	3.8%	Economic freedom index	2.45

Origins of GDP		**Components of GDP**	
	% of total		*% of total*
Agriculture	1.9	Private consumption	48.5
Industry, of which:	30.8	Public consumption	21.2
manufacturing	12.4	Investment	24.3
Services	67.3	Exports	39.0
		Imports	-33.0

Structure of employment

	% of total		*% of labour force*
Agriculture	4	Unemployed 1999	3.2
Industry	24	Av. ann. rate 1990–99	4.8
Services	72		

Energy

	m TCE		
Total output	303.389	% output exported	89.6
Total consumption	34.708	% consumption imported	25.1
Consumption per head,			
kg coal equivalent	7,886		

Inflation and finance

Consumer price			*av. ann. increase 1994–99*
inflation 2000	3.0%	Narrow money (M1)	8.2%
Av. ann. inflation 1990–2000	2.3%	Broad money	5.7%
Deposit rate, 2000	6.73%		

Exchange rates

	end 2000		*July 2000*
Nkr per $	8.85	Effective rates	1995 = 100
Nkr per SDR	11.53	– nominal	93.1
Nkr per euro	8.23	– real	112.1

Trade

Principal exports		Principal imports	
	$bn fob		*$bn cif*
Oil, gas & products	20.7	Machinery & equipment	12.8
Machinery & equipment	5.9	Chemicals	3.4
Metals	4.3	Metals	2.6
Food, drink & tobacco	3.1	Textiles & clothing	2.3
Total incl. others	**45.6**	Total incl. others	**35.0**

Main export destinations		Main origins of imports	
	% of total		*% of total*
United Kingdom	17.1	Sweden	14.7
Germany	11.3	Germany	12.5
Netherlands	9.7	United States	10.0
Sweden	9.3	United Kingdom	9.0
United States	5.4	Denmark	6.7
EU15	72.6	EU15	66.2

Balance of payments, reserves and aid, $bn

Visible exports fob	45.6	Capital balance	-0.2
Visible imports fob	-35.1	Overall balance	6.0
Trade balance	10.5	Change in reserves	1.8
Invisibles inflows	21.5	Level of reserves	
Invisibles outflows	-24.5	end Dec.	20.7
Net transfers	-1.6	No. months of import cover	4.2
Current account balance	6.0	Aid given	1.37
– as % of GDP	3.9	– as % of GDP	0.94

Health and education

Health spending, % of GDP	8.9	Education spending, % of GDP	7.4
Doctors per 1,000 pop.	2.5	Enrolment, %: primary	100
Hospital beds per 1,000 pop.	14.7	secondary	119
Improved-water source access,		tertiary	62
% of pop.	100		

Society

No. of households	2.0m	Colour TVs per 100 households	92.8
Av. no. per household	2.3	Telephone lines per 100 pop.	72.9
Marriages per 1,000 pop.	5.3	Mobile telephone subscribers	
Divorces per 1,000 pop.	2.4	per 100 pop.	70.3
Cost of living, Dec. 1999		Computers per 100 pop.	49.1
New York = 100	99	Internet hosts per 100 pop.	117.9

PAKISTAN

Area	803,940 sq km	Capital	Islamabad
Arable as % of total land	28	Currency	Pakistan rupee (PRs)

People

Population	134.8m	Life expectancy: men	61.2 yrs
Pop. per sq km	175	women	60.9 yrs
Av. ann. growth		Adult literacy	40.9%
in pop. 1995–2000	2.66%	Fertility rate (per woman)	5.4
Pop. under 15	41.8%	Urban population	36.0%
Pop. over 65	5.8%		*per 1,000 pop.*
No. of men per 100 women	106.6	Crude birth rate	36.2
Human Development Index	52.2	Crude death rate	9.7

The economy

GDP[a]	PRs3,026bn	GDP per head	$430
GDP	$58.2bn	GDP per head in purchasing	
Av. ann. growth in real		power parity (USA=100)	5.8
GDP 1990–99	3.8%	Economic freedom index	3.45

Origins of GDP		**Components of GDP[a]**	
	% of total		*% of total*
Agriculture	27	Private consumption	72.5
Industry, of which:	23	Public consumption	11.4
manufacturing	16	Investment	16.0
Other	49	Exports	15.2
		Imports	-15.3

Structure of employment[b]

	% of total[c]		*% of labour force*
Agriculture	44	Unemployed 1997	6.1
Industry	18	Av. ann. rate 1990–97	5.5
Services	38		

Energy

	m TCE		
Total output	31.278	% output exported	2.2
Total consumption	50.506	% consumption imported	41.9
Consumption per head,			
kg coal equivalent	351		

Inflation and finance

Consumer price			*av. ann. increase 1994–99*
inflation 2000	4.3%	Narrow money (M1)	12.8%
Av. ann. inflation 1990–2000	9.2%	Broad money	13.0%
Money market rate, 2000	8.57%		

Exchange rates

	end 2000		*December 2000*
PRs per $	58.03	Effective rates	1995 = 100
PRs per SDR	75.61	– nominal	67.85
PRs per euro	53.97	– real	90.57

Trade

Principal exports[d]		**Principal imports**[d]	
	$bn fob		*$bn cif*
Textile yarn & fabrics	2.1	Machinery	2.0
Apparel & clothing accessories	1.4	Petroleum & products	1.3
Rice	0.6	Palm oil	0.6
		Wheat	0.4
Total incl. others	**8.1**	Total incl. others	**9.0**

Main export destinations[d]		**Main origins of imports**[d]	
	% of total		*% of total*
United States	21.4	United States	9.8
Hong Kong	7.0	Japan	8.0
United Kingdom	6.7	Malaysia	7.8
Germany	6.5	Saudi Arabia	6.4

Balance of payments[e], reserves and debt, $bn

Visible exports fob	8.4	Overall balance	0.5
Visible imports fob	-10.8	Change in reserves	0.5
Trade balance	-2.4	Level of reserves	
Invisibles inflows	1.8	end Dec.	2.1
Invisibles outflows	-5.0	No. months of import cover	1.7
Net transfers	3.9	Foreign debt	34.4
Current account balance	-1.7	– as % of GDP	59
– as % of GDP	-2.8	Debt service paid	3.0
Capital balance	2.3	Debt service ratio	30

Health and education

Health spending, % of GDP	4.0	Education spending, % of GDP	2.7
Doctors per 1,000 pop.	0.6	Enrolment, %: primary	...
Hospital beds per 1,000 pop.	0.7	secondary	...
Improved-water source access,		tertiary	4
% of pop.	88		

Society

No. of households	21.0m	Colour TVs per 100 households	32.4
Av. no. per household	7.1	Telephone lines per 100 pop.	2.2
Marriages per 1,000 pop.	...	Mobile telephone subscribers	
Divorces per 1,000 pop.	...	per 100 pop.	0.2
Cost of living, Dec. 1999		Computers per 100 pop.	0.4
New York = 100	46	Internet hosts per 100 pop.	...

a Fiscal year ending June 30, 1999.
b Fiscal year ending June 30, 1995.
c Employed labour force.
d 1998
e 1997

PERU

Area	1,285,216 sq km	Capital	Lima
Arable as % of total land	3	Currency	Nuevo Sol (New Sol)

People

Population	25.2m	Life expectancy: men	67.3 yrs
Pop. per sq km	20	women	72.4 yrs
Av. ann. growth		Adult literacy[a]	88.7%
in pop. 1995–2000	1.73%	Fertility rate (per woman)	3.0
Pop. under 15	33.4%	Urban population	72.0%
Pop. over 65	7.2%		*per 1,000 pop.*
No. of men per 100 women	98.4	Crude birth rate	22.5
Human Development Index	73.7	Crude death rate	6.2

The economy

GDP	New Soles 176bn	GDP per head	$2,060
GDP	$51.9bn	GDP per head in purchasing	
Av. ann. growth in real		power parity (USA=100)	14.0
GDP 1990–99	5.0%	Economic freedom index	2.50

Origins of GDP		**Components of GDP**	
	% of total		*% of total*
Agriculture	14.5	Private consumption	58.2
Industry, of which:	41.8	Public consumption	7.7
manufacturing	21.9	Investment	26.0
Services	43.7	Exports	29.6
		Imports	-21.5

Structure of employment

	% of total		*% of labour force*
Agriculture	7	Unemployed 1998[b]	8.0
Industry	21	Av. ann. rate 1996–99[b]	7.6
Services	72		

Energy

	m TCE		
Total output	10.677	% output exported	43.7
Total consumption	13.738	% consumption imported	60.3
Consumption per head,			
kg coal equivalent	564		

Inflation and finance

Consumer price		*av. ann. increase 1994–99*	
inflation 2000	3.7%	Narrow money (M1)	31.9%
Av. ann. inflation 1990–2000	38.1%	Broad money	25.5%
Deposit rate, 2000	13.3%		

Exchange rates

	end 2000		*December 2000*
New Soles per $	3.53	Effective rates	1995 = 100
New Soles per SDR	4.60	– nominal	...
New Soles per Ecu	3.28	– real	...

Trade

Principal exports		Principal imports	
	$bn fob		*$bn fob*
Gold	1.2	Industrial supplies	3.0
Copper	0.8	Capital goods	2.1
Fish & fish products	0.8	Consumer goods	1.4
Textiles	0.6		
Zinc	0.5		
Total incl. others	**6.1**	Total incl. others	**6.7**

Main export destinations		Main origins of imports	
	% of total		*% of total*
United States	28.3	United States	22.4
Japan	4.2	Japan	5.8
Germany	4.0	Colombia	5.3
China	3.5	Chile	3.7
Brazil	2.8	Venezuela	2.7

Balance of payments, reserves and debt, $bn

Visible exports fob	6.1	Overall balance	-0.8
Visible imports fob	-6.7	Change in reserves	-0.8
Trade balance	-0.6	Level of reserves	
Invisibles inflows	2.2	end Dec.	9.0
Invisibles outflows	-4.3	No. months of import cover	9.8
Net transfers	0.9	Foreign debt	32.3
Current account balance	-1.8	– as % of GDP	64
– as % of GDP	-3.5	Debt service paid	2.9
Capital balance	0.6	Debt service ratio	33

Health and education

Health spending, % of GDP	6.1	Education spending, % of GDP	2.9
Doctors per 1,000 pop.	0.9	Enrolment, %: primary	123
Hospital beds per 1,000 pop.	1.5	secondary	73
Improved-water source access,		tertiary	26
% of pop.	77		

Society

No. of households	5.4m	Colour TVs per 100 households	44.3
Av. no. per household	4.6	Telephone lines per 100 pop.	6.7
Marriages per 1,000 pop.	4.1	Mobile telephone subscribers	
Divorces per 1,000 pop.	...	per 100 pop.	4.0
Cost of living, Dec. 1999		Computers per 100 pop.	3.6
New York = 100	66	Internet hosts per 100 pop.	0.4

a Excluding indigenous jungle population.
b Urban areas.

PHILIPPINES

Area	300,000 sq km	Capital	Manila
Arable as % of total land	18	Currency	Philippine peso (P)

People

Population	76.8m	Life expectancy: men	68.0 yrs
Pop. per sq km	249	women	72.0 yrs
Av. ann. growth		Adult literacy	94.6%
in pop. 1995–2000	2.03%	Fertility rate (per woman)	3.6
Pop. under 15	37.5%	Urban population	58.0%
Pop. over 65	5.5%		*per 1,000 pop.*
No. of men per 100 women	101	Crude birth rate	25.9
Human Development Index	74.4	Crude death rate	5.2

The economy

GDP	P2,996bn	GDP per head	$1,000
GDP	$76.6bn	GDP per head in purchasing	
Av. ann. growth in real		power parity (USA=100)	12.5
GDP 1990–99	3.2%	Economic freedom index	3.05

Origins of GDP		**Components of GDP**	
	% of total		*% of total*
Agriculture	17.5	Private consumption	72.4
Industry, of which:	30.5	Public consumption	13.0
manufacturing	21.4	Investment	18.8
Services	52.0	Exports	51.3
		Imports	-50.9

Structure of employment

	% of total		*% of labour force*
Agriculture	37	Unemployed 1999	9.4
Industry	16	Av. ann. rate 1990–99	8.6
Services	47		

Energy

	m TCE		
Total output	9.964	% output exported	11.2
Total consumption	39.197	% consumption imported	82.9
Consumption per head,			
kg coal equivalent	549		

Inflation and finance

Consumer price			*av. ann. increase 1994–99*
inflation 2000	4.4%	Narrow money (M1)	19.9%
Av. ann. inflation 1990–2000	8.6%	Broad money	27.7%
Treasury bill rate, 2000	9.91%		

Exchange rates

	end 2000		*December 2000*
P per $	50.00	Effective rates	1995 = 100
P per SDR	65.14	– nominal	63.1
P per euro	46.50	– real	83.5

Trade

Principal exports	$bn fob	Principal imports	$bn cif
Electrical & electronic equipment	21.2	Semi-processed raw materials	11.1
Machinery & transport equipment	5.0	Telecom & electrical machinery	6.9
Clothing	2.3	Electrical equipment parts	4.7
Coconut products	0.5	Semi-processed manufactures	2.5
		Power equipment & specialised machines	2.4
Total incl. others	**35.0**	Total incl. others	**30.7**

Main export destinations	% of total	Main origins of imports	% of total
United States	29.8	United States	20.7
Japan	13.3	Japan	20.0
Netherlands	8.2	South Korea	8.9
Singapore	7.0	Singapore	5.7
United Kingdom	5.6	Taiwan	5.3

Balance of payments, reserves and debt, $bn

Visible exports fob	34.2	Overall balance	3.7
Visible imports fob	-29.3	Change in reserves	4.2
Trade balance	5.0	Level of reserves	
Invisibles inflows	12.9	end Dec.	15.0
Invisibles outflows	-10.4	No. months of import cover	4.5
Net transfers	0.5	Foreign debt	52.0
Current account balance	7.9	– as % of GDP	65
– as % of GDP	10.3	Debt service paid	6.7
Capital balance	-0.9	Debt service ratio	14

Health and education

Health spending, % of GDP	3.7	Education spending, % of GDP	3.4
Doctors per 1,000 pop.	0.1	Enrolment, %: primary	117
Hospital beds per 1,000 pop.	1.1	secondary	78
Improved-water source access, % of pop.	87	tertiary	35

Society

No. of households	13.8m	Colour TVs per 100 households	61.3
Av. no. per household	5.3	Telephone lines per 100 pop.	3.9
Marriages per 1,000 pop.	6.9	Mobile telephone subscribers per 100 pop.	3.8
Divorces per 1,000 pop.	...	Computers per 100 pop.	2.0
Cost of living, Dec. 1999 New York = 100	46	Internet hosts per 100 pop.	0.3

POLAND

Area	312,683 sq km	Capital	Warsaw
Arable as % of total land	46	Currency	Zloty (Zl)

People

Population	38.7m	Life expectancy: men	69.8 yrs
Pop. per sq km	123	women	78.0 yrs
Av. ann. growth		Adult literacy	99.0%
in pop. 1995–2000	0.01%	Fertility rate (per woman)	1.5
Pop. under 15	19.2%	Urban population	65.0%
Pop. over 65	16.6%		*per 1,000 pop.*
No. of men per 100 women	95	Crude birth rate	9.5
Human Development Index	81.4	Crude death rate	9.9

The economy

GDP	Zl616bn	GDP per head	$4,010
GDP	$155bn	GDP per head in purchasing	
Av. ann. growth in real		power parity (USA=100)	26.3
GDP 1990–99	4.5%	Economic freedom index	2.75

Origins of GDP		**Components of GDP**	
	% of total		*% of total*
Agriculture	3.8	Private consumption	64.6
Industry, of which:	36.6	Public consumption	15.4
manufacturing	...	Investment	26.4
Services	59.6	Exports	26.1
		Imports	-32.5

Structure of employment

	% of total		*% of labour force*
Agriculture	21	Unemployed 1998	10.5
Industry	32	Av. ann. rate 1992–97	12.7
Services	47		

Energy

	m TCE		
Total output	136.125	% output exported	22.1
Total consumption	142.281	% consumption imported	30.6
Consumption per head,			
kg coal equivalent	3,677		

Inflation and finance

Consumer price			*av. ann. increase 1994–99*
inflation 2000	10.1%	Narrow money (M1)	26.3%
Av. ann. inflation 1990–2000	27.0%	Broad money	27.8%
Money market rate, 2000	18.2%		

Exchange rates

	end 2000		*December 2000*
Zl per $	4.14	Effective rates	1995 = 100
Zl per SDR	5.40	– nominal	79.6
Zl per euro	3.85	– real	128.2

Trade

Principal exports	$bn fob	Principal imports	$bn cif
Machinery & transport equipment	8.3	Machinery & transport equipment	17.5
Semi-manufactured goods	7.0	Chemicals	6.6
Other manufactured goods	5.8	Semi-manufactured goods	6.6
Agric. products & foodstuffs	2.3	Other manufactured goods	4.4
Chemicals	1.7	Agric. products & foodstuffs	3.3
Total incl. others	**27.4**	Total incl. others	**45.9**

Main export destinations	% of total	Main origins of imports	% of total
Germany	36.1	Germany	25.2
Italy	6.5	Italy	9.4
Netherlands	5.3	France	6.8
France	4.8	Russia	5.8
United Kingdom	4.0	United Kingdom	4.6
Czech Republic	3.8	Netherlands	3.7

Balance of payments, reserves and debt, $bn

Visible exports fob	30.1	Overall balance	0.2
Visible imports fob	-45.1	Change in reserves	-1.9
Trade balance	-15.1	Level of reserves end Dec.	25.5
Invisibles inflows	10.3	No. months of import cover	5.6
Invisibles outflows	-9.9	Foreign debt	54.3
Net transfers	2.2	– as % of GDP	36
Current account balance	-12.5	Debt service paid	8.4
– as % of GDP	-8.0	Debt service ratio	20
Capital balance	10.5		

Health and education

Health spending, % of GDP	6.4	Education spending, % of GDP	7.5
Doctors per 1,000 pop.	2.3	Enrolment, %: primary	96
Hospital beds per 1,000 pop.	5.3	secondary	98
Improved-water source access, % of pop.	...	tertiary	24

Society

No. of households	11.8m	Colour TVs per 100 households	81.9
Av. no. per household	3.9	Telephone lines per 100 pop.	26.3
Marriages per 1,000 pop.	3.7	Mobile telephone subscribers per 100 pop.	10.2
Divorces per 1,000 pop.	1.2	Computers per 100 pop.	6.9
Cost of living, Dec. 1999 New York = 100	59	Internet hosts per 100 pop.	9.6

PORTUGAL

Area	88,940 sq km	Capital	Lisbon
Arable as % of total land	21	Currency	Escudo (Esc)

People

Population	10.0m	Life expectancy: men	72.6 yrs
Pop. per sq km	112	women	79.6 yrs
Av. ann. growth		Adult literacy	90.8%
in pop. 1995–2000	0.20%	Fertility rate (per woman)	1.4
Pop. under 15	16.7%	Urban population	63.0%
Pop. over 65	20.8%		*per 1,000 pop.*
No. of men per 100 women	92.7	Crude birth rate	11.0
Human Development Index	86.4	Crude death rate	10.8

The economy

GDP	Esc21,313bn	GDP per head	$11,380
GDP	$114bn	GDP per head in purchasing	
Av. ann. growth in real		power parity (USA=100)	49.7
GDP 1990–99	2.5%	Economic freedom index	2.30

Origins of GDP[a]		**Components of GDP**	
	% of total		*% of total*
Agriculture	3.6	Private consumption	64.8
Industry, of which:	35.5	Public consumption	20.0
manufacturing	...	Investment	25.6
Services	60.9	Exports	29.9
		Imports	-40.2

Structure of employment

	% of total		*% of labour force*
Agriculture	13	Unemployed 1999	4.5
Industry	35	Av. ann. rate 1990–99	5.7
Services	52		

Energy

	m TCE		
Total output	1.688	% output exported[a]	185.9
Total consumption	23.410	% consumption imported[a]	119.0
Consumption per head,			
kg coal equivalent	2,373		

Inflation and finance

Consumer price			*av. ann. increase 1994–99*
inflation 2000	2.9%	Euro area:	
Av. ann. inflation 1990–2000	4.9%	Narrow money (M1)	7.9%
Money market rate, 1999	2.71%	Broad money	5.9%

Exchange rates

	end 2000		*December 2000*
Esc per $	217.1	Effective rates	1995 = 100
Esc per SDR	282.2	– nominal	92.8
Esc per euro	200.5	– real	97.2

Trade

Principal exports	*$bn fob*
Consumer goods	9.9
Capital goods	7.3
Raw materials & semi-manufactures	6.9
Energy products	0.4
Total incl. others	**24.5**

Principal imports	*$bn cif*
Capital goods	15.3
Raw materials & semi-manufactures	12.4
Consumer goods	9.5
Energy products	2.7
Total incl. others	**39.9**

Main export destinations	*% of total*
Germany	19.8
Spain	18.1
France	13.9
United Kingdom	12.0
United States	5.0
EU15	83.2

Main origins of imports	*% of total*
Spain	25.3
Germany	14.7
France	11.4
Italy	7.7
United Kingdom	6.8
EU15	78.1

Balance of payments, reserves and debt, $bn

Visible exports fob	25.7
Visible imports fob	-39.8
Trade balance	-14.2
Invisibles inflows	12.7
Invisibles outflows	-12.7
Net transfers	3.9
Current account balance	-10.2
– as % of GDP	-8.9
Capital balance	12.9

Overall balance	0.2
Change in reserves	-0.4
Level of reserves end Dec.	14.5
No. months of import cover	3.3
Aid given	0.28
– as % of GDP	0.26

Health and education

Health spending, % of GDP	7.5
Doctors per 1,000 pop.	3.1
Hospital beds per 1,000 pop.	4.0
Improved-water source access, % of pop.	...

Education spending, % of GDP	5.8
Enrolment, %: primary	128
secondary[a]	111
tertiary	38

Society

No. of households	3.7m
Av. no. per household	2.7
Marriages per 1,000 pop.	6.7
Divorces per 1,000 pop.	1.6
Cost of living, Dec. 1999 New York = 100	63

Colour TVs per 100 households	97.2
Telephone lines per 100 pop.	42.3
Mobile telephone subscribers per 100 pop.	66.5
Computers per 100 pop.	10.5
Internet hosts per 100 pop.	17.8

a 1998
a Includes training for unemployed.

ROMANIA

Area	237,500 sq km	Capital	Bucharest
Arable as % of total land	41	Currency	Leu (L)

People

Population	22.5m	Life expectancy: men	66.5 yrs
Pop. per sq km	94	women	73.3 yrs
Av. ann. growth		Adult literacy	97.8%
in pop. 1995–2000	-0.22%	Fertility rate (per woman)	1.3
Pop. under 15	18.3%	Urban population	56.2%
Pop. over 65	18.8%		*per 1,000 pop.*
No. of men per 100 women	96.4	Crude birth rate	10.4
Human Development Index	77.0	Crude death rate	12.8

The economy

GDP	L521,736bn	GDP per head	$1,520
GDP	$34.0bn	GDP per head in purchasing	
Av. ann. growth in real		power parity (USA=100)	18.7
GDP 1990–99	-0.8%	Economic freedom index	3.65

Origins of GDP		**Components of GDP**	
	% of total		*% of total*
Agriculture	13.9	Private consumption	69.6
Industry, of which:	32.6	Public consumption	14.7
manufacturing	...	Investment	20.0
Services	43.5	Exports	30.1
		Imports	-34.3

Structure of employment[a]

	% of total		*% of labour force*
Agriculture	39	Unemployed 1999	6.8
Industry	31	Av. ann. rate 1991–99	7.0
Services	30		

Energy

	m TCE		
Total output	39.746	% output exported	10.3
Total consumption	55.797	% consumption imported	45.0
Consumption per head,			
kg coal equivalent	3,474		

Inflation and finance

Consumer price			*av. ann. increase 1994–99*
inflation 2000	45.7%	Narrow money (M1)	45.9%
Av. ann. inflation 1990–2000	105.9%	Broad money	66.0%
Treasury bill rate, 2000	51.9%		

Exchange rates

	end 2000		*December 2000*
L per $	25,926	Effective rates	1995 = 100
L per SDR	33,779	– nominal	10.8
L per euro	24,111	– real	126.4

Trade

Principal exports		Principal imports	
	$bn fob		*$bn cif*
Textiles & footwear	2.2	Machinery & equipment	2.2
Basic metals & products	1.3	Textiles & footwear	1.8
Machinery & equipment	1.0	Fuels & minerals	1.2
Minerals & fuels	0.5	Chemicals	0.9
Total incl. others	**8.5**	Total incl. others	**9.6**

Main export destinations		Main origins of imports	
	% of total		*% of total*
Italy	23.4	Italy	19.6
Germany	18.2	Germany	18.6
France	6.2	France	7.2
Turkey	5.0	Russia	5.7
EU15	65.5	EU15	60.4

Balance of payments, reserves and debt, $bn

Visible exports fob	8.5	Overall balance	0.2
Visible imports fob	-9.6	Change in reserves	-0.1
Trade balance	-1.1	Level of reserves	
Invisibles inflows	1.5	end Dec.	3.7
Invisibles outflows	-2.3	No. months of import cover	3.7
Net transfers	0.6	Foreign debt	9.4
Current account balance	-1.3	– as % of GDP	28
– as % of GDP	-3.8	Debt service paid	3.1
Capital balance	0.7	Debt service ratio	31

Health and education

Health spending, % of GDP	4.1	Education spending, % of GDP	3.6
Doctors per 1,000 pop.	1.8	Enrolment, %: primary	104
Hospital beds per 1,000 pop.	7.6	secondary	78
Improved-water source access,		tertiary	23
% of pop.	58		

Society

No. of households	7.6m	Colour TVs per 100 households	47.2
Av. no. per household	3.0	Telephone lines per 100 pop.	16.7
Marriages per 1,000 pop.	6.0	Mobile telephone subscribers	
Divorces per 1,000 pop.	1.9	per 100 pop.	6.1
Cost of living, Dec. 1999		Computers per 100 pop.	2.7
New York = 100	46	Internet hosts per 100 pop.	1.8

a 1997

RUSSIA

Area	17,075,400 sq km	Capital	Moscow
Arable as % of total land	8	Currency	Rouble (Rb)

People

Population	146.5m	Life expectancy: men	60.0 yrs
Pop. per sq km	9	women	72.5 yrs
Av. ann. growth		Adult literacy	99.0%
in pop. 1995–2000	-0.36%	Fertility rate (per woman)	1.2
Pop. under 15	18.0%	Urban population	77.7%
Pop. over 65	18.5%		*per 1,000 pop.*
No. of men per 100 women	87.8	Crude birth rate	8.5
Human Development Index	77.1	Crude death rate	15.3

The economy

GDP[a]	Rb4,545bn	GDP per head	$2,740
GDP	$401bn	GDP per head in purchasing	
Av. ann. growth in real		power parity (USA=100)	21.9
GDP 1990–99	-6.1%	Economic freedom index	3.70

Origins of GDP		**Components of GDP**	
	% of total		*% of total*
Agriculture	6.7	Private consumption	54.8
Industry, of which:	38.4	Public consumption	15.9
manufacturing	...	Investment	15.5
Services	54.9	Net exports	16.8

Structure of employment

	% of total		*% of labour force*
Agriculture	18	Unemployed 1999	13.4
Industry	31	Av. ann. rate 1992–99	9.6
Services	51		

Energy

	m TCE		
Total output	1,365.411	% output exported	38.4
Total consumption	832.247	% consumption imported	3.4
Consumption per head,			
kg coal equivalent	5,636		

Inflation and finance

Consumer price			*av. ann. increase 1994–99*
inflation 2000	20.75%	Narrow money (M1)	50.4%
Av. ann. inflation 1990–2000	166.4%	Broad money	50.0%
Money market rate, 2000	7.1%		

Exchange rates

	end 2000		*December 2000*
Rb per $	28.16	Effective rates	1995 = 100
Rb per SDR	36.69	– nominal	36.81
Rb per euro	26.19	– real	100.74

Trade

Principal exports		Principal imports	
	$bn fob		*$bn fob*
Fuels & energy	33.2	Machinery & equipment	12.8
Metals	15.5	Food products	11.2
Machinery & equipment	8.0	Chemicals	6.5
Chemicals	6.3	Metals	2.8
Total incl. others	**75.8**	Total incl. others	**39.5**

Main export destinations		Main origins of imports	
	% of total		*% of total*
United States	8.8	Germany	13.8
Germany	8.5	Belarus	10.7
Ukraine	6.5	Ukraine	8.3
Belarus	5.1	United States	7.9
Italy	5.0	Kazakhstan	4.6
Netherlands	4.8	Italy	3.8

Balance of payments, reserves and debt, $bn

Visible exports fob	75.8	Overall balance	-1.7
Visible imports fob	-39.6	Change in reserves	0.3
Trade balance	36.2	Level of reserves	
Invisibles inflows	12.9	end Dec.	12.3
Invisibles outflows	-24.4	No. months of import cover	2.3
Net transfers	0.5	Foreign debt	173.9
Current account balance	25.3	– as % of GDP	46
– as % of GDP	6.3	Debt service paid	11.5
Capital balance	-19.4	Debt service ratio	13

Health and education

Health spending, % of GDP	4.6	Education spending, % of GDP	3.5
Doctors per 1,000 pop.	4.6	Enrolment, %: primary	107
Hospital beds per 1,000 pop.	12.1	secondary	...
Improved-water source access,		tertiary	41
% of pop.	99		

Society

No. of households	51.9m	Colour TVs per 100 households	79.5
Av. no. per household	2.8	Telephone lines per 100 pop.	21.0
Marriages per 1,000 pop.	5.2	Mobile telephone subscribers	
Divorces per 1,000 pop.	3.2	per 100 pop.	0.9
Cost of living, Dec. 1999		Computers per 100 pop.	4.3
New York = 100	85	Internet hosts per 100 pop.	2.0

a Production based.

SAUDI ARABIA

Area	2,200,000 sq km	Capital	Riyadh
Arable as % of total land	2	Currency	Riyal (SR)

People

Population	21.4m	Life expectancy: men	71.1 yrs
Pop. per sq km	9	women	73.7 yrs
Av. ann. growth		Adult literacy	73.4%
in pop. 1995–2000	3.49%	Fertility rate (per woman)	6.1
Pop. under 15	42.9%	Urban population	85.0%
Pop. over 65	4.8%		*per 1,000 pop.*
No. of men per 100 women	115	Crude birth rate	33.7
Human Development Index	74.7	Crude death rate	4.1

The economy

GDP	SR535bn	GDP per head	$6,500
GDP	$139bn	GDP per head in purchasing	
Av. ann. growth in real		power parity (USA=100)	34.6
GDP 1990–99	1.6%	Economic freedom index	3.00

Origins of GDP[a]		**Components of GDP**	
	% of total		*% of total*
Agriculture	7.0	Private consumption	38.5
Industry, of which:	46.8	Public consumption	29.2
manufacturing	9.7	Investment	18.9
Services	46.2	Exports	40.6
		Imports	-27.2

Structure of employment[b]

	% of total		*% of labour force*
Agriculture	5	Unemployed 1998	...
Industry	26	Av. ann. rate 1990–98	...
Services	69		

Energy

	m TCE		
Total output	664.512	% output exported	74.6
Total consumption	123.838	% consumption imported	0.2
Consumption per head,			
kg coal equivalent	6,358		

Inflation and finance

Consumer price			*av. ann. increase 1994–99*
inflation 2000	-0.8%	Narrow money (M1)	4.5%
Av. ann. inflation 1990–2000	1.0%	Broad money	5.2%
Deposit rate, 2000	6.67%		

Exchange rates

	end 2000		*December 2000*
SR per $	3.75	Effective rates	1995 = 100
SR per SDR	4.88	– nominal	125.3
SR per euro	3.49	– real	110.3

Trade

Principal exports[c]		Principal imports[a]	
	$bn fob		*$bn cif*
Crude oil & refined petroleum	52.3	Machinery	6.0
Petrochemicals	2.6	Transport equipment	5.5
		Chemical products	2.5
		Textiles & clothing	2.0
Total incl. others	**60.7**	Total incl. others	**30.0**

Main export destinations		Main origins of imports	
	% of total		*% of total*
United States	18.2	United States	18.9
Japan	17.5	Japan	9.2
France	3.7	United Kingdom	8.1
Italy	2.4	Germany	7.3
		France	4.2
		Italy	4.2

Balance of payments, reserves and aid, $bn

Visible exports fob	50.8	Overall balance	2.8
Visible imports fob	-25.7	Change in reserves	2.8
Trade balance	25.0	Level of reserves end Dec.	18.3
Invisibles inflows	11.2	No. months of import cover	4.6
Invisibles outflows	-21.7	Aid given	0.19
Net transfers	-14.1	– as % of GDP	0.14
Current account balance	0.4		
– as % of GDP	0.3		
Capital balance	2.4		

Health and education

Health spending, % of GDP	8.0	Education spending, % of GDP	7.5
Doctors per 1,000 pop.	1.7	Enrolment, %: primary	76
Hospital beds per 1,000 pop.	2.3	secondary	61
Improved-water source access, % of pop.	95	tertiary	16

Society

No. of households	3.2m	Colour TVs per 100 households	97.3
Av. no. per household	6.3	Telephone lines per 100 pop.	13.0
Marriages per 1,000 pop.	3.1	Mobile telephone subscribers per 100 pop.	4.0
Divorces per 1,000 pop.	...	Computers per 100 pop.	5.7
Cost of living, Dec. 1999 New York = 100	72	Internet hosts per 100 pop.	0.3

a 1998
b % of workers, 1994.
c 1997

SINGAPORE

Area	639 sq km	Capital	Singapore
Arable as % of total land	2	Currency	Singapore dollar (S$)

People

Population	3.2m	Life expectancy: men	75.9 yrs
Pop. per sq km	6,384	women	80.3 yrs
Av. ann. growth		Adult literacy	91.4%
in pop. 1995–2000	2.90%	Fertility rate (per woman)	1.6
Pop. under 15	21.9%	Urban population	100.0%
Pop. over 65	10.6%		*per 1,000 pop.*
No. of men per 100 women	101.5	Crude birth rate	10.8
Human Development Index	88.1	Crude death rate	5.3

The economy

GDP	S$144bn	GDP per head	$26,360
GDP	$84.9bn	GDP per head in purchasing	
Av. ann. growth in real		power parity (USA=100)	69.9
GDP 1990–99	8.0%	Economic freedom index	1.55

Origins of GDP		**Components of GDP**	
	% of total		*% of total*
Agriculture	0.2	Private consumption	40.4
Industry, of which:	35.7	Public consumption	9.7
manufacturing	25.8	Investment	32.8
Services	64.1	Exports less imports	19.0

Structure of employment

	% of total		*% of labour force*
Agriculture	0	Unemployed 1999	4.6
Industry	29	Av. ann. rate 1990–99	2.8
Services	71		

Energy

	m TCE		
Total output	...	% output exported	...
Total consumption	35.382	% consumption imported[a]	345.4
Consumption per head,			
kg coal equivalent	10,324		

Inflation and finance

Consumer price			*av. ann. increase 1994–99*
inflation 2000	1.4%	Narrow money (M1)	5.9%
Av. ann. inflation 1990–2000	1.8%	Broad money	13.2%
Money market rate, 2000	2.57%		

Exchange rates

	end 2000		*December 2000*
S$ per $	1.73	Effective rates	1995 = 100
S$ per SDR	2.26	– nominal	103.5
S$ per euro	1.61	– real	97.5

Trade

Principal exports	*$bn fob*	**Principal imports**	*$bn cif*
Machinery & equipment	75.3	Machinery & equipment	78.6
Chemicals	9.0	Mineral fuels	10.0
Mineral fuels	9.0	Manufactured products	8.8
Manufactured products	8.5	Chemicals	6.6
Agric. products & foodstuffs	1.8	Agric. products & foodstuffs	2.9
Crude materials	0.9	Crude minerals	0.9
Total incl. others	**114.7**	Total incl. others	**111.2**

Main export destinations	*% of total*	**Main origins of imports**	*% of total*
United States	19.2	United States	17.0
Malaysia	16.6	Japan	16.6
Hong Kong	7.7	Malaysia	15.6
Japan	7.4	China	5.1
Taiwan	4.8	Thailand	4.7
Thailand	4.4	Taiwan	4.0
China	3.4	Germany	3.2

Balance of payments, reserves and debt[b], $bn

Visible exports fob	115.6	Overall balance	4.2
Visible imports fob	-104.3	Change in reserves	1.9
Trade balance	11.3	Level of reserves	
Invisibles inflows	39.1	end Dec.	76.8
Invisibles outflows	-28.0	No. months of import cover	7.0
Net transfers	-1.2	Foreign debt	10.7
Current account balance	21.3	– as % of GDP	12.6
– as % of GDP	25.0	Debt service	3.2
Capital balance	-17.9	Debt service ratio	2.1

Health and education

Health spending, % of GDP	3.2	Education spending, % of GDP	3.0
Doctors per 1,000 pop.	1.4	Enrolment, %: primary	94
Hospital beds per 1,000 pop.	3.6	secondary	74
Improved-water source access,		tertiary	39
% of pop.	100		

Society

No. of households	0.9m	Colour TVs per 100 households	98.4
Av. no. per household	4.1	Telephone lines per 100 pop.	48.2
Marriages per 1,000 pop.	6.6	Mobile telephone subscribers	
Divorces per 1,000 pop.	1.9	per 100 pop.	60.8
Cost of living, Dec. 1999		Computers per 100 pop.	48.3
New York = 100	97	Internet hosts per 100 pop.	54.5

a Energy trade data are distorted by transitory and oil refining activities.
b 1997

SLOVAKIA

Area	49,035 sq km	Capital	Bratislava
Arable as % of total land	31	Currency	Koruna (Kc)

People

Population	5.4m	Life expectancy: men	69.8 yrs
Pop. per sq km	110	women	77.6 yrs
Av. ann. growth		Adult literacy	99.0%
in pop. 1995–2000	0.13%	Fertility rate (per woman)	1.4
Pop. under 15	19.5%	Urban population	57.4%
Pop. over 65	15.4%		*per 1,000 pop.*
No. of men per 100 women	95.0	Crude birth rate	10.2
Human Development Index	82.5	Crude death rate	9.8

The economy

GDP	Kc815bn	GDP per head	$3,650
GDP	$19.7bn	GDP per head in purchasing	
Av. ann. growth in real		power parity (USA=100)	32.7
GDP 1990–99	1.8%	Economic freedom index	2.85

Origins of GDP		**Components of GDP**	
	% of total		*% of total*
Agriculture	4.5	Private consumption	53.5
Industry, of which:	35.1	Public consumption	20.0
manufacturing	...	Investment	31.9
Services	60.4	Exports	61.5
		Imports	-66.9

Structure of employment

	% of total		*% of labour force*
Agriculture	7	Unemployed 1999	16.2
Industry	37	Av. ann. rate 1991–99	12.1
Services	56		

Energy

	m TCE		
Total output	6.603	% output exported	48.1
Total consumption	22.629	% consumption imported	93.3
Consumption per head,			
kg coal equivalent	4,212		

Inflation and finance

Consumer price			*av. ann. increase 1994–99*
inflation 2000	12.0%	Narrow money (M1)	4.3%
Av. ann. inflation 1990–2000	15.0%	Broad money	11.9%
Deposit rate, 2000	8.45%		

Exchange rates

	end 2000		*December 2000*
Kc per $	51.32	Effective rates	1995 = 100
Kc per SDR	66.74	– nominal	89.65
Kc per euro	47.63	– real	105.59

Trade

Principal exports		Principal imports	
	$bn fob		*$bn fob*
Machinery & transport equipment	4.0	Machinery & transport equipment	4.3
Intermediate manufactured goods	2.8	Intermediate manufactured goods	2.1
Other manufactured goods	1.3	Fuels	1.5
Chemicals	0.8	Chemicals	1.3
Fuels	0.5		
Total incl. others	**10.2**	Total incl. others	**11.3**

Main export destinations		Main origins of imports	
	% of total		*% of total*
Germany	27.8	Germany	26.0
Czech Republic	18.1	Czech Republic	16.6
Italy	8.9	Russia	11.9
Austria	8.0	Italy	7.1
EU15	59.7	EU15	51.4

Balance of payments, reserves and debt, $bn

Visible exports fob	10.2	Overall balance	0.8
Visible imports fob	-11.3	Change in reserves	0.5
Trade balance	-1.1	Level of reserves	
Invisibles inflows	2.1	end Dec.	3.7
Invisibles outflows	-2.4	No. months of import cover	3.3
Net transfers	0.2	Foreign debt	9.1
Current account balance	-1.2	– as % of GDP	47
– as % of GDP	-5.9	Debt service paid	1.7
Capital balance	2.0	Debt service ratio	14

Health and education

Health spending, % of GDP	7.2	Education spending, % of GDP	5.0
Doctors per 1,000 pop.	3.0	Enrolment, %: primary	102
Hospital beds per 1,000 pop.	7.5	secondary	94
Improved-water source access,		tertiary	22
% of pop.	100		

Society

No. of households	1.4m	Colour TVs per 100 households	85.7
Av. no. per household	3.9	Telephone lines per 100 pop.	30.7
Marriages per 1,000 pop.	5.0	Mobile telephone subscribers	
Divorces per 1,000 pop.	1.6	per 100 pop.	17.0
Cost of living, Dec. 1999		Computers per 100 pop.	10.9
New York = 100	...	Internet hosts per 100 pop.	6.8

SLOVENIA

Area	20,253 sq km	Capital	Ljubljana
Arable as % of total land	12	Currency	Tolars (SIT)

People

Population	2.0m	Life expectancy: men	72.3 yrs
Pop. per sq km	99	women	79.6 yrs
Av. ann. growth		Adult literacy	99.5%
in pop. 1995–2000	-0.02%	Fertility rate (per woman)	1.2
Pop. under 15	15.9%	Urban population	50.4%
Pop. over 65	19.2%		*per 1,000 pop.*
No. of men per 100 women	94.5	Crude birth rate	8.2
Human Development Index	86.1	Crude death rate	9.9

The economy

GDP	SIT3,648bn	GDP per head	$10,100
GDP	$20.0bn	GDP per head in purchasing	
Av. ann. growth in real		power parity (USA=100)	50.3
GDP 1990–99	2.4%	Economic freedom index	2.90

Origins of GDP		**Components of GDP**	
	% of total		*% of total*
Agriculture	3.7	Private consumption	55.7
Industry, of which:	38.4	Public consumption	20.6
manufacturing	27.9	Investment	28.3
Services	57.8	Exports	52.7
		Imports	-57.1

Structure of employment

	% of total		*% of labour force*
Agriculture	12	Unemployed 1999	7.4
Industry	40	Av. ann. rate 1990–99	7.9
Services	48		

Energy

	m TCE		
Total output	3.802	% output exported	8.4
Total consumption	8.805	% consumption imported	62.5
Consumption per head,			
kg coal equivalent	4,414		

Inflation and finance

Consumer price			*av. ann. increase 1994–99*
inflation 2000	10.9%	Narrow money (M1)	22.6%
Av. ann. inflation 1990–2000	36.2%	Broad money	22.1%
Money market rate, 2000	6.95%		

Exchange rates

	end 2000		*December 2000*
SIT per $	227.4	Effective rates	1995 = 100
SIT per SDR	296.3	– nominal	...
SIT per euro	211.5	– real	...

Trade

Principal exports	$bn fob	Principal imports	$bn fob
Manufactures	4.0	Machinery & transport equipment	3.7
Machinery & transport equipment	3.0	Manufactures	3.4
Chemicals	0.9	Chemicals	1.2
Food & live animals	0.2	Food & live animals	0.5
Total incl. others	**8.6**	Total incl. others	**9.9**

Main export destinations	% of total	Main origins of imports	% of total
Germany	30.7	Germany	20.6
Italy	13.8	Italy	16.7
Croatia	7.9	France	10.9
Austria	7.3	Austria	8.0
France	5.7	Croatia	4.4

Balance of payments, reserves and debt[a], $bn

Visible exports fob	8.6	Overall balance	-0.1
Visible imports fob	-9.9	Change in reserves	-0.5
Trade balance	-1.2	Level of reserves end Dec.	3.2
Invisibles inflows	3.3	No. months of import cover	3.2
Invisibles outflows	-2.0	Foreign debt	5.4
Net transfers	0.1	– as % of GDP	26.9
Current account balance	-0.8	Debt service paid	0.8
– as % of GDP	-3.9	Debt service ratio	7.7
Capital balance	0.7		

Health and education

Health spending, % of GDP	7.6	Education spending, % of GDP	5.7
Doctors per 1,000 pop.	2.1	Enrolment, %: primary	98
Hospital beds per 1,000 pop.	5.7	secondary	92
Improved-water source access, % of pop.	100	tertiary	36

Society

No. of households	0.5m	Colour TVs per 100 households	90.5
Av. no. per household	3.8	Telephone lines per 100 pop.	37.8
Marriages per 1,000 pop.	3.7	Mobile telephone subscribers per 100 pop.	30.9
Divorces per 1,000 pop.	1.1	Computers per 100 pop.	25.1
Cost of living, Dec. 1999 New York = 100	...	Internet hosts per 100 pop.	11.9

a 1996

SOUTH AFRICA

Area	1,225,815 sq km	Capital	Pretoria
Arable as % of total land	12	Currency	Rand (R)

People

Population	42.1m	Life expectancy: men	46.5 yrs
Pop. per sq km	34	women	48.3 yrs
Av. ann. growth		Adult literacy	84.0%
in pop. 1995–2000	1.57%	Fertility rate (per woman)	3.1
Pop. under 15	34.0%	Urban population	55.0%
Pop. over 65	5.7%		*per 1,000 pop.*
No. of men per 100 women	96.5	Crude birth rate	24.6
Human Development Index	69.7	Crude death rate	17.1

The economy

GDP	R796bn	GDP per head	$3,110
GDP	$131.1bn	GDP per head in purchasing	
Av. ann. growth in real		power parity (USA=100)	27.3
GDP 1990–99	1.9%	Economic freedom index	3.05

Origins of GDP		**Components of GDP**	
	% of total		*% of total*
Agriculture	4.5	Private consumption	62.6
Industry, of which:	29.3	Public consumption	19.2
manufacturing	19.9	Investment	15.1
Services	66.2	Exports	25.4
		Imports	-22.9

Structure of employment

	% of total		*% of labour force*
Agriculture	9	Unemployed 1997	5.4
Industry	25	Av. ann. rate 1994–97	4.9
Services	66		

Energy

	m TCE		
Total output	184.144	% output exported	39.0
Total consumption	127.739	% consumption imported	16.9
Consumption per head,			
kg coal equivalent	2,847		

Inflation and finance

Consumer price			*av. ann. increase 1994–99*
inflation 2000	5.3%	Narrow money (M1)	22.4%
Av. ann. inflation 1990–2000	8.9%	Broad money	14.5%
Money market rate, 2000	9.54%		

Exchange rates

	end 2000		*December 2000*
R per $	7.57	Effective rates	1995 = 100
R per SDR	9.86	– nominal	60.8
R per euro	7.04	– real	78.5

Trade

Principal exports[a]	$bn fob	Principal imports[a]	$bn cif
Metals & metal products	6.3	Machinery & appliances	8.9
Gold	6.0	Mineral products	3.7
Diamonds	2.9	Chemicals	3.4
Machinery & transport equipment	2.6	Transport & equipment	1.7
Total incl. others	**23.5**	Total incl. others	**28.4**

Main export destinations[b]	% of total	Main origins of imports[b]	% of total
United States	8.1	United States	13.1
Japan	6.5	Germany	13.0
Germany	6.1	United Kingdom	9.2
United Kingdom	6.0	Japan	6.5
Italy	5.8		

Balance of payments, reserves and debt, $bn

Visible exports fob	28.6	Overall balance	4.2
Visible imports fob	-24.5	Change in reserves	2.0
Trade balance	4.2	Level of reserves end Dec.	7.5
Invisibles inflows	6.6	No. months of import cover	2.6
Invisibles outflows	-10.4	Foreign debt	24.2
Net transfers	-0.9	– as % of GDP	19
Current account balance	-0.6	Debt service	4.8
– as % of GDP	-0.4	Debt service ratio	14
Capital balance	3.6		

Health and education

Health spending, % of GDP	7.1	Education spending, % of GDP	7.9
Doctors per 1,000 pop.	0.6	Enrolment, %: primary	133
Hospital beds per 1,000 pop.	...	secondary	95
Improved-water source access, % of pop.	86	tertiary	17

Society

No. of households	8.5m	Colour TVs per 100 households	62.6
Av. no. per household	5.6	Telephone lines per 100 pop.	12.5
Marriages per 1,000 pop.	4.0	Mobile telephone subscribers per 100 pop.	12.0
Divorces per 1,000 pop.	0.9	Computers per 100 pop.	6.2
Cost of living, Dec. 1999 New York = 100	51	Internet hosts per 100 pop.	4.5

a 1997
b 1998

SOUTH KOREA

Area	99,274 sq km	Capital	Seoul
Arable as % of total land	17	Currency	Won (W)

People

Population	46.8m	Life expectancy: men	71.8 yrs
Pop. per sq km	475	women	79.1 yrs
Av. ann. growth		Adult literacy	97.2%
in pop. 1995–2000	0.78%	Fertility rate (per woman)	1.5
Pop. under 15	20.8%	Urban population	81.0%
Pop. over 65	11.0%		*per 1,000 pop.*
No. of men per 100 women	101	Crude birth rate	12.7
Human Development Index	85.4	Crude death rate	5.9

The economy

GDP	W484trn	GDP per head	$8,690
GDP	$406.9bn	GDP per head in purchasing	
Av. ann. growth in real		power parity (USA=100)	48.7
GDP 1990–99	5.7%	Economic freedom index	2.25

Origins of GDP		**Components of GDP**	
	% of total		*% of total*
Agriculture	5.0	Private consumption	55.7
Industry, of which:	43.6	Public consumption	10.1
manufacturing	31.8	Investment	26.9
Services	51.4	Exports	42.1
		Imports	-35.3

Structure of employment

	% of total		*% of labour force*
Agriculture	11	Unemployed 1999	6.3
Industry	31	Av. ann. rate 1990–99	3.2
Services	58		

Energy

	m TCE		
Total output	32.248	% output exported	117.5
Total consumption	210.559	% consumption imported	121.6
Consumption per head,			
kg coal equivalent	4,604		

Inflation and finance

Consumer price			*av. ann. increase 1994–99*
inflation 2000	2.3%	Narrow money (M1)	6.4%
Av. ann. inflation 1990–2000	5.1%	Broad money	19.8%
Money market rate, 2000	5.2%		

Exchange rates

	end 2000		*December 2000*
W per $	1,237	Effective rates	1995 = 100
W per SDR	1,608	– nominal	...
W per euro	1,150	– real	...

Trade

Principal exports	$bn fob	Principal imports	$bn cif
Electronic products	45.8	Electrical machinery	31.7
Machinery	11.6	Mineral fuels & lubricants	22.7
Metal goods	10.3	Other machinery & equipment	13.5
Chemicals	9.4	Chemicals	9.8
Motor vehicles	9.4	Consumer durables	6.4
Total incl. others	**143.7**	Total incl. others	**119.8**

Main export destinations	% of total	Main origins of imports	% of total
United States	20.5	United States	20.8
Japan	11.0	Japan	20.2
China	9.5	China	7.4
Hong Kong	6.3	Saudi Arabia	4.7
Taiwan	4.4	Australia	3.9

Balance of payments, reserves and debt, $bn

Visible exports fob	145.2	Overall balance	33.3
Visible imports fob	-116.8	Change in reserves	22.0
Trade balance	28.4	Level of reserves	
Invisibles inflows	29.8	end Dec.	74.1
Invisibles outflows	-35.6	No. months of import cover	5.8
Net transfers	1.5	Foreign debt	129.8
Current account balance	24.5	– as % of GDP	32
– as % of GDP	6.0	Debt service paid	43.0
Capital balance	12.3	Debt service ratio	25

Health and education

Health spending, % of GDP	5.1	Education spending, % of GDP	3.7
Doctors per 1,000 pop.	1.3	Enrolment, %: primary	94
Hospital beds per 1,000 pop.	5.1	secondary	102
Improved-water source access,		tertiary	68
% of pop.	92		

Society

No. of households	13.9m	Colour TVs per 100 households	92.5
Av. no. per household	3.3	Telephone lines per 100 pop.	46.4
Marriages per 1,000 pop.	6.8	Mobile telephone subscribers	
Divorces per 1,000 pop.	1.5	per 100 pop.	56.7
Cost of living, Dec. 1999		Computers per 100 pop.	19.0
New York = 100	102	Internet hosts per 100 pop.	8.5

a 1995

SPAIN

Area	504,782 sq km	Capital	Madrid
Arable as % of total land	29	Currency	Peseta (Pta)

People

Population	39.4m	Life expectancy: men	75.4 yrs
Pop. per sq km	78	women	82.3 yrs
Av. ann. growth		Adult literacy	97.2%
in pop. 1995–2000	0.09%	Fertility rate (per woman)	1.1
Pop. under 15	14.7%	Urban population	77.6%
Pop. over 65	21.8%		*per 1,000 pop.*
No. of men per 100 women	95.7	Crude birth rate	8.8
Human Development Index	89.9	Crude death rate	9.8

The economy

GDP	Pta93,010bn	GDP per head	$15,120
GDP	$595.9bn	GDP per head in purchasing	
Av. ann. growth in real		power parity (USA=100)	55.9
GDP 1990–99	2.2%	Economic freedom index	2.40

Origins of GDP		**Components of GDP**	
	% of total		*% of total*
Agriculture	4.2	Private consumption	59.3
Industry, of which:	30.5	Public consumption	17.3
manufacturing	...	Investment	24.7
Services	65.3	Exports	27.3
		Imports	-28.7

Structure of employment

	% of total		*% of labour force*
Agriculture	8	Unemployed 1999	15.9
Industry	30	Av. ann. rate 1990–99	19.8
Services	62		

Energy

	m TCE		
Total output	39.345	% output exported[a]	19.7
Total consumption	132.873	% consumption imported[a]	91.3
Consumption per head,			
kg coal equivalent	3,354		

Inflation and finance

Consumer price			*av. ann. increase 1994–99*
inflation 2000	3.5%	Euro area:	
Av. ann. inflation 1990–2000	3.9%	Narrow money (M1)	7.9%
Money market rate, 2000	4.11%	Broad money	5.9%

Exchange rates

	end 2000		*July 2000*
Pta per $	180.2	Effective rates	1995 = 100
Pta per SDR	234.3	– nominal	92.2
Pta per euro	166.4	– real	106.1

Trade

Principal exports	$bn fob	Principal imports	$bn cif
Raw materials & intermediate products	47.6	Raw materials & intermediate products (excl. fuels)	68.4
Consumer goods	45.1	Consumer goods	39.2
Capital goods	15.5	Capital goods	27.9
Energy products	2.2	Energy products	9.7
Total incl. others	**110.4**	Total incl. others	**145.2**

Main export destinations	% of total	Main origins of imports	% of total
France	19.5	France	18.1
Germany	13.2	Germany	15.7
Portugal	9.8	Italy	9.2
Italy	9.1	United Kingdom	7.5
United Kingdom	8.4	United States	5.4
EU15	72.3	EU15	67.7

Balance of payments, reserves and aid, $bn

Visible exports fob	111.0	Capital balance	-4.2
Visible imports fob	-140.2	Overall balance	-22.8
Trade balance	-29.2	Change in reserves	-22.8
Invisibles inflows	65.8	Level of reserves end Dec.	38.0
Invisibles outflows	-52.4	No. months of import cover	2.4
Net transfers	3.2	Aid given	1.36
Current account balance	-12.6	– as % of GDP	0.24
– as % of GDP	-2.1		

Health and education

Health spending, % of GDP	7.1	Education spending, % of GDP	5.0
Doctors per 1,000 pop.	4.2	Enrolment, %: primary	107
Hospital beds per 1,000 pop.	3.9	secondary	120
Improved-water source access, % of pop.	...	tertiary	53

Society

No. of households	14.8m	Colour TVs per 100 households	98.1
Av. no. per household	2.7	Telephone lines per 100 pop.	42.1
Marriages per 1,000 pop.	5.2	Mobile telephone subscribers per 100 pop.	30.6
Divorces per 1,000 pop.	0.8	Computers per 100 pop.	14.3
Cost of living, Dec. 1999 New York = 100	67	Internet hosts per 100 pop.	16.8

a Energy trade data are distorted by transitory and oil refining activities.

SWEDEN

Area	449,964 sq km	Capital	Stockholm
Arable as % of total land	7	Currency	Swedish krona (Skr)

People

Population	8.9m	Life expectancy: men	77.6 yrs
Pop. per sq km	22	women	82.6 yrs
Av. ann. growth		Adult literacy	99.0%
in pop. 1995–2000	0.03%	Fertility rate (per woman)	1.5
Pop. under 15	18.2%	Urban population	83.3%
Pop. over 65	22.4%		*per 1,000 pop.*
No. of men per 100 women	98.4	Crude birth rate	8.2
Human Development Index	92.6	Crude death rate	10.6

The economy

GDP	Skr1,972bn	GDP per head	$26,950
GDP	$238.7bn	GDP per head in purchasing	
Av. ann. growth in real		power parity (USA=100)	69.4
GDP 1990–99	1.6%	Economic freedom index	2.25

Origins of GDP		**Components of GDP**	
	% of total		*% of total*
Agriculture	2.8	Private consumption	50.5
Industry, of which:	26.5	Public consumption	27.0
manufacturing	...	Investment	16.3
Services	70.7	Exports	43.8
		Imports	-38.2

Structure of employment

	% of total		*% of labour force*
Agriculture	3	Unemployed 1999	5.6
Industry	26	Av. ann. rate 1990–99	6.2
Services	71		

Energy

	m TCE		
Total output	34.912	% output exported	44.5
Total consumption	57.487	% consumption imported	74.6
Consumption per head,			
kg coal equivalent	6,491		

Inflation and finance

Consumer price			*av. ann. increase 1994–99*
inflation 2000	1.0%	Narrow money (M1)	...
Av. ann. inflation 1990–2000	2.3%	Broad money	4.2%
Money market rate, 2000	3.81%		

Exchange rates

	end 2000		*July 2000*
Skr per $	9.54	Effective rates	1995 = 100
Skr per SDR	12.42	– nominal	103.2
Skr per euro	8.83	– real	98.2

Trade

Principal exports	$bn fob	Principal imports	$bn cif
Electrical machinery & transport equipment	29.5	Electrical machinery & transport equipment	21.3
Non-electrical machinery	24.6	Non-electrical machinery	7.7
Wood & paper products	10.4	Chemicals	7.1
Chemicals	8.0	Food, beverages & tobacco	4.5
Total incl. others	**84.7**	Total incl. others	**68.4**

Main export destinations	% of total	Main origins of imports	% of total
Germany	10.9	Germany	17.7
United Kingdom	9.5	United Kingdom	10.3
United States	9.4	Norway	7.9
Norway	8.0	Denmark	6.9
Denmark	5.7	France	6.3
EU15	55.1	EU15	67.2

Balance of payments, reserves and aid, $bn

Visible exports fob	87.6	Capital balance	-3.6
Visible imports fob	-71.9	Overall balance	1.9
Trade balance	15.7	Change in reserves	1.3
Invisibles inflows	39.8	Level of reserves end Dec.	16.7
Invisibles outflows	-45.9	No. months of import cover	1.7
Net transfers	-3.6	Aid given	1.63
Current account balance	6.0	– as % of GDP	0.72
– as % of GDP	2.5		

Health and education

Health spending, % of GDP	8.0	Education spending, % of GDP	8.3
Doctors per 1,000 pop.	3.1	Enrolment, %: primary	107
Hospital beds per 1,000 pop.	3.8	secondary[a]	140
Improved-water source access, % of pop.	100	tertiary	50

Society

No. of households	4.0m	Colour TVs per 100 households	97.1
Av. no. per household	2.2	Telephone lines per 100 pop.	66.5
Marriages per 1,000 pop.	4.7	Mobile telephone subscribers per 100 pop.	58.3
Divorces per 1,000 pop.	2.3	Computers per 100 pop.	50.7
Cost of living, Dec. 1999 New York = 100	85	Internet hosts per 100 pop.	86.3

a Includes training for unemployed.

SWITZERLAND

Area	41,293 sq km	Capital	Berne
Arable as % of total land	11	Currency	Swiss franc (SFr)

People

Population	7.1m	Life expectancy: men	75.9 yrs
Pop. per sq km	180	women	82.3 yrs
Av. ann. growth		Adult literacy	99.0%
in pop. 1995–2000	0.15%	Fertility rate (per woman)	1.4
Pop. under 15	16.7%	Urban population	67.7%
Pop. over 65	21.3%		*per 1,000 pop.*
No. of men per 100 women	97.8	Crude birth rate	8.5
Human Development Index	91.5	Crude death rate	9.8

The economy

GDP	SFr407bn	GDP per head	$36,310
GDP	$258.6bn	GDP per head in purchasing	
Av. ann. growth in real		power parity (USA=100)	90.1
GDP 1990–99	0.6%	Economic freedom index	1.90

Origins of GDP[a]	*% of total*	**Components of GDP**	*% of total*
Agriculture	1.6	Private consumption	60.3
Industry, of which:	33.8	Public consumption	14.5
manufacturing	...	Investment	20.0
Services	64.6	Exports	42.1
		Imports	-37.0

Structure of employment

	% of total		*% of labour force*
Agriculture	5	Unemployed 1999	3.1
Industry	27	Av. ann. rate 1990–99	3.0
Services	68		

Energy

	m TCE		
Total output	13.777	% output exported	29.3
Total consumption	32.758	% consumption imported	76.4
Consumption per head,			
kg coal equivalent	4,498		

Inflation and finance

Consumer price			*av. ann. increase 1996–99*
inflation 2000	1.6%	Narrow money (M1)	5.0%
Av. ann. inflation 1990–2000	1.9%	Broad money	4.9%
Money market rate, 2000	3.50%		

Exchange rates

	end 2000		*July 2000*
SFr per $	1.64	Effective rates	1995 = 100
SFr per SDR	2.13	– nominal	93.7
SFr per euro	1.53	– real	98.2

Trade

Principal exports	$bn fob	Principal imports	$bn cif
Chemicals	22.7	Machinery	18.0
Machinery	21.8	Chemicals	12.9
Precision instruments, watches & jewellery	11.7	Motor vehicles	9.6
Metals & metal manufactures	6.3	Agricultural products	6.4
Textiles & clothing	1.7	Metals & metals manufactures	6.1
Total incl. others	**76.3**	Total incl. others	**75.6**

Main export destinations	% of total	Main origins of imports	% of total
Germany	23.3	Germany	32.5
United States	11.4	France	12.5
France	9.4	Italy	10.2
Italy	8.0	United States	6.1
United Kingdom	5.4	Netherlands	5.2
Japan	3.6	United Kingdom	4.4
EU15	62.6	EU15	79.7

Balance of payments, reserves and aid, $bn

Visible exports fob	91.7	Capital balance	-38.0
Visible imports fob	-91.0	Overall balance	-2.7
Trade balance	0.7	Change in reserves	-4.7
Invisibles inflows	76.2	Level of reserves end Dec.	60.5
Invisibles outflows	-43.7	No. months of import cover	5.4
Net transfers	-4.2	Aid given	0.97
Current account balance	29.1	– as % of GDP	0.37
– as % of GDP	11.3		

Health and education

Health spending, % of GDP	10.4	Education spending, % of GDP	5.4
Doctors per 1,000 pop.	1.9	Enrolment, %: primary	97
Hospital beds per 1,000 pop.	18.1	secondary	100
Improved-water source access, % of pop.	100	tertiary	34

Society

No. of households	3.0m	Colour TVs per 100 households	97.0
Av. no. per household	2.5	Telephone lines per 100 pop.	69.4
Marriages per 1,000 pop.	5.2	Mobile telephone subscribers per 100 pop.	63.6
Divorces per 1,000 pop.	2.6	Computers per 100 pop.	50.3
Cost of living, Dec. 1999 New York = 100	96	Internet hosts per 100 pop.	64.8

a 1998

TAIWAN

Area	36,179 sq km	Capital	Taipei
Arable as % of total land	25	Currency	Taiwan dollar (T$)

People

Population	21.9m	Life expectancy: men	...
Pop. per sq km	612	women	...
Av. ann. growth		Adult literacy	...
in pop. 1995–98	0.87%	Fertility rate (per woman)	1.8
Pop. under 15	22.0%	Urban population	...
Pop. over 65	8.3%		*per 1,000 pop.*
No. of men per 100 women	105.2	Crude birth rate	12.9
Human Development Index	...	Crude death rate[a]	6.0

The economy

GDP	T$9,289bn	GDP per head	$13,200
GDP	$288.7bn	GDP per head in purchasing	
Av. ann. growth in real		power parity (USA=100)	66.2
GDP 1990–99	6.2%	Economic freedom index	2.10

Origins of GDP		**Components of GDP**	
	% of total		*% of total*
Agriculture	2.6	Private consumption	60.8
Industry, of which:	33.0	Public consumption	13.1
manufacturing	26.4	Investment	24.2
Services	64.4	Exports	47.2
		Imports	-45.4

Structure of employment

	% of total		*% of labour force*
Agriculture	8	Unemployed 1997	2.7
Industry	37	Av. ann. rate 1990–97	1.9
Services	55		

Energy

	m TCE		
Total output	...	% output exported	3.3
Total consumption	...	% consumption imported	76.7
Consumption per head, kg coal equivalent	...		

Inflation and finance

Consumer price			*av. ann. increase 1994–99*
inflation 2000	1.3%	Narrow money (M1)	2.1%
Av. ann. inflation 1990–2000	1.6%	Broad money	9.2%

Exchange rates

	end 2000		*December 2000*
T$ per $	33.2	Effective rates	1995 = 100
T$ per SDR	43.2	– nominal	...
T$ per euro	30.9	– real	...

Trade

Principal exports	$bn fob	Principal imports	$bn fob
Machinery & electrical equipment	64.2	Machinery & electrical equipment	50.6
Textiles & clothing	14.2	Chemicals	10.6
Base metals & manufactures	11.6	Metals	9.5
Plastics and rubber products	7.5	Precision instruments, clocks & watches	6.2
Vehicles, aircraft & ships	5.2	Crude petroleum	4.6
Total incl. others	**121.5**	Total incl. others	**110.6**

Main export destinations	% of total	Main origins of imports	% of total
United States	25.4	Japan	27.6
Hong Kong	21.4	United States	17.8
Japan	9.8	South Korea	6.5
Netherlands	3.5	Germany	4.8
Germany	3.4	Malaysia	3.5
Singapore	3.1	Australia	2.7
United Kingdom	3.1	Indonesia	2.1

Balance of payments, reserves and debt, $bn

Visible exports fob	121.1	Overall balance[c]	4.8
Visible imports fob	-106.1	Change in reserves	15.9
Trade balance	15.0	Level of reserves end Dec.	106.2
Invisibles inflows	24.3	No. months of import cover	9.5
Invisibles outflows	-28.7	Foreign debt	31.5
Net transfers	-2.2	– as % of GDP	11.0
Current account balance	8.4	Debt service paid	1.0
– as % of GDP	2.9	Debt service ratio	2.1
Capital balance[c]	1.6		

Health and education

Health spending, % of GDP	6.2	Education spending, % of GDP	...
Doctors per 1,000 pop.	0.4	Enrolment, %: primary	89
Hospital beds per 1,000 pop.	2.0	secondary	59
Improved-water source access, % of pop.	...	tertiary	21

Society

No. of households	6.2m	Colour TVs per 100 households	99.4
Av. no. per household	3.5	Telephone lines per 100 pop.	54.5
Marriages per 1,000 pop.	7.9	Mobile telephone subscribers per 100 pop.	52.2
Divorces per 1,000 pop.	1.8	Computers per 100 pop.	22.5
Cost of living, Dec. 1999 New York = 100	102	Internet hosts per 100 pop.	50.1

a 1995–2000.
b 1997
c 1998

THAILAND

Area	513,115 sq km	Capital	Bangkok
Arable as % of total land	33	Currency	Baht (Bt)

People

Population	61.7m	Life expectancy: men	67.9 yrs
Pop. per sq km	120	women	73.8 yrs
Av. ann. growth		Adult literacy	94.7%
in pop. 1995–2000	1.34%	Fertility rate (per woman)	2.1
Pop. under 15	26.7%	Urban population	21.6%
Pop. over 65	8.1%		*per 1,000 pop.*
No. of men per 100 women	98	Crude birth rate	17.7
Human Development Index	74.5	Crude death rate	6.2

The economy

GDP	Bt4,615bn	GDP per head	$2,020
GDP	$124.4bn	GDP per head in purchasing	
Av. ann. growth in real		power parity (USA=100)	18.6
GDP 1990–99	4.7%	Economic freedom index	2.20

Origins of GDP		**Components of GDP**	
	% of total		*% of total*
Agriculture	11.4	Private consumption	53.8
Industry, of which:	42.6	Public consumption	9.3
manufacturing	34.5	Investment	19.3
Services	46.0	Exports	58.0
		Imports	-41.1

Structure of employment

	% of total		*% of labour force*
Agriculture	48	Unemployed 1999	3.0
Industry	19	Av. ann. rate 1990–99	1.9
Services	33		

Energy

	m TCE		
Total output	41.761	% output exported	19.4
Total consumption	86.704	% consumption imported	68.0
Consumption per head,			
kg coal equivalent	1,451		

Inflation and finance

Consumer price		*av. ann. increase 1994–99*	
inflation 2000	1.6%	Narrow money (M1)	16.4%
Av. ann. inflation 1990–2000	4.5%	Broad money	12.1%
Money market rate, 2000	1.95%		

Exchange rates

	end 2000		*December 2000*
Bt per $	42.27	Effective rates	1995 = 100
Bt per SDR	55.07	– nominal	...
Bt per euro	39.31	– real	...

Trade

Principal exports		Principal imports	
	$bn fob		*$bn cif*
Computers & parts	9.2	Capital goods	24.0
Textiles & clothing	4.4	Raw materials & intermediates	14.1
Integrated circuits	3.0	Consumer goods	5.6
Rice	2.0	Petroleum & products	4.3
Total incl. others	**58.6**	Total incl. others	**50.4**

Main export destinations		Main origins of imports	
	% of total		*% of total*
United States	23.4	Japan	24.9
Japan	13.8	Singapore	11.0
Singapore	8.2	United States	10.9
Hong Kong	4.5	Malaysia	6.0
Netherlands	3.8	Germany	3.4

Balance of payments, reserves and debt, $bn

Visible exports fob	56.8	Overall balance	1.4
Visible imports fob	-42.8	Change in reserves	5.2
Trade balance	14.0	Level of reserves	
Invisibles inflows	17.7	end Dec.	34.8
Invisibles outflows	-19.7	No. months of import cover	6.7
Net transfers	0.4	Foreign debt	96.3
Current account balance	12.4	– as % of GDP	80
– as % of GDP	10.0	Debt service paid	16.4
Capital balance	-11.1	Debt service ratio	22

Health and education

Health spending, % of GDP	6.0	Education spending, % of GDP	4.8
Doctors per 1,000 pop.	0.4	Enrolment, %: primary	89
Hospital beds per 1,000 pop.	2.0	secondary	59
Improved-water source access,		tertiary	21
% of pop.	80		

Society

No. of households	13.4m	Colour TVs per 100 households	80.3
Av. no. per household	4.5	Telephone lines per 100 pop.	8.6
Marriages per 1,000 pop.	7.0	Mobile telephone subscribers	
Divorces per 1,000 pop.	1.2	per 100 pop.	3.8
Cost of living, Dec. 1999		Computers per 100 pop.	2.4
New York = 100	57	Internet hosts per 100 pop.	1.0

TURKEY

Area	779,452 sq km	Capital	Ankara
Arable as % of total land	32	Currency	Turkish Lira (L)

People

Population	64.3m	Life expectancy: men	68.0 yrs
Pop. per sq km	82	women	73.2 yrs
Av. ann. growth		Adult literacy	83.2%
in pop. 1995–2000	1.62%	Fertility rate (per woman)	2.7
Pop. under 15	30.0%	Urban population	74.0%
Pop. over 65	8.4%		*per 1,000 pop.*
No. of men per 100 women	102.0	Crude birth rate	20.1
Human Development Index	73.2	Crude death rate	6.2

The economy

GDP	L82,926trn	GDP per head	$2,890
GDP	$185.7bn	GDP per head in purchasing	
Av. ann. growth in real		power parity (USA=100)	20.2
GDP 1990–99	3.8%	Economic freedom index	2.90

Origins of GDP		**Components of GDP**	
	% of total		*% of total*
Agriculture	15.0	Private consumption	67.6
Industry, of which:	28.8	Public consumption	14.1
manufacturing	...	Investment	21.7
Services	56.2	Exports	21.6
		Imports	-25.0

Structure of employment

	% of total		*% of labour force*
Agriculture	42	Unemployed 1999	7.3
Industry	23	Av. ann. rate 1990–99	7.3
Services	35		

Energy

	m TCE		
Total output	28.983	% output exported	4.9
Total consumption	85.620	% consumption imported	74.3
Consumption per head,			
kg coal equivalent	1,350		

Inflation and finance

Consumer price			*av. ann. increase 1994–99*
inflation 2000	54.9%	Narrow money (M1)	79.9%
Av. ann. inflation 1990–2000	76.1%	Broad money	101.1%
Money market rate, 2000	56.72%		

Exchange rates

	end 2000		*December 2000*
L per $	673,385	Effective rates	1995 = 100
L per SDR	877,360	– nominal	...
L per euro	626,248	– real	...

Trade

Principal exports	$bn fob	Principal imports	$bn cif
Clothing & textiles	8.3	Machinery	11.5
Electrical machinery	1.6	Petroleum & products	5.4
Iron & steel	1.5	Vehicles	3.1
Vegetables, fruit & nuts	1.5	Iron & steel	2.1
Total incl. others	**26.6**	Total incl. others	**41.7**

Main export destinations	% of total	Main origins of imports	% of total
Germany	20.6	Germany	14.5
United States	9.2	Italy	7.8
United Kingdom	6.9	France	7.7
Italy	6.3	United States	7.6
France	5.9	Russia	5.8
EU15	53.9	EU15	52.6

Balance of payments, reserves and debt, $bn

Visible exports fob	29.3	Overall balance	5.2
Visible imports fob	-39.8	Change in reserves	3.9
Trade balance	-10.4	Level of reserves	
Invisibles inflows	18.7	end Dec.	24.4
Invisibles outflows	-14.8	No. months of import cover	5.4
Net transfers	5.2	Foreign debt	101.8
Current account balance	-1.4	– as % of GDP	54
– as % of GDP	-0.7	Debt service paid	13.8
Capital balance	4.7	Debt service ratio	26

Health and education

Health spending, % of GDP	5.8	Education spending, % of GDP	2.2
Doctors per 1,000 pop.	1.2	Enrolment, %: primary	107
Hospital beds per 1,000 pop.	2.5	secondary	58
Improved-water source access,		tertiary	21
% of pop.	83		

Society

No. of households	14.9m	Colour TVs per 100 households	66.7
Av. no. per household	4.3	Telephone lines per 100 pop.	27.8
Marriages per 1,000 pop.	8.0	Mobile telephone subscribers	
Divorces per 1,000 pop.	0.5	per 100 pop.	12.5
Cost of living, Dec. 1999		Computers per 100 pop.	3.8
New York = 100	61	Internet hosts per 100 pop.	1.8

UKRAINE

Area	603,700 sq km	Capital	Kiev
Arable as % of total land	57	Currency	Hryvnya (UAH)

People

Population	49.9m	Life expectancy: men	62.7 yrs
Pop. per sq km	83	women	73.5 yrs
Av. ann. growth		Adult literacy	98.0%
in pop. 1995–2000	-0.78%	Fertility rate (per woman)	1.2
Pop. under 15	17.8%	Urban population	68.0%
Pop. over 65	20.5%		*per 1,000 pop.*
No. of men per 100 women	87.2	Crude birth rate	8.1
Human Development Index	74.4	Crude death rate	15.4

The economy

GDP	UAH127.1bn	GDP per head	$770
GDP	$38.7bn	GDP per head in purchasing	
Av. ann. growth in real		power parity (USA=100)	10.5
GDP 1990–99	-10.7%	Economic freedom index	3.85

Origins of GDP		**Components of GDP**[a]	
	% of total		*% of total*
Agriculture	13	Private consumption	60.1
Industry, of which:	38	Public consumption	19.0
manufacturing	33	Investment	19.8
Services	49	Exports	52.6
		Imports	-51.5

Structure of employment[a]

	% of total		*% of labour force*
Agriculture	22.0	Unemployed 1999	11.9
Industry	22.8	Av. ann. rate 1995–99	9.1
Services	55.6		

Energy

	m TCE		
Total output	117.408	% output exported	5.8
Total consumption	220.931	% consumption imported	51.0
Consumption per head,			
kg coal equivalent	4,327		

Inflation and finance

Consumer price			*av. ann. increase 1994–99*
inflation 2000	28.2%	Narrow money (M1)	49.9%
Av. ann. inflation 1990–2000	240.2%	Broad money	46.4%
Money market rate, 2000	18.34%		

Exchange rates

	end 2000		*December 2000*
UAH per $	5.43	Effective rates	1995 = 100
UAH per SDR	7.08	– nominal	116.6
UAH per euro	5.05	– real	119.1

Trade

Principal exports	*$bn fob*	Principal imports	*$bn cif*
Metals	4.3	Fuels, mineral products	5.4
Food & agricultural produce	1.3	Machinery & transport equipment	2.3
Chemicals	1.2	Chemicals	1.5
Machinery & transport equipment	1.2	Food & agricultural produce	0.9
Total incl. others	**11.6**	Total incl. others	**11.8**

Main export destinations	*% of total*	Main origins of imports	*% of total*
Russia	20.7	Russia	47.6
China	6.3	Germany	8.0
Turkey	5.8	Turkmenistan	4.1
Germany	4.8	United States	3.4

Balance of payments, reserves and debt, $bn

Visible exports fob	13.2	Overall balance	-0.2
Visible imports fob	-12.9	Change in reserves	0.3
Trade balance	0.2	Level of reserves end Dec.	1.1
Invisibles inflows	4.0	No. months of import cover	0.8
Invisibles outflows	-3.2	Foreign debt	14.1
Net transfers	0.7	– as % of GDP	38
Current account balance	1.7	Debt service paid	2.8
– as % of GDP	4.3	Debt service ratio	16
Capital balance	-0.9		

Health and education

Health spending, % of GDP	5.1	Education spending, % of GDP	7.3
Doctors per 1,000 pop.	4.5	Enrolment, %: primary	...
Hospital beds per 1,000 pop.	11.8	secondary	...
Improved-water source access, % of pop.	...	tertiary	42

Society

No. of households	9.0m	Colour TVs per 100 households	71.4
Av. no. per household	5.7	Telephone lines per 100 pop.	19.9
Marriages per 1,000 pop.	6.1	Mobile telephone subscribers per 100 pop.	0.4
Divorces per 1,000 pop.	3.6	Computers per 100 pop.	1.6
Cost of living, Dec. 1999 New York = 100	56	Internet hosts per 100 pop.	0.8

a 1997
a 1996

UNITED KINGDOM

Area	242,534 sq km	Capital	London
Arable as % of total land	26	Currency	Pound (£)

People

Population	59.1m	Life expectancy: men	75.7 yrs
Pop. per sq km	246	women	80.7 yrs
Av. ann. growth		Adult literacy	99.0%
in pop. 1995–2000	0.27%	Fertility rate (per woman)	1.7
Pop. under 15	19.0%	Urban population	89.5%
Pop. over 65	20.6%		*per 1,000 pop.*
No. of men per 100 women	97	Crude birth rate	10.6
Human Development Index	91.8	Crude death rate	10.5

The economy

GDP	£891bn	GDP per head	$24,390
GDP	$1,442bn	GDP per head in purchasing	
Av. ann. growth in real		power parity (USA=100)	69.6
GDP 1990–99	2.5%	Economic freedom index	1.80

Origins of GDP		**Components of GDP**	
	% of total		*% of total*
Agriculture	1.7	Private consumption	65.9
Industry, of which:	24.9	Public consumption	18.3
manufacturing	19.9	Investment	17.6
Services	73.4	Exports	25.8
		Imports	-27.5

Structure of employment

	% of total		*% of labour force*
Agriculture	2	Unemployed 1999	6.0
Industry	27	Av. ann. rate 1990–99	8.1
Services	71		

Energy

	m TCE		
Total output	381.896	% output exported	38.7
Total consumption	320.087	% consumption imported	32.9
Consumption per head,			
kg coal equivalent	5,448		

Inflation and finance

Consumer price			*av. ann. increase 1994–99*
inflation 2000	2.9%	Narrow money (M0)	7.0%
Av. ann. inflation 1990–2000	3.0%	Broad money	7.5%
Money market rate, 2000	5.71%		

Exchange rates

	end 2000		*July 2000*
£ per $	0.67	Effective rates	1995 = 100
£ per SDR	0.87	– nominal	124.5
£ per euro	0.62	– real	152.7

Trade

Principal exports	*$bn fob*	Principal imports	*$bn cif*
Finished manufactured products	163.7	Finished manufactured products	197.7
Chemicals	38.1	Semi-manufactured products	45.2
Semi-manufactured products	33.5	Chemicals	31.5
Food, beverages & tobacco	16.1	Food, beverages & tobacco	28.1
Fuels	14.9	Basic materials	9.4
Total incl. others	**267.3**	Total incl. others	**310.0**

Main export destinations	*% of total*	Main origins of imports	*% of total*
United States	14.8	Germany	13.5
Germany	12.2	United States	12.9
France	10.0	France	9.1
Netherlands	7.9	Netherlands	6.9
Ireland	6.4	Japan	4.9
EU15	58.0	EU15	53.0

Balance of payments, reserves and aid, $bn

Visible exports fob	268.9	Capital balance	18.8
Visible imports fob	-311.3	Overall balance	-1.0
Trade balance	-42.4	Change in reserves	3.0
Invisibles inflows	285.1	Level of reserves end Dec.	41.8
Invisibles outflows	-252.1	No. months of import cover	0.9
Net transfers	-6.7	Aid given	3.40
Current account balance	-16.0	– as % of GDP	0.25
– as % of GDP	-1.1		

Health and education

Health spending, % of GDP	6.7	Education spending, % of GDP	5.3
Doctors per 1,000 pop.	1.7	Enrolment, %: primary	116
Hospital beds per 1,000 pop.	4.2	secondary[a]	129
Improved-water source access, % of pop.	100	tertiary	52

Society

No. of households	22.0m	Colour TVs per 100 households	98.3
Av. no. per household	2.7	Telephone lines per 100 pop.	56.7
Marriages per 1,000 pop.	10.7	Mobile telephone subscribers per 100 pop.	67.0
Divorces per 1,000 pop.	3.4	Computers per 100 pop.	33.8
Cost of living, Dec. 1999 New York = 100	99	Internet hosts per 100 pop.	38.8

a Includes training for unemployed.

UNITED STATES

Area	9,372,610 sq km	Capital	Washington DC
Arable as % of total land	19	Currency	US dollar ($)

People

Population	272.9m	Life expectancy: men	74.6 yrs
Pop. per sq km	29	women	80.4 yrs
Av. ann. growth		Adult literacy	99.0%
in pop. 1995–2000	1.05%	Fertility rate (per woman)	2.0
Pop. under 15	21.7%	Urban population	77.2%
Pop. over 65	16.1%		*per 1,000 pop.*
No. of men per 100 women	97.2	Crude birth rate	13.0
Human Development Index	92.9	Crude death rate	8.4

The economy

GDP	$9,152bn	GDP per head	$33,540
Av. ann. growth in real		GDP per head in purchasing	
GDP 1990–99	3.3%	power parity (USA=100)	100
		Economic freedom index	1.75

Origins of GDP		**Components of GDP**	
	% of total		*% of total*
Agriculture	1.3	Private consumption	67.4
Industry, of which:	21.8	Public consumption	17.6
manufacturing	16.1	Investment	17.7
Services[a]	76.9	Exports	10.7
		Imports	-13.4

Structure of employment

	% of total		*% of labour force*
Agriculture	3	Unemployed 1999	4.2
Industry	24	Av. ann. rate 1990–99	5.8
Services	73		

Energy

	m TCE		
Total output	2,506.364	% output exported	5.0
Total consumption	3,123.599	% consumption imported	27.1
Consumption per head,			
kg coal equivalent	11,493		

Inflation and finance

Consumer price			*av. ann. increase 1994–99*
inflation 2000	3.4%	Narrow money (M1)	-0.5%
Av. ann. inflation 1990–2000	2.8%	Broad money	8.4%
Treasury bill rate, 2000	5.84%		

Exchange rates

	end 2000		*July 2000*
$ per SDR	1.30	Effective rates	1995 = 100
$ per euro	0.93	– nominal	120.2
		– real	130.7

Trade

Principal exports	$bn fob	Principal imports	$bn fob
Capital goods, excl. vehicles	311.4	Capital goods, excl. vehicles	297.1
Industrial supplies	147.0	Consumer goods, excl. vehicles	239.5
Consumer goods, excl. vehicles	80.8	Industrial supplies	222.0
Vehicles & products	75.8	Vehicles & products	179.4
Food & beverages	45.5	Food & beverages	43.6
Total incl. others	**695.8**	Total incl. others	**1,024.6**

Main export destinations	% of total	Main origins of imports	% of total
Canada	23.9	Canada	19.3
Mexico	12.5	Japan	12.8
Japan	8.3	Mexico	10.7
United Kingdom	5.5	China	8.0
Germany	3.9	Germany	5.4
EU15	21.8	EU15	19.1

Balance of payments, reserves and aid, $bn

Visible exports fob	686.7	Capital balance	311.1
Visible imports fob	-1,029.9	Overall balance	-8.7
Trade balance	-343.3	Change in reserves	-9.6
Invisibles inflows	545.8	Level of reserves	
Invisibles outflows	-486.0	end Dec.	136.4
Net transfers	-48.0	No. months of import cover	1.1
Current account balance	-331.5	Aid given	9.15
– as % of GDP	-3.6	– as % of GDP	0.11

Health and education

Health spending, % of GDP	13.0	Education spending, % of GDP	5.4
Doctors per 1,000 pop.	2.7	Enrolment, %: primary	102
Hospital beds per 1,000 pop.	3.7	secondary	97
Improved-water source access,		tertiary	81
% of pop.	100		

Society

No. of households	101.0m	Colour TVs per 100 households	99.2
Av. no. per household	2.7	Telephone lines per 100 pop.	67.3
Marriages per 1,000 pop.	8.6	Mobile telephone subscribers	
Divorces per 1,000 pop.	4.7	per 100 pop.	31.6
Cost of living, Dec. 1999		Computers per 100 pop.	58.5
New York = 100	100	Internet hosts per 100 pop.	266.1

a Including utilities.

VENEZUELA

Area	912,050 sq km	Capital	Caracas
Arable as % of total land	3	Currency	Bolivar (Bs)

People

Population	23.7m	Life expectancy: men	70.9 yrs
Pop. per sq km	26	women	76.7 yrs
Av. ann. growth		Adult literacy	92.0%
in pop. 1995–2000	2.02%	Fertility rate (per woman)	3.0
Pop. under 15	34.0%	Urban population	86.9%
Pop. over 65	6.6%		*per 1,000 pop.*
No. of men per 100 women	101.3	Crude birth rate	22.8
Human Development Index	77.0	Crude death rate	4.7

The economy

GDP	Bs62,577bn	GDP per head	$4,310
GDP	$102.2bn	GDP per head in purchasing	
Av. ann. growth in real		power parity (USA=100)	17.0
GDP 1990–99	1.7%	Economic freedom index	3.55

Origins of GDP		**Components of GDP**	
	% of total		*% of total*
Agriculture	4.8	Private consumption	70.2
Industry, of which:	37.5	Public consumption	7.6
manufacturing	26.5	Investment	15.6
Services	57.7	Exports	22.0
		Imports	-15.4

Structure of employment

	% of total		*% of labour force*
Agriculture	11	Unemployed 1999	14.9
Industry	24	Av. ann. rate 1990–99	10.2
Services	65		

Energy

	m TCE		
Total output	313.281	% output exported	65.9
Total consumption	110.999	% consumption imported	0.4
Consumption per head,			
kg coal equivalent	4,173		

Inflation and finance

Consumer price			*av. ann. increase 1994–99*
inflation 2000	16.2%	Narrow money (M1)	45.9%
Av. ann. inflation 1990–2000	43.3%	Broad money	36.5%
Money market rate, 2000	8.14%		

Exchange rates

	end 2000		*December 2000*
Bs per $	670	Effective rates	1995 = 100
Bs per SDR	912	– nominal	31.1
Bs per euro	623	– real	167.3

Trade

Principal exports		Principal imports[a]	
	$bn fob		*$bn fob*
Oil	17.1	Machinery & transport equipment	6.8
Metals	1.5	Chemicals	1.8
Chemicals	0.6	Food, beverages & tobacco	1.5
Plastics	0.3		
Total incl. others	**21.1**	Total incl. others	**14.3**

Main export destinations		Main origins of imports	
	% of total		*% of total*
United States	50.4	United States	42.0
Colombia	7.3	Colombia	6.7
Brazil	3.7	Italy	5.5
Germany	1.4	Germany	4.8

Balance of payments, reserves and debt, $bn

Visible exports fob	20.8	Overall balance	1.0
Visible imports fob	-13.2	Change in reserves	0.4
Trade balance	7.6	Level of reserves end Dec.	15.1
Invisibles inflows	3.4	No. months of import cover	8.8
Invisibles outflows	-7.4	Foreign debt	35.8
Net transfers	0.1	– as % of GDP	36
Current account balance	3.7	Debt service paid	5.6
– as % of GDP	3.6	Debt service ratio	23
Capital balance	-1.7		

Health and education

Health spending, % of GDP	4.2	Education spending, % of GDP	5.2
Doctors per 1,000 pop.	2.4	Enrolment, %: primary	91
Hospital beds per 1,000 pop.	1.5	secondary	40
Improved-water source access, % of pop.	84	tertiary	25

Society

No. of households	4.1m	Colour TVs per 100 households	89.2
Av. no. per household	5.6	Telephone lines per 100 pop.	10.9
Marriages per 1,000 pop.	3.8	Mobile telephone subscribers per 100 pop.	14.3
Divorces per 1,000 pop.	1.0	Computers per 100 pop.	4.6
Cost of living, Dec. 1999 New York = 100	76	Internet hosts per 100 pop.	0.7

a 1998

VIETNAM

Area	331,114 sq km	Capital	Hanoi
Arable as % of total land	18	Currency	Dong (D)

People

Population	77.5m	Life expectancy: men	66.9 yrs
Pop. per sq km	238	women	71.9 yrs
Av. ann. growth		Adult literacy	91.9%
in pop. 1995–2000	1.4%	Fertility rate (per woman)	2.5
Pop. under 15	33.4%	Urban population	19.7%
Pop. over 65	7.5%		*per 1,000 pop.*
No. of men per 100 women	99	Crude birth rate	19.7
Human Development Index	67.1	Crude death rate	6.4

The economy

GDP	D400trn	GDP per head	$370
GDP	$28.7bn	GDP per head in purchasing	
Av. ann. growth in real		power parity (USA=100)	5.8
GDP 1990–99	8.1%	Economic freedom index	4.10

Origins of GDP	*% of total*	**Components of GDP**[a]	*% of total*
Agriculture	25.8	Private consumption	70.3
Industry, of which:	33.5	Public consumption	13.7
manufacturing	...	Investment	27.9
Services	40.7	Exports	42.9
		Imports	-56.5

Structure of employment

	% of total		*% of labour force*
Agriculture	...	Unemployed 1998	...
Industry	...	Av. ann. rate 1990–98	...
Services	...		

Energy

	m TCE		
Total output	28.560	% output exported	60.3
Total consumption	18.040	% consumption imported	45.7
Consumption per head,			
kg coal equivalent	236		

Inflation and finance

		av. ann. increase 1995–99	
Consumer price			
inflation 2000	-1.6%	Narrow money (M1)	26.5
Av. ann. inflation 1990–2000	15.4%	Broad money	33.9
Treasury bill rate, 2000	5.42%		

Exchange rates

	end 2000		*December 2000*
D per $	14,508	Effective rates	1995 = 100
D per SDR	18,860	– nominal	...
D per euro	13,492	– real	...

Trade

Principal exports	$bn fob	Principal imports	$bn cif
Crude oil	2.1	Machinery & parts	2.0
Textiles & garments	1.8	Petroleum products	1.1
Footwear	1.4	Computers & electronics	0.6
Rice	1.0	Steel	0.6
Total incl. others	**11.5**	Total incl. others	**11.6**

Main export destinations	% of total	Main origins of imports	% of total
Japan	15.5	Singapore	16.2
China	7.5	Japan	12.9
Australia	7.1	Taiwan	12.7
Singapore	7.1	South Korea	12.4
Taiwan	5.9	Sweden	6.8
Germany	5.7	Thailand	5.9

Balance of payments[b], reserves and debt, $bn

Visible exports fob	9.4	Overall balance	...
Visible imports fob	-10.4	Change in reserves	1.3
Trade balance	-1.0	Level of reserves	
Invisibles inflows	2.7	end Dec.	3.3
Invisibles outflows	-4.0	No. months of import cover	2.3
Net transfers[a]	1.2	Foreign debt	23.2
Current account balance[a]	-2.4	– as % of GDP	81
– as % of GDP	-9.2	Debt service paid	1.4
Capital balance	...	Debt service ratio	10

Health and education

Health spending, % of GDP	4.8	Education spending, % of GDP	3.0
Doctors per 1,000 pop.	0.6	Enrolment, %: primary	114
Hospital beds per 1,000 pop.	1.7	secondary	57
Improved-water source access,		tertiary	7
% of pop.	56		

Society

No. of households	16.8m	Colour TVs per 100 households	35.2
Av. no. per household	4.6	Telephone lines per 100 pop.	2.7
Marriages per 1,000 pop.	...	Mobile telephone subscribers	
Divorces per 1,000 pop.	...	per 100 pop.	0.4
Cost of living, Dec. 1999		Computers per 100 pop.	0.9
New York = 100	68	Internet hosts per 100 pop.	...

a 1996
b 1998

ZIMBABWE

Area	390,759 sq km	Capital	Harare
Arable as % of total land	8	Currency	Zimbabwe dollar (Z$)

People

Population	11.9m	Life expectancy: men	43.3 yrs
Pop. per sq km	30	women	42.4 yrs
Av. ann. growth		Adult literacy	90.9%
in pop. 1995–2000	1.91%	Fertility rate (per woman)	5.00
Pop. under 15	45.2%	Urban population	35.3%
Pop. over 65	4.7%		*per 1,000 pop.*
No. of men per 100 women	100	Crude birth rate	35.0
Human Development Index	55.5	Crude death rate	17.8

The economy

GDP	Z$215bn	GDP per head	$470
GDP	$5.6bn	GDP per head in purchasing	
Av. ann. growth in real		power parity (USA=100)	8.4
GDP 1990–99	2.8%	Economic freedom index	4.25

Origins of GDP		**Components of GDP**[a]	
	% of total		*% of total*
Agriculture	20	Private consumption	69.5
Industry, of which:	25	Public consumption	17.8
manufacturing	17	Investment	19.8
Services	55	Exports	38.5
		Imports	-45.7

Structure of employment[b]

	% of total		*% of labour force*
Agriculture	68	Unemployed 1998	...
Industry	8	Av. ann. rate 1990–98	...
Services	24		

Energy

	m TCE		
Total output	5.368	% output exported	2.3
Total consumption	7.732	% consumption imported	32.2
Consumption per head,			
kg coal equivalent	689		

Inflation and finance

Consumer price			*av. ann. increase 1994–99*
inflation 2000	55.7%	Narrow money (M1)	36.8%
Av. ann. inflation 1990–2000	31.7%	Broad money	29.0%
Money market rate, 2000	64.98%		

Exchange rates

	end 2000		*December 2000*
Z$ per $	54.95	Effective rates	1995 = 100
Z$ per SDR	71.94	– nominal	...
Z$ per euro	51.10	– real	...

Trade

Principal exports	$m fob	Principal imports	$m cif
Tobacco	624	Machinery & transport equipment	754
Gold	149	Manufactured products	385
Ferro-alloys	130	Chemicals	363
Cotton	102	Petroleum products & electricity	237
Total incl. others	**2,131**	Total incl. others	**2,137**

Main export destinations[c]	% of total	Main origins of imports	% of total
South Africa	10.4	South Africa	46.0
United Kingdom	9.0	United Kingdom	5.6
Malawi	8.1	China	3.8
Botswana	7.5	Germany	3.6
Japan	6.8	United States	2.9

Balance of payments[d], reserves and debt, $bn

Visible exports fob	1.9	Overall balance	-0.05
Visible imports fob	-1.7	Change in reserves	0.2
Trade balance	0.2	Level of reserves end Dec.	0.5
Invisibles inflows	0.7	No. months of import cover	2.3
Invisibles outflows	-0.8	Foreign debt	4.6
Net transfers	0.2	– as % of GDP	87
Current account balance	0.03	Debt service paid	0.6
– as % of GDP	0.5	Debt service ratio	25
Capital balance	-0.02		

Health and education

Health spending, % of GDP	6.6	Education spending, % of GDP	9.0
Doctors per 1,000 pop.	0.1	Enrolment, %: primary	112
Hospital beds per 1,000 pop.	0.5	secondary	50
Improved-water source access, % of pop.	85	tertiary	7

Society

No. of households	3.0m	Colour TVs per 100 households	3.0
Av. no. per household	3.8	Telephone lines per 100 pop.[a]	2.1
Marriages per 1,000 pop.	...	Mobile telephone subscribers per 100 pop.	1.5
Divorces per 1,000 pop.	...	Computers per 100 pop.	1.3
Cost of living, Dec. 1999 New York = 100	46	Internet hosts per 100 pop.	0.2

a 1997
b 1990
c Excluding gold.
d Provisional, does not sum to total.

Glossary

Balance of payments The record of a country's transactions with the rest of the world. The **current account** of the balance of payments consists of: visible trade (goods); "invisible" trade (services and income); private transfer payments (eg, remittances from those working abroad); official transfers (eg, payments to international organisations, famine relief). Visible imports and exports are normally compiled on rather different definitions to those used in the trade statistics (shown in principal imports and exports) and therefore the statistics do not match. The **capital account** consists of long- and short-term transactions relating to a country's assets and liabilities (eg, loans and borrowings). Adding the current to the capital account gives the **overall balance**. This is compensated by net monetary movements and changes in reserves. In practice methods of statistical recording are neither complete nor accurate and an errors and omissions item, sometimes quite large, will appear. In the country pages of this book this item is included in the overall balance. **Changes in reserves** exclude revaluation effects and are shown without the practice often followed in balance of payments presentations of reversing the sign.

CFA Communauté Financière Africaine. Its members, most of the francophone African nations, share a common currency, the CFA franc, which is maintained at a fixed rate of 1FFr = 100 CFAfr by the French treasury.

Cif/fob Measures of the value of merchandise trade. Imports include the cost of "carriage, insurance and freight" (cif) from the exporting country to the importing. The value of exports des not include these elements and is recorded 'free on board" (fob). Balance of payments statistics are generally adjusted so that both exports and imports are shown fob; the cif elements are included in invisibles.

Commonwealth of Independent States All former Soviet Union Republics, excluding Estonia, Latvia and Lithuania. It was established January 1 1992; Azerbaijan joined in September 1993 and Georgia in December 1993.

Crude birth rate The number of live births in a year per 1,000 population. The crude rate will automatically be relatively high if a large proportion of the population is of childbearing age.

Crude death rate The number of deaths in a year per 1,000 population. Also affected by the population's age structure.

Debt, foreign Financial obligations owed by a country to the rest of the world and repayable in foreign currency. **Debt service paid** is the sum of principal repayments and interest payments actually made. **The debt service ratio** is debt service expressed as a percentage of the country's earnings from exports of goods and services.

EU European Union. Members are: Belgium, Denmark, France, Germany, Greece, Ireland, Italy, Luxembourg, Netherlands, Portugal, Spain and the United Kingdom and, since January 1 1995, Austria, Finland and Sweden.

Effective exchange rate This measures a currency's depreciation (figures below 100) or appreciation (figures over 100) from a base date against a trade weighted basket of the currencies of the country's main trading partners.

Euro Replaced the ecu (European currency unit), on a one-to-one basis on January 1 1999. The currencies of the 11 euro area members have irrevocably fixed conversion rates for the euro. Notes and coins will begin circulation on January 1 2002.

Euro area (EU11) Members are those of the EU except Denmark, Sweden and the

United Kingdom. Greece joined on January 1 2001 so is not included in the Euro zone figures in this book.

Fertility rate The average number of children born to a woman who completes her childbearing years.

GDP Gross domestic product. The sum of all output produced by economic activity within a country. GNP (gross national product) includes net income from abroad eg, rent, profits.

Import cover The number of months of imports covered by reserves, ie reserves ÷ 1/12 annual imports (visibles and invisibles).

Inflation The annual rate at which prices are increasing. The most common measure and the one shown here is the increase in the consumer price index.

Internet hosts Websites and other computers that sit permanently on the Internet.

Life expectancy The average length of time a baby born today can expect to live.

Literacy is defined by UNESCO as the ability to read and write a simple sentence, but definitions can vary from country to country.

Median age Divides the age distribution into two halves. Half of the population is above and half below the median age.

Money supply A measure of the "money" available to buy goods and services. Various definitions exist. The measures shown here are based on definitions used by the IMF and may differ from measures used nationally. Narrow money (M1) consists of cash in circulation and demand deposits (bank deposits that can be withdrawn on demand). "Quasi-money" (time, savings and foreign currency deposits) is added to this to create broad money.

OECD Organisation for Economic Co-operation and Development. The "rich countries" club was established in 1961 to promote economic growth and the expansion of world trade. It is based in Paris and now has 29 members.

Opec Organisation of Petroleum Exporting Countries. Set up in 1960 and based in Vienna, Opec is mainly concerned with oil pricing and production issues. Members are; Algeria, Indonesia, Iran, Iraq, Kuwait, Libya, Nigeria, Qatar, Saudi Arabia, United Arab Emirates and Venezuela.

PPP Purchasing power parity. PPP statistics adjust for cost of living differences by replacing normal exchange rates with rates designed to equalise the prices of a standard "basket"of goods and services. These are used to obtain PPP estimates of GDP per head. PPP estimates are normally shown on a scale of 1 to 100, taking the United States as 100.

Real terms Figures adjusted to exclude the effect of inflation.

Reserves The stock of gold and foreign currency held by a country to finance any calls that may be made for the settlement of foreign debt.

SDR Special drawing right. The reserve currency, introduced by the IMF in 1970, was intended to replace gold and national currencies in settling international transactions. The IMF uses SDRs for book-keeping purposes and issues them to member countries. Their value is based on a basket of the US dollar (with a weight of 45%), the euro (29%), the Japanese yen (15%) and the pound sterling (11%).

List of countries

Whenever data is available, the world rankings consider 173 countries: all those which had (in 1999) or have recently had a population of at least 1m or a GDP of at least $1bn. Here is a list of them.

	Population	GDP	GDP per head	Area	Median age
	m	*$bn*	*$PPP*	*'000 sq km*	*years*
Afghanistan	25.9	21.0[a]	810[a]	652	18.5
Albania	3.4	3.7	3,240	29	26.7
Algeria	30.0	47.9	4,840	2,382	21.1
Angola	12.4	8.6	1,100	1,247	16.2
Argentina	36.6	283.2	11,940	2,767	27.8
Armenia	3.8	1.8	2,360	30	30.4
Australia	19.0	404.0	23,850	7,682	35.3
Austria	8.1	208.2	24,600	84	37.8
Azerbaijan	8.0	4.0	2,450	87	27.0
Bahamas	0.3	4.6	15,500	14	26.4
Bahrain	0.7	6.6	11,530[c]	1	28.6
Bangladesh	127.7	46.0	1,530	144	20.9
Barbados	0.3	2.3	14,010	0.4	32.5
Belarus	10.2	26.8	6,880	208	36.4
Belgium	10.2	248.4	25,710	31	39.3
Benin	6.1	2.4	920	113	16.8
Bermuda	0.1	2.6	23,300[c]	1	...
Bhutan	0.8	0.4	1,260	47	18.7
Bolivia	8.1	8.3	2,300	1,099	20.0
Bosnia	3.9	4.4	1,130[d]	51	35.1
Botswana	1.6	6.0	6,540	581	18.3
Brazil	168.1	751.5	6,840	8,512	25.7
Brunei	0.3	4.9[a]	24,820[c]	6	25.4
Bulgaria	8.2	12.4	5,070	111	38.8
Burkina Faso	11.0	2.6	960	274	16.2
Burundi	6.7	0.7	570	28	16.7
Cambodia	11.8	3.1	1,350	181	19.3
Cameroon	14.7	9.2	1,490	475	18.0
Canada	30.6	634.9	25,440	9,971	36.8
Central African Rep	3.5	1.1	1,150	622	18.5
Chad	7.5	1.5	840	1,284	17.1
Chile	15.0	67.5	8,410	757	28.3
China	1,249.7	989.5	3,550	9,561	30.0
Colombia	41.4	86.6	5,580	1,142	24.0
Congo	49.8	5.6	730[c]	2,345	15.8
Congo-Brazzaville	2.9	2.2	540	342	16.7
Costa Rica	3.6	15.1	7,880	51	24.2
Côte d'Ivoire	14.7	11.2	1,540	322	17.7
Croatia	4.5	20.4	7,260	57	38.8
Cuba	11.2	18.6[a]	1,670[a]	111	32.9
Cyprus	0.8	9.1	19,080	9	33.3
Czech Republic	10.3	53.1	12,840	79	37.5
Denmark	5.3	174.3	25,600	43	39.0
Dominican Republic	8.4	17.4	5,210	48	23.9

	Population	GDP	GDP per head	Area	Median age
	m	*$bn*	*$PPP*	*'000 sq km*	*years*
Ecuador	12.4	19.0	2,820	272	22.9
Egypt	62.4	89.1	3,460	1,000	22.0
El Salvador	6.2	12.5	4,260	21	21.8
Eritrea	4.0	0.6	1,040	117	17.8
Estonia	1.4	5.2	8,190	45	37.5
Ethiopia	62.8	6.4	620	1,134	16.9
Fiji	0.8	1.8	4,780	18	23.6
Finland	5.2	129.7	22,600	338	39.4
France	60.8	1432.3[b]	23,020	544	37.6
French Polynesia	0.2	3.9	22,200	3	24.3
Gabon	1.2	4.4	5,280	268	20.4
Gambia, The	1.3	0.4	1,550	11	20.1
Georgia	5.5	2.7	2,540	70	34.1
Germany	82.0	2,111.9	23,510	358	40.0
Ghana	18.9	7.8	1,850	239	18.1
Greece	10.5	125.1	15,800	132	39.4
Guadeloupe	0.5	5.5[c]	11,870[c]	2	30.0
Guatemala	11.1	18.2	3,630	109	17.8
Guinea	7.2	3.5	1,870	246	17.7
Guinea-Bissau	1.2	0.2	630	36	18.6
Haiti	7.8	4.3	1,470	28	18.9
Honduras	6.3	5.4	2,270	112	18.8
Hong Kong	6.9	158.9	22,570	1	35.9
Hungary	10.1	48.4	11,050	93	38.1
Iceland	0.3	8.2	27,210	103	32.9
India	997.5	447.3	2,230	3,287	23.8
Indonesia	207.0	142.5	2,660	1,904	24.8
Iran	63.0	110.8	5,520	1,648	20.7
Iraq	22.8	19.3[a]	850[ad]	438	19.0
Ireland	3.7	93.4	22,460	70	32.3
Israel	6.1	100.8	18,070	21	28.4
Italy	57.6	1,171.0	22,000	301	40.6
Jamaica	2.6	6.9	3,390	11	25.0
Japan	126.6	4,346.9	25,170	378	41.2
Jordan	4.7	8.1	3,880	89	18.8
Kazakhstan	15.4	15.8	4,790	2,717	27.9
Kenya	29.4	10.6	1,010	583	17.9
Kirgizstan	4.7	1.3	2,420	199	22.7
Kuwait	1.9	29.6	15,370[d]	18	22.8
Laos	5.1	1.4	1,430	237	18.0
Latvia	2.4	6.3	6,220	64	37.7
Lebanon	4.3	17.2	4,030d	10	24.4
Lesotho	2.1	0.9	2,350	30	19.9
Liberia	3.0	0.4[a]	130[ad]	111	18.1
Libya	5.4	32.3	5,960[d]	1,760	20.0
Lithuania	3.7	10.6	6,490	65	36.0
Luxembourg	0.4	18.5	41,230	3	37.8

	Population	GDP	GDP per head	Area	Median age
	m	*$bn*	*$PPP*	*'000 sq km*	*years*
Macau	0.5	6.2	16,940	0.02	33.5
Macedonia	2.0	3.5	4,590	26	32.2
Madagascar	15.1	3.7	790	587	17.9
Malawi	10.8	1.8	570	118	16.3
Malaysia	22.7	79.0	7,640	333	23.3
Mali	10.9	2.7	740	1,240	16.6
Malta	0.4	3.5	9,210[d]	0.3	36.1
Martinique	0.4	5.7[c]	13,540[c]	1	32.3
Mauritania	2.6	1.0	1,550	1,031	18.0
Mauritius	1.2	4.2	8,950	2	29.1
Mexico	97.4	483.7	8,070	1,973	23.3
Moldova	4.3	1.2	2,100	34	31.6
Mongolia	2.6	0.9	1,610	1,565	22.1
Morocco	28.2	35.0	3,320	447	23.2
Mozambique	17.3	4.0	810	799	17.4
Myanmar	45.0	5.7[a]	130[d]	677	25.5
Namibia	1.7	3.1	5,580	824	19.0
Nepal	23.4	5.0	1,280	147	19.1
Netherlands	15.8	393.7	24,410	42	37.8
Netherlands Antilles	0.2	2.4[a]	11,160[ad]	1	31.8
New Caledonia	0.2	3.2	21,130	19	26.1
New Zealand	3.8	54.7	17,630	271	34.0
Nicaragua	4.9	2.3	2,060	130	18.1
Niger	10.5	2.0	740	1,267	15.9
Nigeria	123.9	35.0	770	924	18.1
North Korea	23.4	22.6[a]	970[a]	121	28.8
Norway	4.5	152.9	28,140	324	37.4
Oman	2.3	15.6	6,640[d]	310	17.7
Pakistan	134.8	58.2	1,860	804	19.0
Panama	2.8	9.6	5,450	77	25.2
Papua New Guinea	4.7	3.6	2,260	463	20.5
Paraguay	5.4	7.7	4,380	407	19.8
Peru	25.2	51.9	4,480	1,285	23.1
Philippines	76.8	76.6	3,990	300	21.5
Poland	38.7	155.2	8,390	313	35.1
Portugal	10.0	113.7	15,860	89	37.3
Puerto Rico	3.9	38.2	9,820[d]	9	30.4
Qatar	0.8	14.1[a]	18,630[ad]	11	35.0
Réunion	0.7	8.2[c]	11,320[c]	3	27.9
Romania	22.5	34.0	5,970	238	34.9
Russia	146.5	401.4	6,990	17,075	36.7
Rwanda	8.3	2.0	880	26	17.0
Saudi Arabia	21.4	139.4	11,050	2,200	19.7
Senegal	9.3	4.8	1,400	197	17.5
Serbia & Montenegro	10.6	20.6[a]	1,940[a]	102	35.6
Sierra Leone	4.9	0.7	440	72	17.9
Singapore	3.2	84.9	22,310	1	34.4

	Population	GDP	GDP per head	Area	Median age
	m	*$bn*	*$PPP*	*'000 sq km*	*years*
Slovakia	5.4	19.7	10,430	49	34.0
Slovenia	2.0	20.0	16,050	20	38.1
Somalia	9.4	4.3[a]	460[a]	638	16.0
South Africa	42.1	131.1	8,710	1,226	22.5
South Korea	46.8	406.9	15,530	99	31.4
Spain	39.4	595.9	17,850	505	37.9
Sri Lanka	19.0	16.0	3,230	66	27.5
Sudan	29.0	9.7	1,300	2,506	19.5
Suriname	0.4	1.6[a]	3,780	164	24.0
Swaziland	1.0	1.4	4,200	17	18.3
Sweden	8.9	238.7	22,150	450	39.9
Switzerland	7.1	258.6	28,760	41	38.3
Syria	15.7	19.4	3,450	185	18.8
Taiwan	21.9	288.7	21,140[a]	36	30.1[a]
Tajikistan	6.2	1.9	980	143	19.5
Tanzania	32.9	8.8	500	945	17.1
Thailand	61.7	124.4	5,950	513	28.0
Togo	4.6	1.4	1,380	57	16.9
Trinidad & Tobago	1.3	6.9	7,690	5	27.7
Tunisia	9.5	20.9	5,700	164	24.4
Turkey	64.3	185.7	6,440	779	25.6
Turkmenistan	4.8	3.2	3,340	488	21.1
Uganda	21.5	6.4	1,160	241	30.5
Ukraine	49.9	38.7	3,360	604	15.0
United Arab Emirates	2.8	47.2	18,820[c]	84	37.6
United Kingdom	59.1	1,441.8	22,220	243	38.2
United States	272.9	9,152.1	31,910	9,373	35.8
Uruguay	3.3	20.8	8,750	176	31.4
Uzbekistan	24.6	17.7	2,230	447	21.0
Venezuela	23.7	102.2	5,420	912	23.1
Vietnam	77.5	28.7	1,860	331	23.1
West Bank and Gaza	2.8	4.2	1,490[d]	6	14.4
Yemen	17.0	6.8	730	528	15.8
Zambia	9.9	3.2	720	753	16.1
Zimbabwe	11.9	5.6	2,690	391	18.6
Euro area (EU11)	293.3	6,535.5	22,180	2,365	38.0

a Estimate.
b Including French Guiana, Guadeloupe, Martinique and Réunion.
c 1998
d At market exchange rates.

Sources

Airports Council International, *Worldwide Airport Traffic Report*
BP, *Statistical Review of World Energy*
British Mountaineering Council
Corporate Resources Group, *Quality of Living Report*
Council of Europe
The Economist Intelligence Unit, *Cost of Living Survey*; *Country Forecasts*; *Country Reports*; *Country Risk Service; Global Outlook – Business Environment Rankings*
ERC Statistics International, *World Cigarette Report*
Euromonitor, *International Marketing Data and Statistics*; *European Marketing Data and Statistics*
Europa Publications, *The Europa World Yearbook*
European Bank for Reconstruction and Development, *Transition Report*
Eurostat, *Statistics in Focus*
FAO, *FAOSTAT database*
Financial Times Business Information, *The Banker*
The Heritage Foundation, *The 2001 Index of Economic Freedom*
ILO, *Year Book of Labour Statistics*
IMD, *World Competitiveness Yearbook*
IMF, *Direction of Trade*; *International Financial Statistics; World Economic Outlook*
International Cocoa Organisation, *Quarterly Bulletin of Cocoa Statistics*
International Civil Aviation Organisation, *Civil Aviation Statistics of the World*
International Coffee Organisation
International Cotton Advisory Committee, *Bulletin*
International Criminal Police Organisation (Interpol), *International Crime Statistics*
International Road Federation, *World Road Statistics*
International Rubber Study Group, *Rubber Statistical Bulletin*
International Federation of the Phonographic Industry
International Grains Council, *The Grain Market Report*
International Sugar Organisation, *Sugar Yearbook*
International Tea Committee, *Annual Bulletin of Statistics*
International Telecommunication Union, *ITU Indicators*
International Wool Textile Organisation
ISTA Mielke, *Oil World*
Lloyd's Register, *Statistical Tables*
William M. Mercer Limited
National statistics offices
Network Wizards
Nobel Foundation
OECD, *Development Assistance Committee Report*; *Environmental Data*
Standard & Poor's *Emerging Stock Markets Factbook*
Swiss Re, *sigma*
Taiwan Statistical Data Book
Taiwanese Directorate of Budget, Accounting and Statistics, website
The Times, *Atlas of the World*
Time Inc Magazines, *Fortune International*
UK Home Office
UN, *Energy Statistics Yearbook*; *Global Urban Indicators Database*; *State of World Population Report*; *Statistical Chart on World Families*; *Urban Agglomerations*; *World Population*; *World Population Prospects*
UN Development Programme, *Human Development Report*
UNESCO, website: unescostat.unesco.org
Union Internationale des Chemins de Fer, *Statistiques Internationales des Chemins de Fer*
US Department of Agriculture, *Rice Report*
University of Michigan, Windows to the Universe website
WHO, *Weekly Epidemiological Record*; *World Health Statistics Annual*
World Bank, *Global Development Finance*; *World Development Indicators*; *World Development Report*
World Bureau of Metal Statistics, *World Metal Statistics*
World Economic Forum/Harvard University, *Global Competitiveness Yearbook*
World Economic Forum/Yale University/Columbia University, *Environmental Sustainability Index*
World Resources Institute, *World Resources*
World Tourist Organisation, *Yearbook of Tourism Statistics*
World Trade Organisation, *Annual Report*

ICELAND
NORWAY
SWEDEN
FINL
ESTON
LAT
LITHUAN
DENMARK
IRELAND
U. K.
NETH.
BELG.
LUX.
GERMANY
POLAND
CZECH
SLOV
AUSTRIA
HUNGARY
FRANCE
SWITZ
SLOV
CRO
BOS
SER
PORTUGAL
SPAIN
ITALY
MON
ALB
CANADA
UNITED STATES
BERMUDA
BAHAMAS
MEXICO
CUBA
DOM. REP.
JAM
HAITI
P. RICO
BEL
HOND
GUATEMALA
EL SALVADOR
NICARAGUA
BARBADOS
TRINIDAD & TOBAGO
COSTA RICA
PANAMA
VENEZUELA
SURINAME
FRENCH GUIANA
COLOMBIA
GUY
ECUADOR
BRAZIL
PERU
BOLIVIA
PARAGUAY
CHILE
URUGUAY
ARGENTINA
MOROCCO
ALG
WESTERN SAHARA
MAURITANIA
MALI
SENEGAL
GAMBIA
GUINEA-BISSAU
GUINEA
BURK F
SIERRA LEONE
GHANA
LIBERIA
CÔTE D'IVOIRE
TOGO
BENIN